THE
BODYGUARD
UNIT

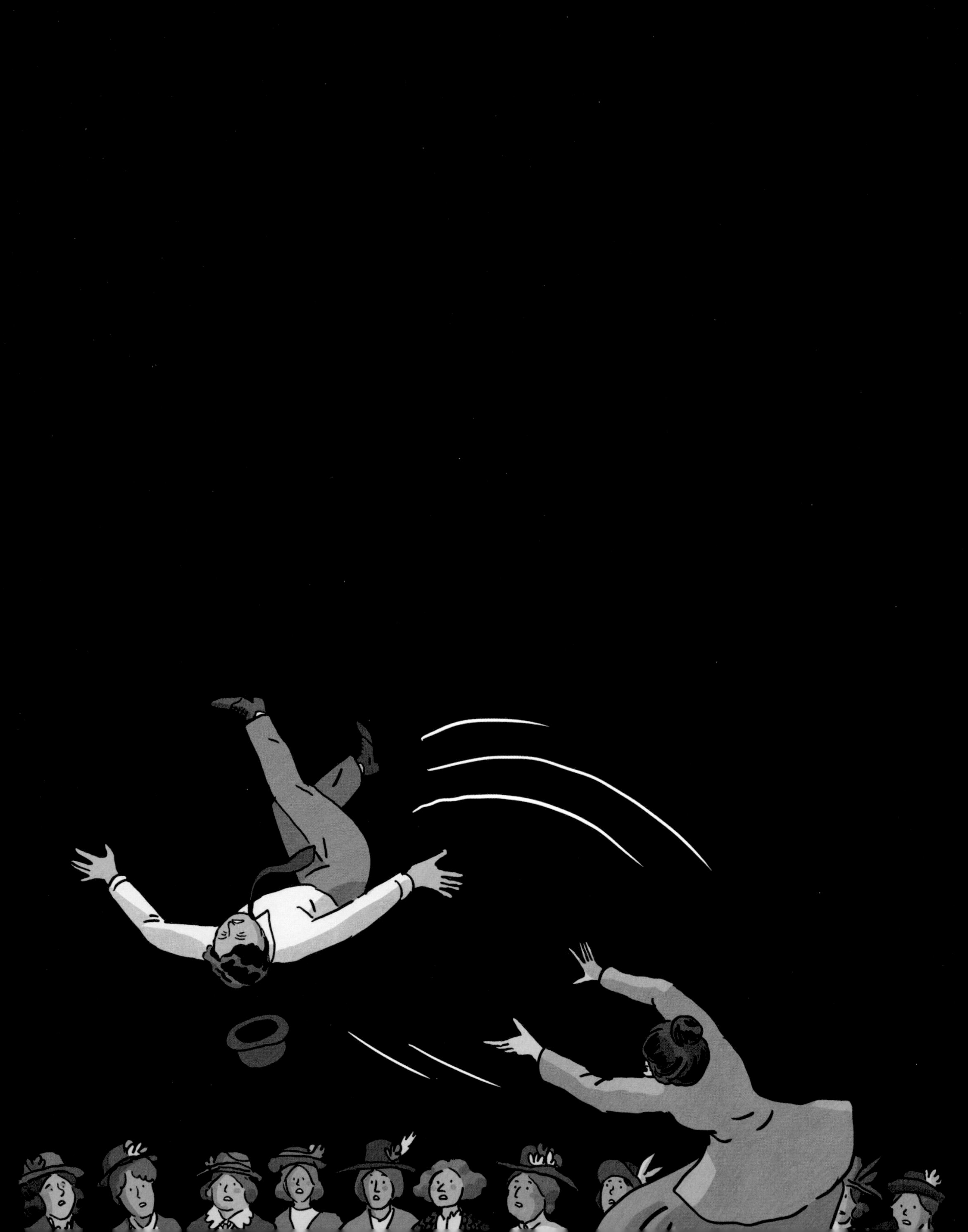

THE BODYGUARD UNIT

Edith Garrud, Women's Suffrage, and Jujitsu

Clément Xavier • Lisa Lugrin • Albertine Ralenti

Edward Gauvin, Translator

Graphic Universe™ • Minneapolis

Text by Clément Xavier
Art by Lisa Lugrin
Coloring by Albertine Ralenti
Translated from the French text by Edward Gauvin

First American edition published in 2023 by Graphic Universe™

Originally published in French under the following title: *Jujitsuffragettes, les Amazones de Londres* by Clément Xavier and Lisa Lugrin © Editions Delcourt, 2020

English-language translation copyright © 2023 by Lerner Publishing Group, Inc.

Graphic Universe™ is a trademark of Lerner Publishing Group, Inc.

Graphic Universe™
An imprint of Lerner Publishing Group, Inc.
241 First Avenue North
Minneapolis, MN 55401 USA

For reading levels and more information, look up this title at www.lernerbooks.com.

Additional photos courtesy of: Richard Gordon Matzene/Library of Congress, p. 132 (top); National Archives of the Netherlands, p. 132 (bottom); Wikipedia Commons, p. 133 (top).

Main body text set in Yekini.
Typeface provided by Adobe Systems.

Library of Congress Cataloging-in-Publication Data

Names: Xavier, Clément, 1981– author. | Lugrin, Lisa, 1983– author. | Ralenti, Albertine, illustrator. | Gauvin, Edward, translator.
Title: The bodyguard unit : Edith Garrud, women's suffrage, and jujitsu / Clement Xavier, Lisa Lugrin ; Albertine Ralenti, colorist ; Edward Gauvin, translator
Other titles: Jujitsuffragettes. English
Description: First American edition. | Minneapolis : Graphic Universe, 2023. | Audience: Ages 14–18 | Audience: Grades 10–12 | Summary: "In the early 20th century, English suffragist group the Women's Social and Political Union formed an all-women security unit. Trained by Edith Garrud, these "jujitsuffragettes" fought against abuse and arrest while pursuing long overdue rights"— Provided by publisher.
Identifiers: LCCN 2022045104 (print) | LCCN 2022045105 (ebook) | ISBN 9781728445656 (library binding) | ISBN 9798765607473 (paperback) | ISBN 9781728494982 (ebook)
Subjects: LCSH: Garrud, Edith Margaret, 1872-1971. | Women—Suffrage—Great Britain—History—Comic books, strips, etc. | Suffragists—Great Britain—Comic books, strips, etc. | Women martial artists—Great Britain—Comic books, strips, etc. | Women's Social and Political Union (Great Britain)—Comic books, strips, etc. | LCGFT: Graphic novels | Biographical comics
Classification: LCC HQ1595.G37 X3813 2023 (print) | LCC HQ1595.G37 (ebook) | DDC 324.6/23092 [B]—dc23/eng/20221122

LC record available at https://lccn.loc.gov/2022045104
LC ebook record available at https://lccn.loc.gov/2022045105

Manufactured in the United States of America
2-1010430-49874-12/13/2023

Self-Defense!

It is a little-known story of English feminism that Lisa Lugrin and Clément Xavier have put into words and images: a history of feminism that we are not used to reading. Not a sentimental portrait of women's rights, it concerns the fight for freedom, because the rights of women were not *given* to them (as people too often say). The story told about the incredible trajectory of Edith Garrud, an instructor of jujitsu who trained dozens of women and activists to defend themselves, is a story about the revolt of the body. A story of the political, physical, even muscular combat of a female uprising. These women understood that those whom they were asking for justice were the same authorities who were maintaining civil and political inequality between men and women, knowingly leaving violence against women unpunished. Women therefore became self-organized, self-determined, and self-emancipated!

Contrary to the highly polished image of women's movements, we see women using hammers, knees, fists, arm locks, and tricks of all kinds to take the rights and freedoms of which they have been unjustly deprived. All the finery surrounding femininity becomes weaponized: perceived to be harmless, restrained within corsets, assigned to the sphere of domesticity, the bodies of women become the bodies of Amazons, taking advantage of the element of surprise. The speeches are insurrectionist and insolent; skirts conceal lit fuses; umbrellas, brooms, and hairpins become clubs and daggers.

This is the tradition of feminist self-defense that Lugrin and Xavier draw upon: a philosophy of life that refuses to submit, a feminism of direct action, sabotage, vandalism. It is a popular, radical feminism, in the face of which the state and its police force deploy fierce, unprecedented repression. The persecution of these activists—imprisonment, beatings, and torture—testifies that the patriarchy of the time had perceived the activists' revolutionary power. By retracing the mobilization of English suffragists—through the jujitsu of Edith Garrud, the philosophy and practice of feminist self-defense, the guidance of the Pankhursts and other activists from the Women's Social and Political Union (WSPU)—we understand how the past, and the way it is shaped into story, in turn shapes the present. It sets precedents, provides toolboxes, and keeps alive a memory of the rebellions that can drive current struggles. By contrast, we also realize how a caricatured image of the suffragists, an image of ridicule that other accounts have transmitted to us, has had the disastrous result of depoliticizing our history, of limiting our bodies, our imaginations, and our rage.

The linework of *The Bodyguard Unit* is lively, fast, and effective. Like a counterattack that hits the mark, it is creative, satisfying. The joy that these pages provide is a muscular joy, which over the story's pages revives the rage lurking in us.

Elsa Dorlin, author of *Self-Defense: A Philosophy of Violence*
July 2020

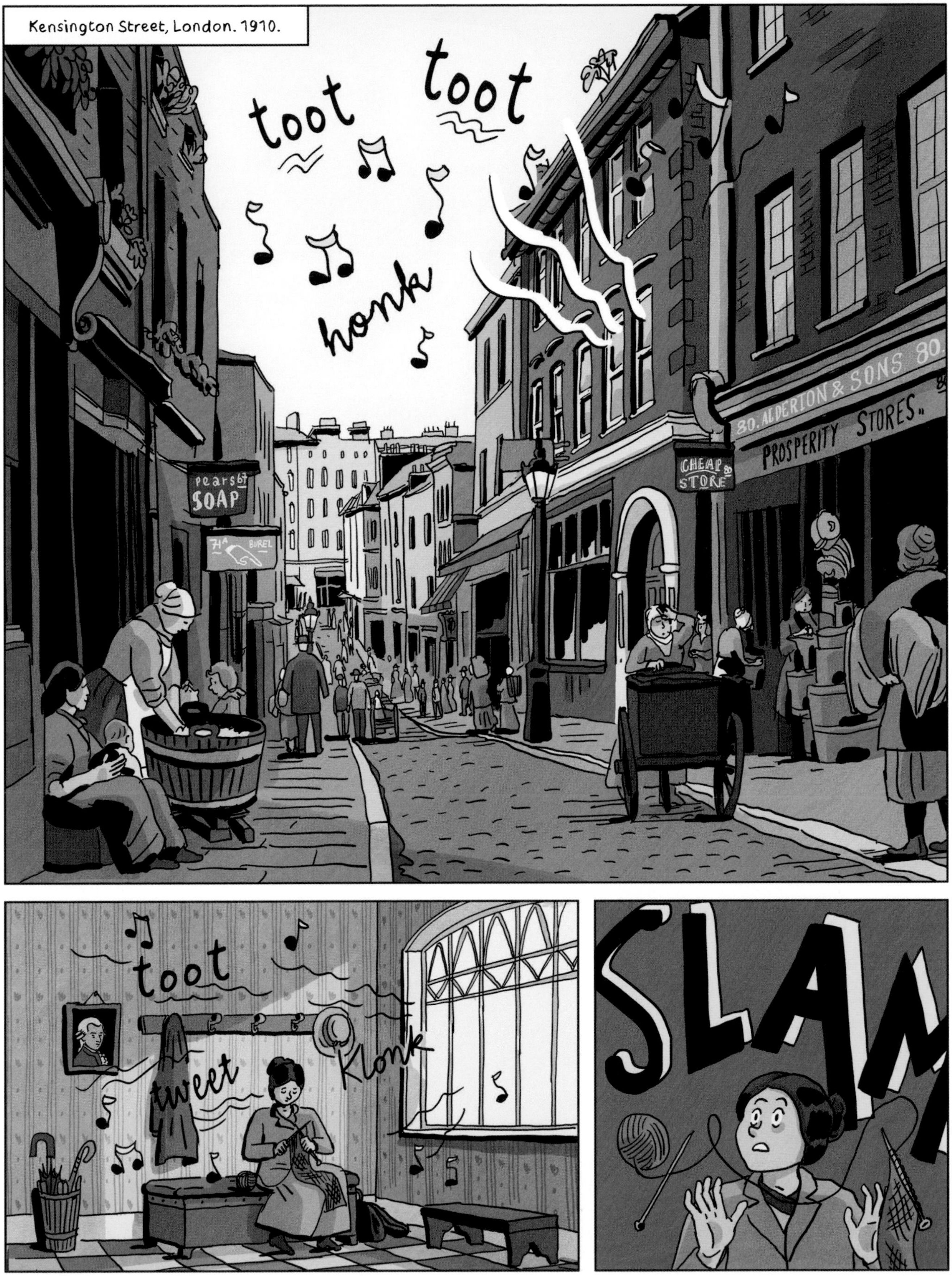
Kensington Street, London. 1910.
toot toot
honk
PEARS SOAP
CHEAP STORE
80. ALDERION & SONS 80.
PROSPERITY STORES.
toot
tweet
Klonk
SLAM

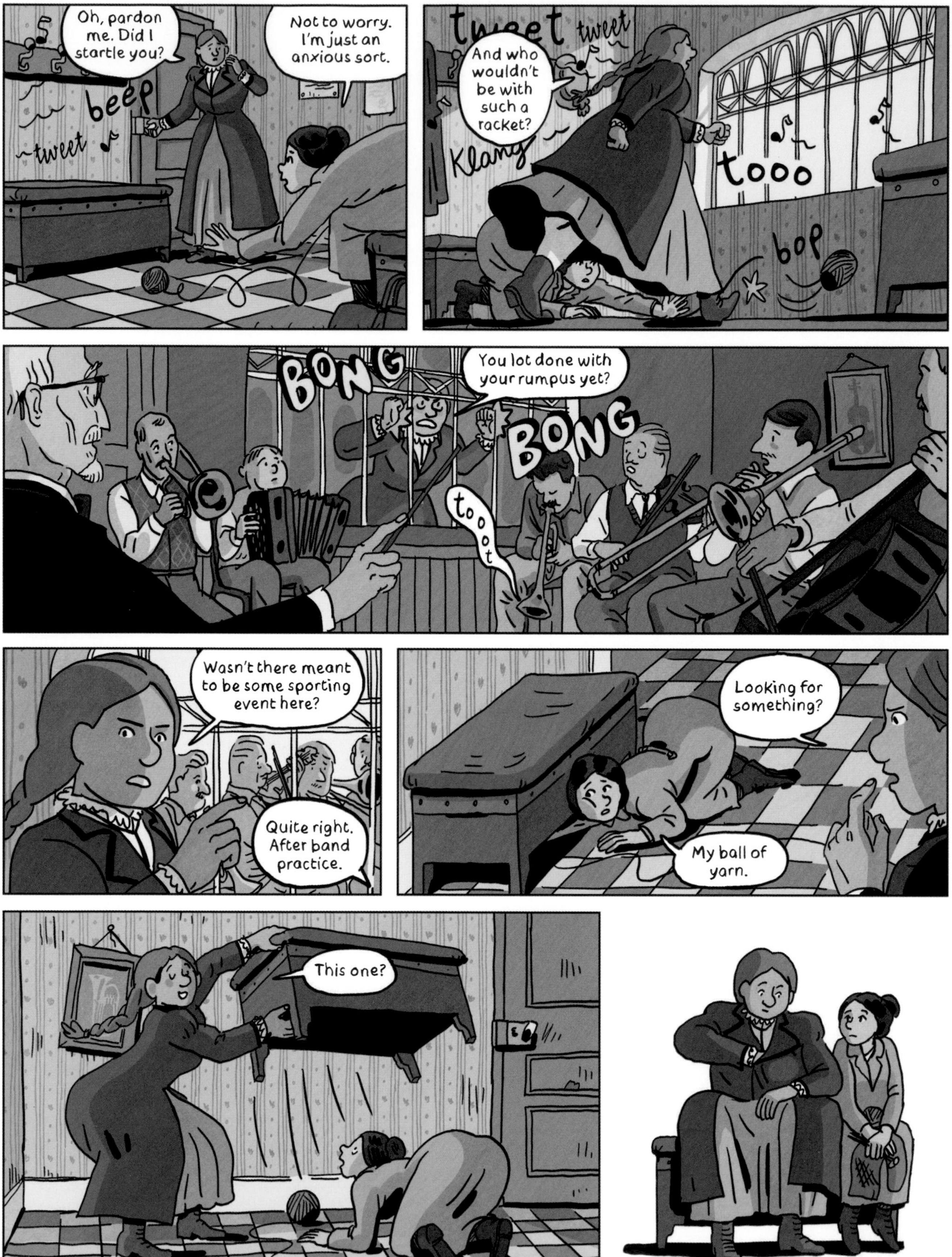

Oh, pardon me. Did I startle you?
Not to worry. I'm just an anxious sort.
beep
tweet
tweet
tweet
And who wouldn't be with such a racket?
Klang
tooo
bop
BONG
You lot done with your rumpus yet?
BONG
toooot
Wasn't there meant to be some sporting event here?
Quite right. After band practice.
Looking for something?
My ball of yarn.
This one?

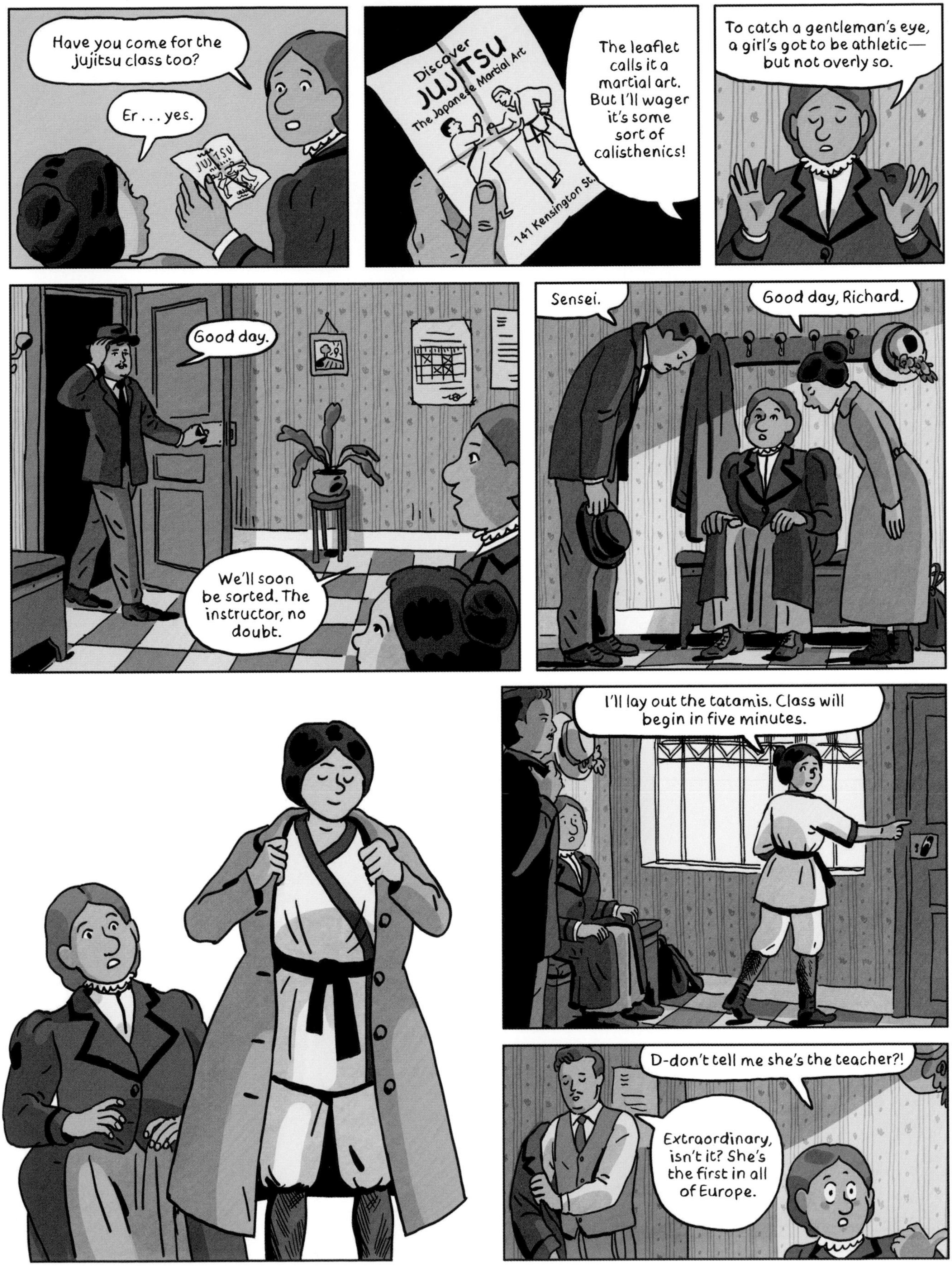
Have you come for the jujitsu class too?
Er . . . yes.
Discover JUJITSU The Japanese Martial Art
141 Kensington St.
The leaflet calls it a martial art. But I'll wager it's some sort of calisthenics!
To catch a gentleman's eye, a girl's got to be athletic— but not overly so.
Good day.
We'll soon be sorted. The instructor, no doubt.
Sensei.
Good day, Richard.
I'll lay out the tatamis. Class will begin in five minutes.
D-don't tell me she's the teacher?!
Extraordinary, isn't it? She's the first in all of Europe.

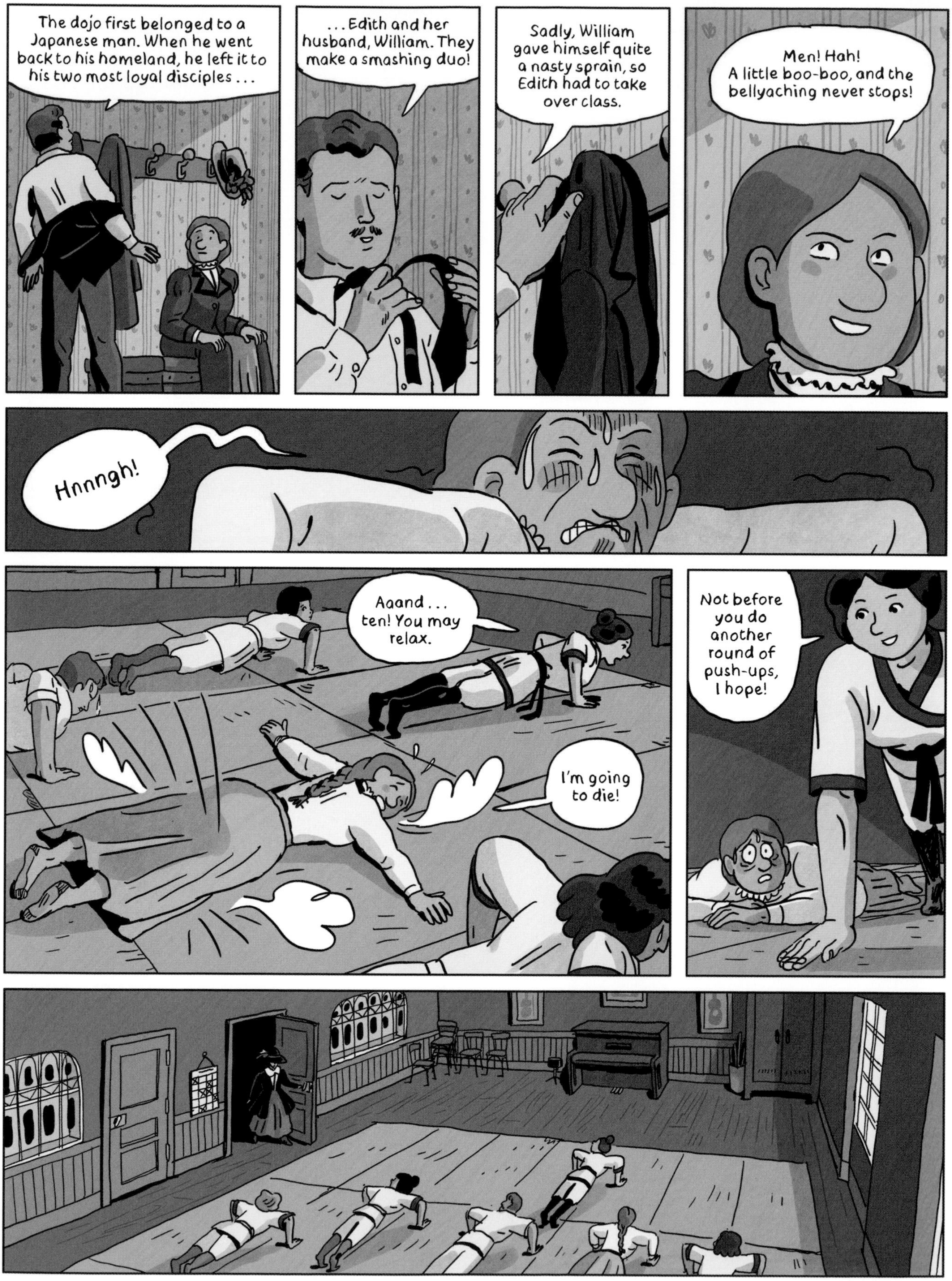
The dojo first belonged to a Japanese man. When he went back to his homeland, he left it to his two most loyal disciples . . .
. . . Edith and her husband, William. They make a smashing duo!
Sadly, William gave himself quite a nasty sprain, so Edith had to take over class.
Men! Hah! A little boo-boo, and the bellyaching never stops!
Hnnngh!
Aaand . . . ten! You may relax.
I'm going to die!
Not before you do another round of push-ups, I hope!

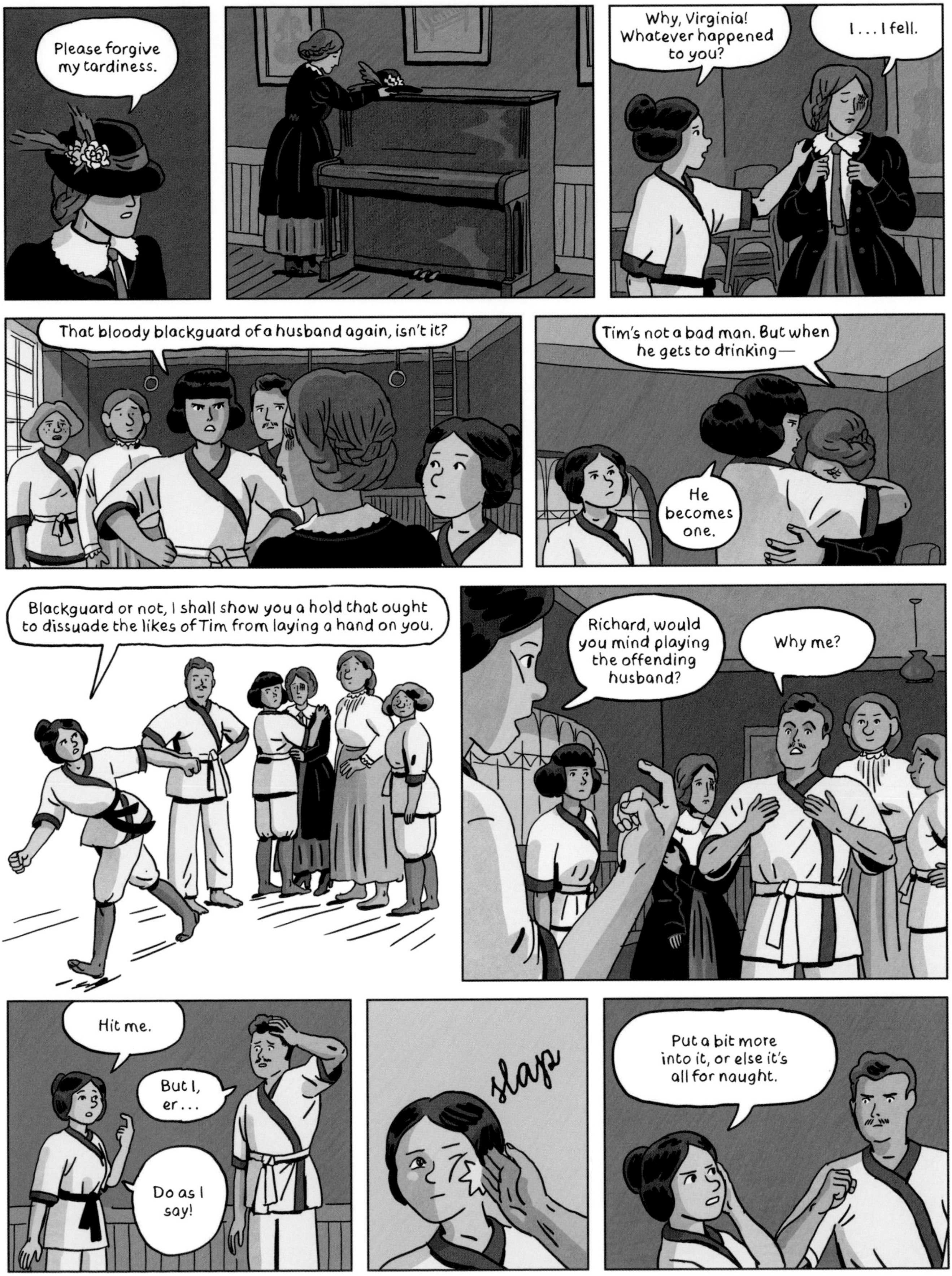
Please forgive my tardiness.
Why, Virginia! Whatever happened to you?
I . . . I fell.
That bloody blackguard of a husband again, isn't it?
Tim's not a bad man. But when he gets to drinking—
He becomes one.
Blackguard or not, I shall show you a hold that ought to dissuade the likes of Tim from laying a hand on you.
Richard, would you mind playing the offending husband?
Why me?
Hit me.
But I, er . . .
Do as I say!
slap
Put a bit more into it, or else it's all for naught.

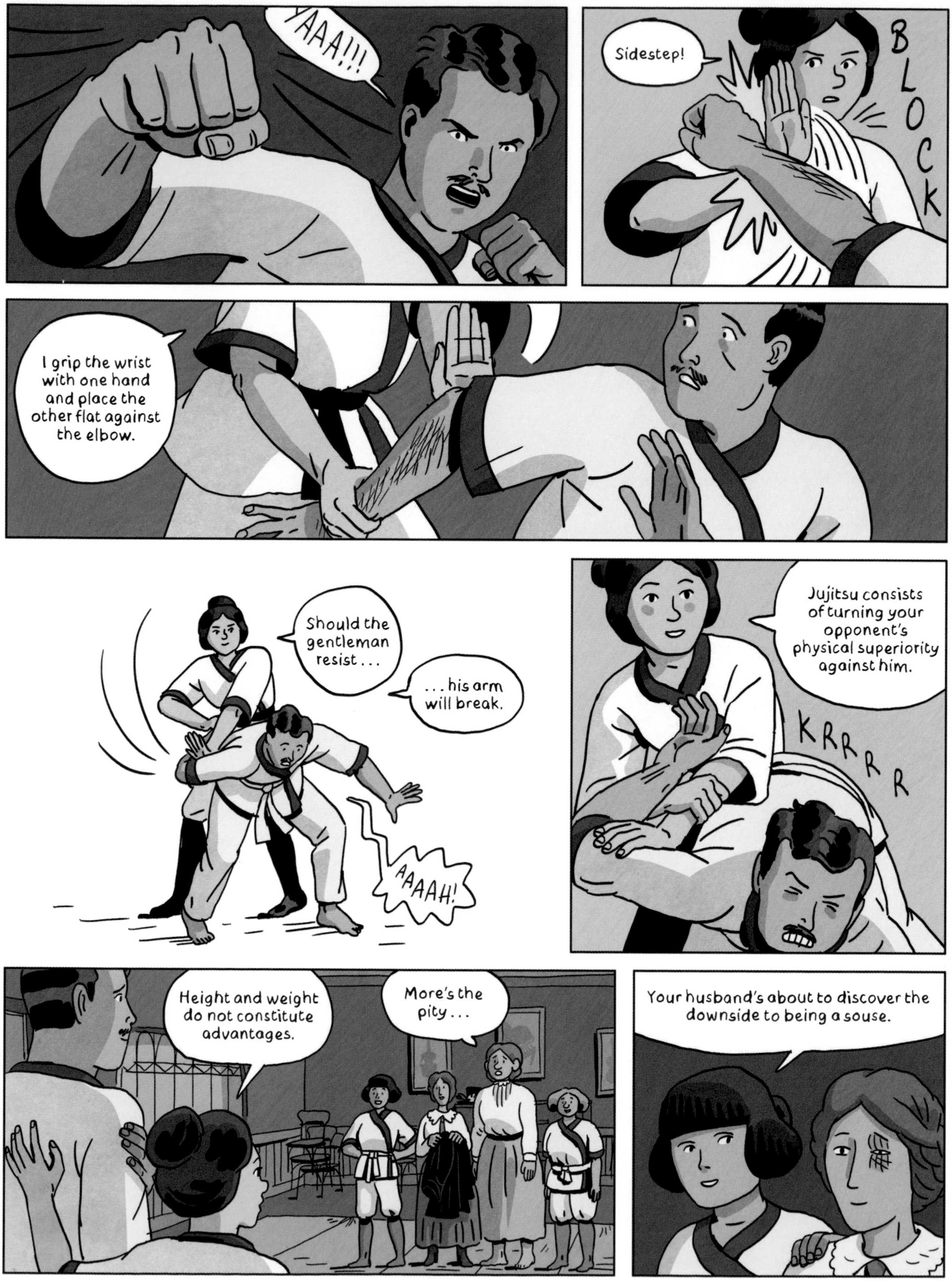
YAAA!!!
Sidestep!
BLOCK
I grip the wrist with one hand and place the other flat against the elbow.
Should the gentleman resist . . .
. . . his arm will break.
AAAAH!
Jujitsu consists of turning your opponent's physical superiority against him.
KRRRRR
Height and weight do not constitute advantages.
More's the pity . . .
Your husband's about to discover the downside to being a souse.

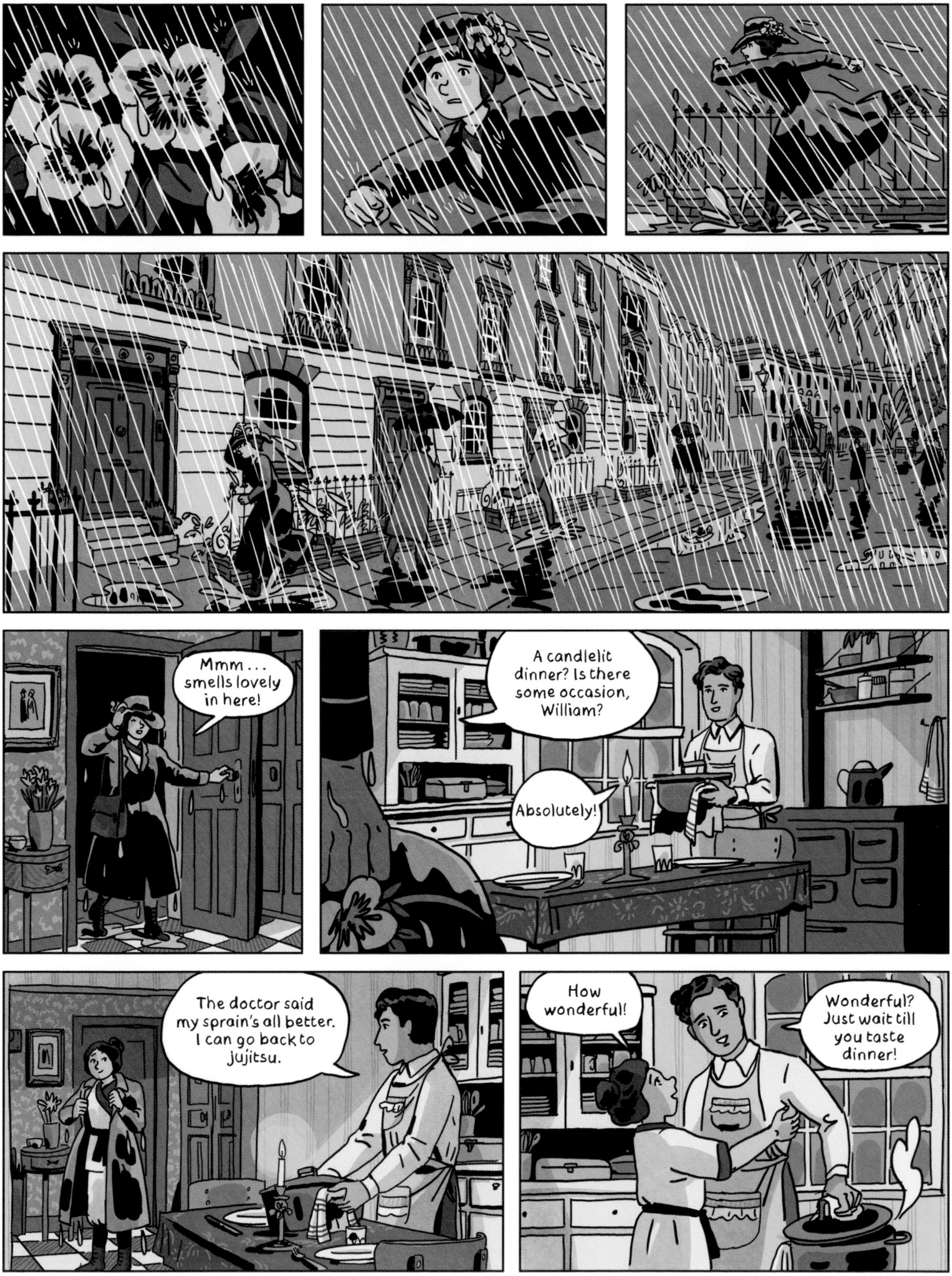
Mmm . . . smells lovely in here!
A candlelit dinner? Is there some occasion, William?
Absolutely!
The doctor said my sprain's all better. I can go back to jujitsu.
How wonderful!
Wonderful? Just wait till you taste dinner!

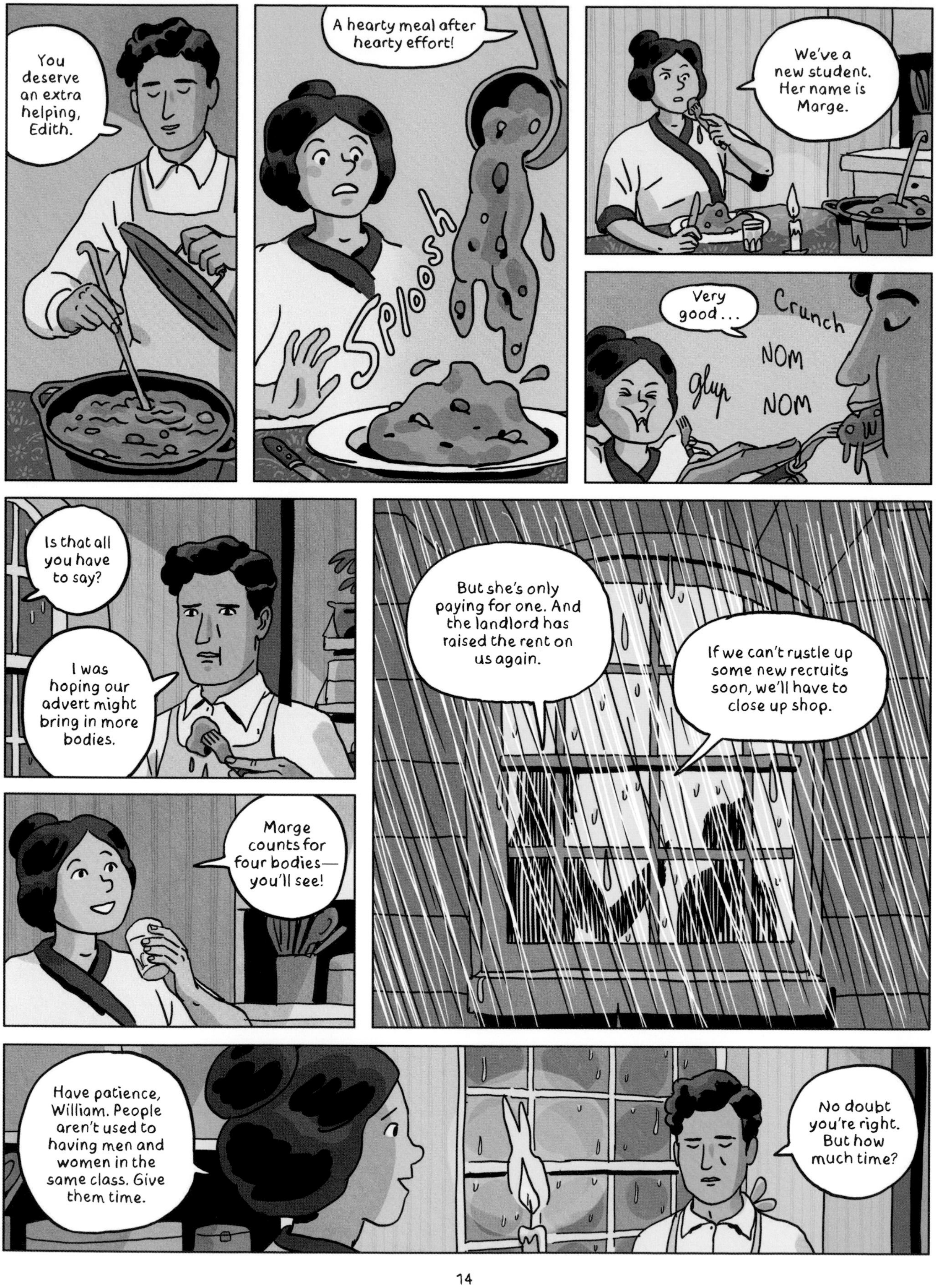
You deserve an extra helping, Edith.
A hearty meal after hearty effort!
Sploosh
We've a new student. Her name is Marge.
Very good...
Crunch
NOM
NOM
glup
Is that all you have to say?
I was hoping our advert might bring in more bodies.
Marge counts for four bodies— you'll see!
But she's only paying for one. And the landlord has raised the rent on us again.
If we can't rustle up some new recruits soon, we'll have to close up shop.
Have patience, William. People aren't used to having men and women in the same class. Give them time.
No doubt you're right. But how much time?

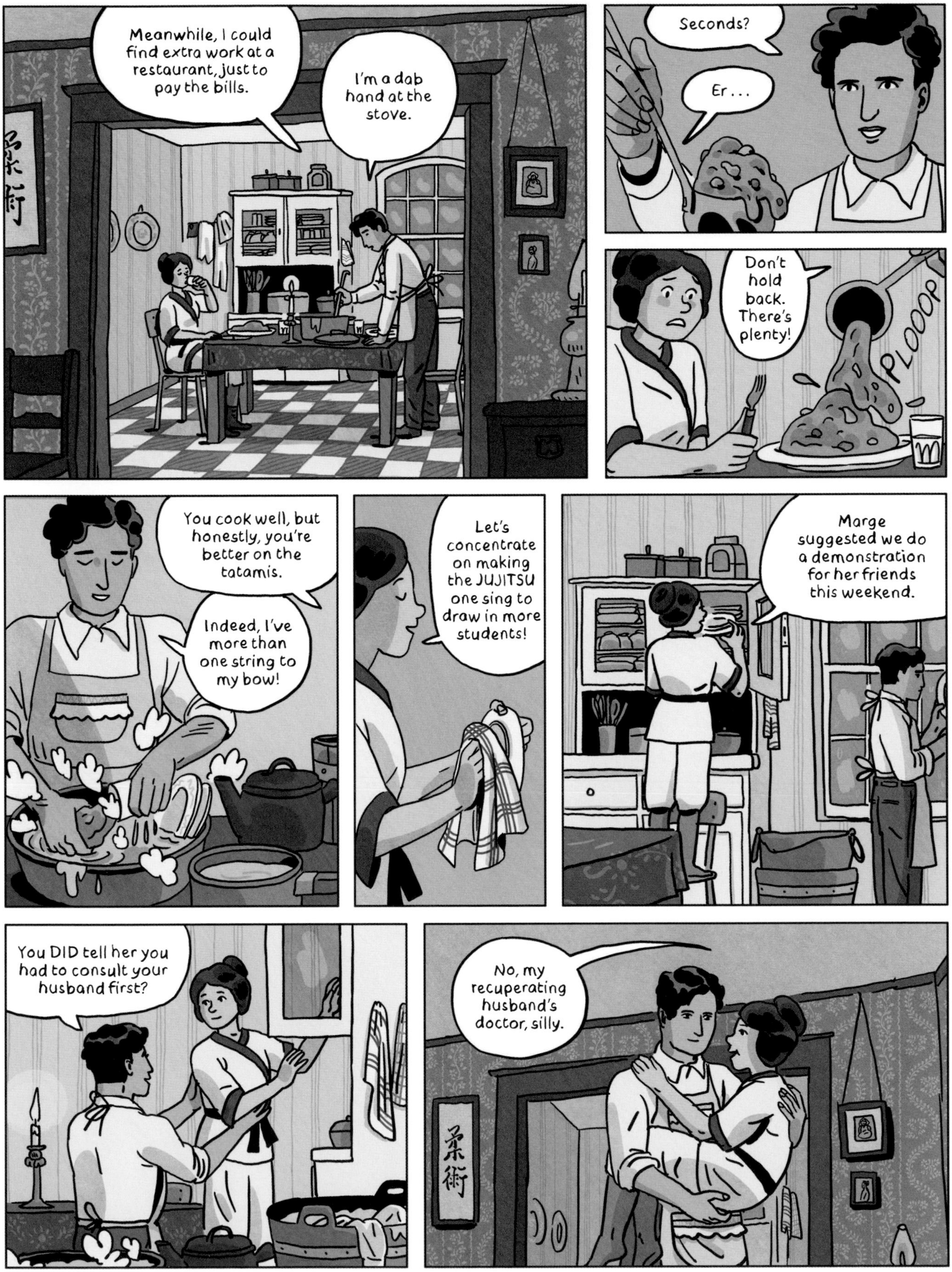

Meanwhile, I could find extra work at a restaurant, just to pay the bills.
I'm a dab hand at the stove.
Seconds?
Er . . .
Don't hold back. There's plenty!
PLOOOP
You cook well, but honestly, you're better on the tatamis.
Indeed, I've more than one string to my bow!
Let's concentrate on making the JUJITSU one sing to draw in more students!
Marge suggested we do a demonstration for her friends this weekend.
You DID tell her you had to consult your husband first?
No, my recuperating husband's doctor, silly.

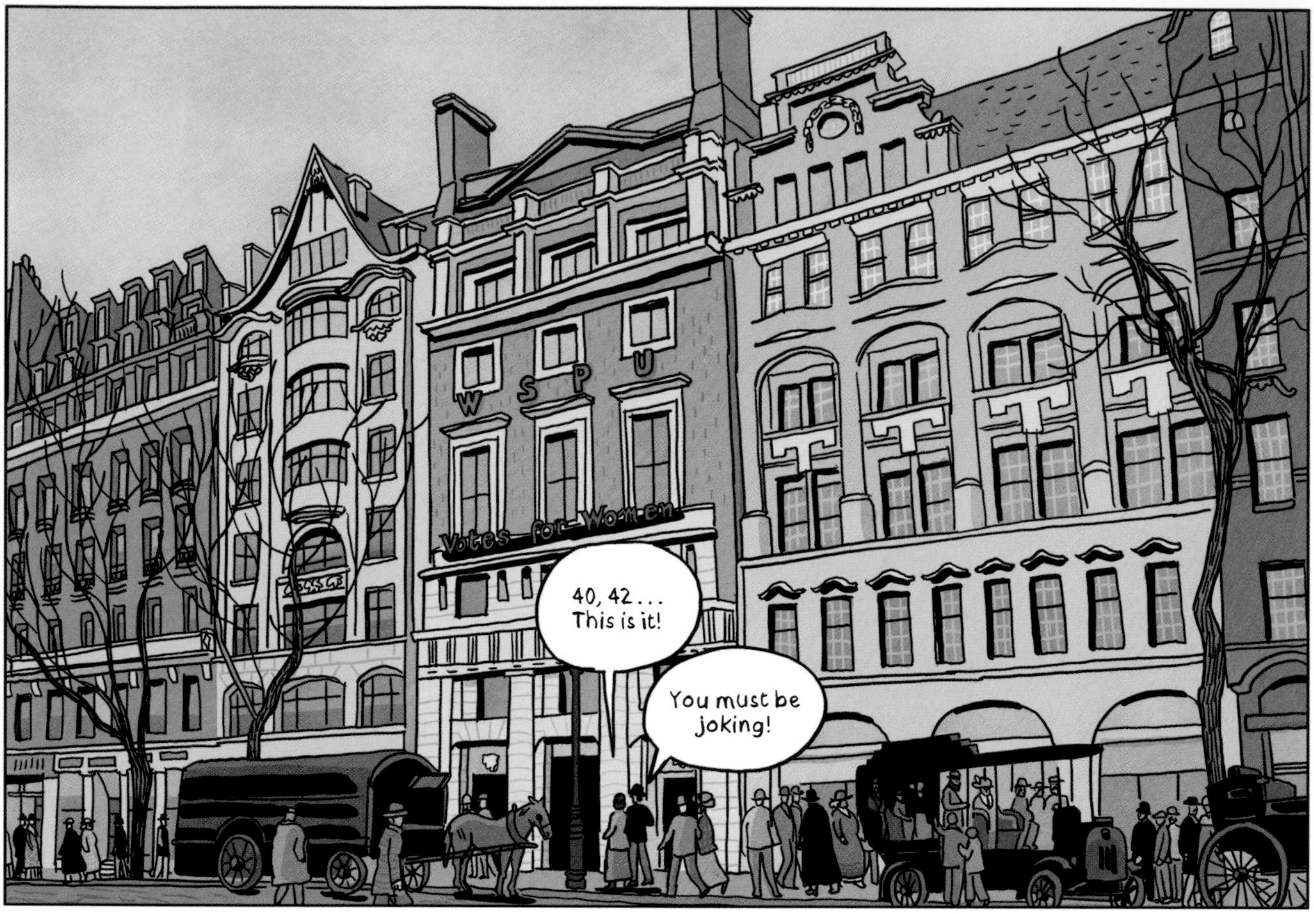
W S P U
Votes for Women
40, 42 . . . This is it!
You must be joking!

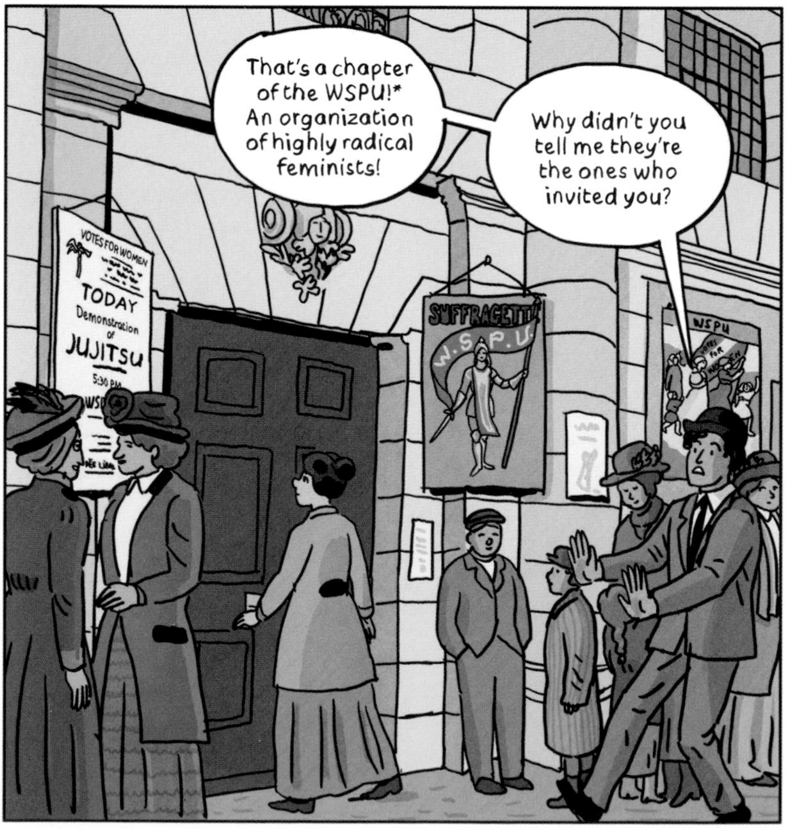
That's a chapter of the WSPU!* An organization of highly radical feminists!
Why didn't you tell me they're the ones who invited you?
VOTES FOR WOMEN
TODAY
Demonstration of
JUJITSU
5:30 PM
SUFFRAGETTE
W.S.P.U.
WSPU

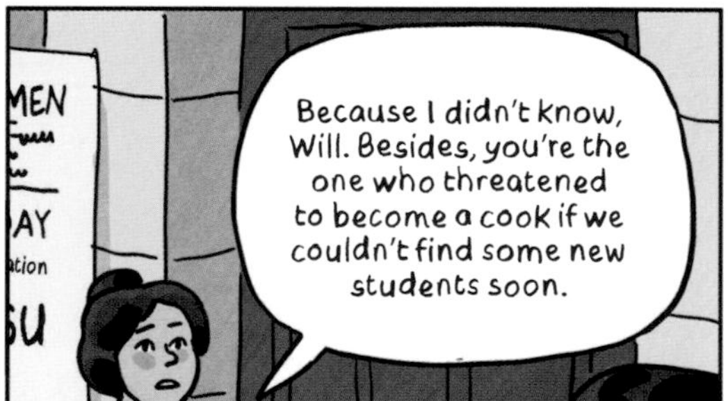
Because I didn't know, Will. Besides, you're the one who threatened to become a cook if we couldn't find some new students soon.

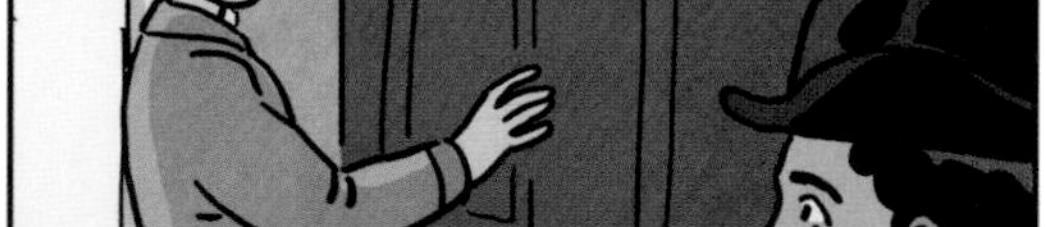
Hey . . . that wasn't a threat!

*WSPU: Women's Social and Political Union

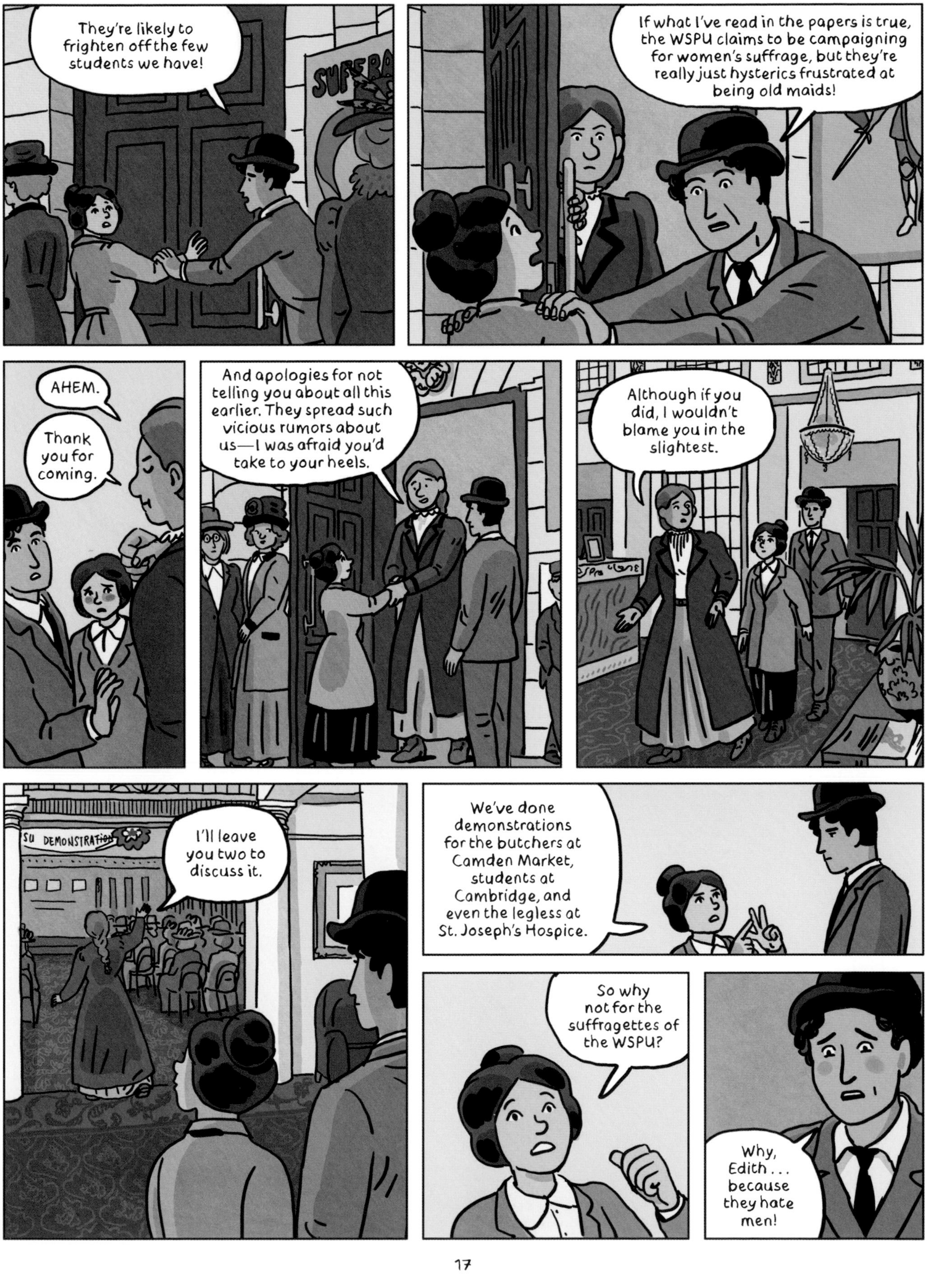
They're likely to frighten off the few students we have!
If what I've read in the papers is true, the WSPU claims to be campaigning for women's suffrage, but they're really just hysterics frustrated at being old maids!
AHEM.
Thank you for coming.
And apologies for not telling you about all this earlier. They spread such vicious rumors about us—I was afraid you'd take to your heels.
Although if you did, I wouldn't blame you in the slightest.
DEMONSTRATION
I'll leave you two to discuss it.
We've done demonstrations for the butchers at Camden Market, students at Cambridge, and even the legless at St. Joseph's Hospice.
So why not for the suffragettes of the WSPU?
Why, Edith . . . because they hate men!

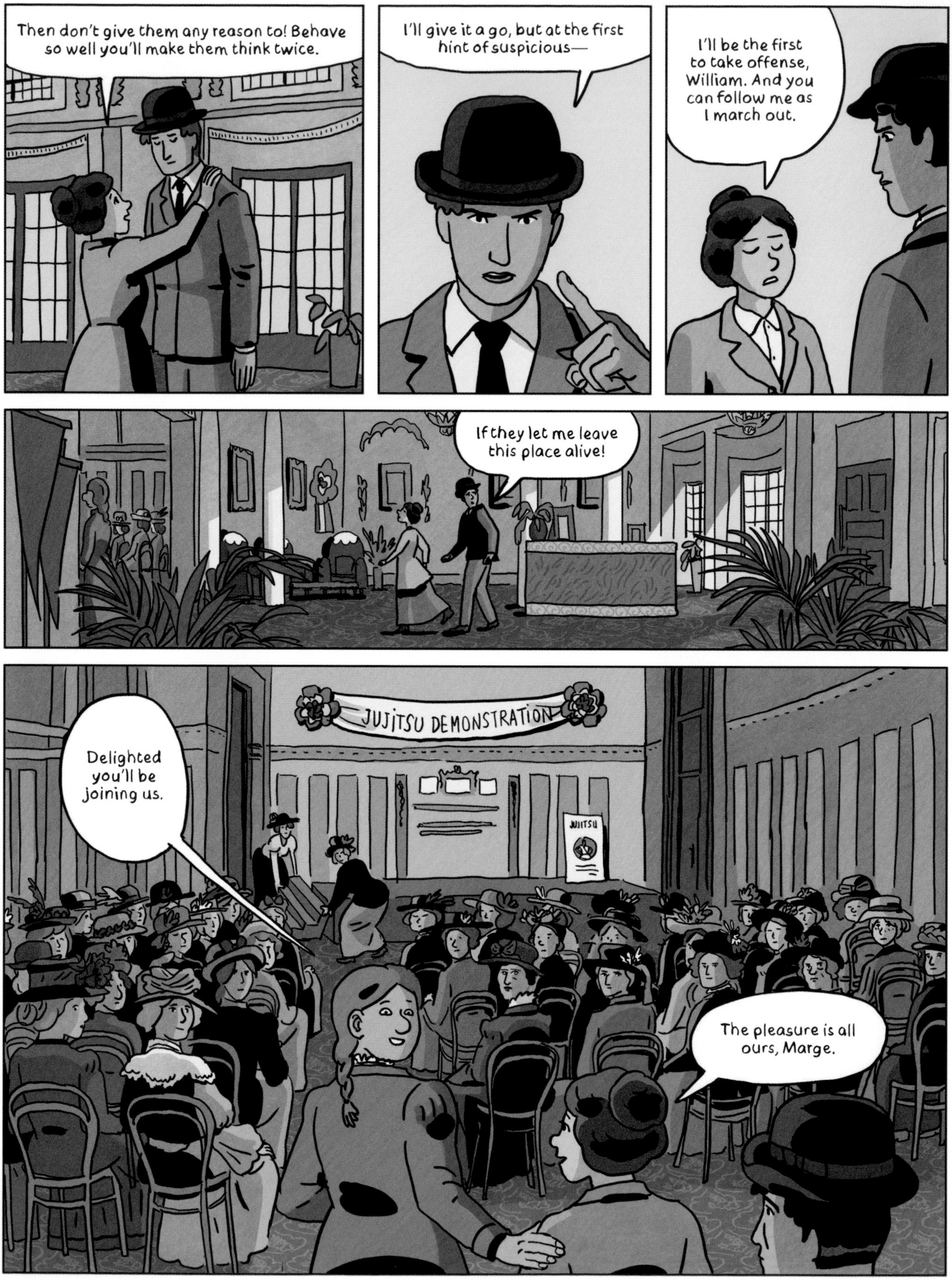
Then don't give them any reason to! Behave so well you'll make them think twice.
I'll give it a go, but at the first hint of suspicious—
I'll be the first to take offense, William. And you can follow me as I march out.
If they let me leave this place alive!
JUJITSU DEMONSTRATION
JUJITSU
Delighted you'll be joining us.
The pleasure is all ours, Marge.

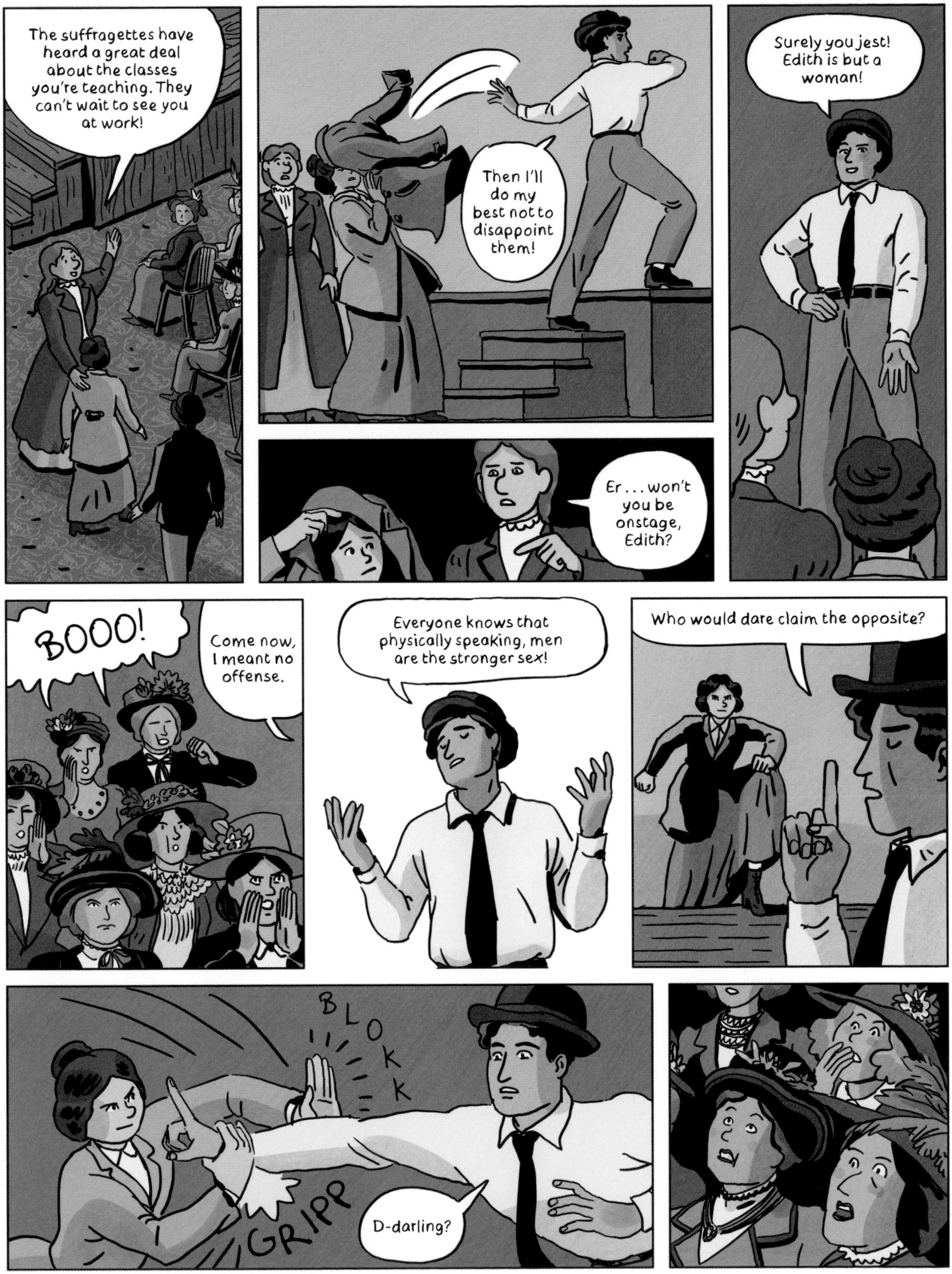
The suffragettes have heard a great deal about the classes you're teaching. They can't wait to see you at work!
Then I'll do my best not to disappoint them!
Er . . . won't you be onstage, Edith?
Surely you jest! Edith is but a woman!
BOOO!
Come now, I meant no offense.
Everyone knows that physically speaking, men are the stronger sex!
Who would dare claim the opposite?
BLOKK
GRIPP
D-darling?

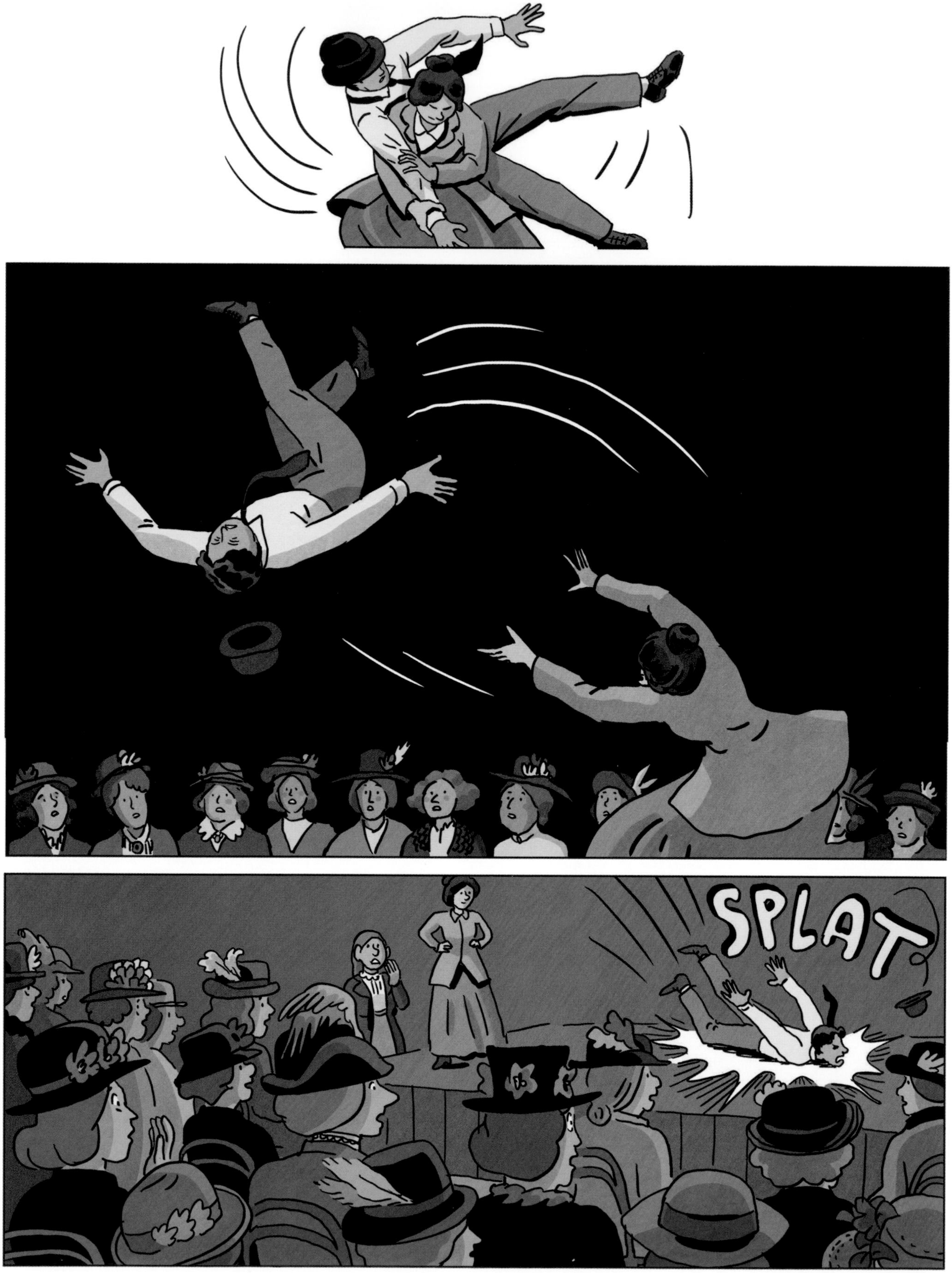
SPLAT

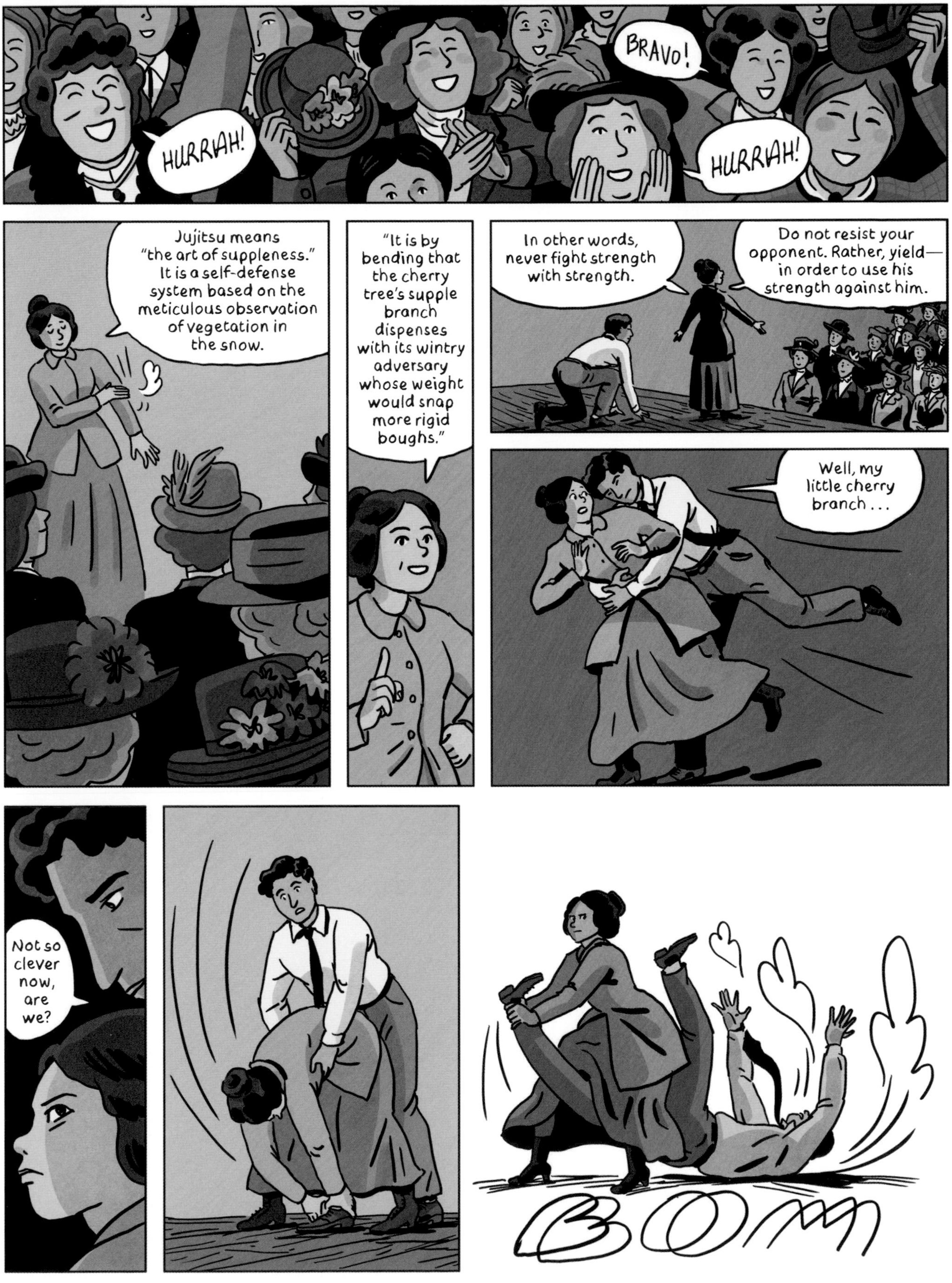
HURRAH!
BRAVO!
HURRAH!
Jujitsu means "the art of suppleness." It is a self-defense system based on the meticulous observation of vegetation in the snow.
"It is by bending that the cherry tree's supple branch dispenses with its wintry adversary whose weight would snap more rigid boughs."
In other words, never fight strength with strength.
Do not resist your opponent. Rather, yield— in order to use his strength against him.
Well, my little cherry branch . . .
Not so clever now, are we?
BOOM

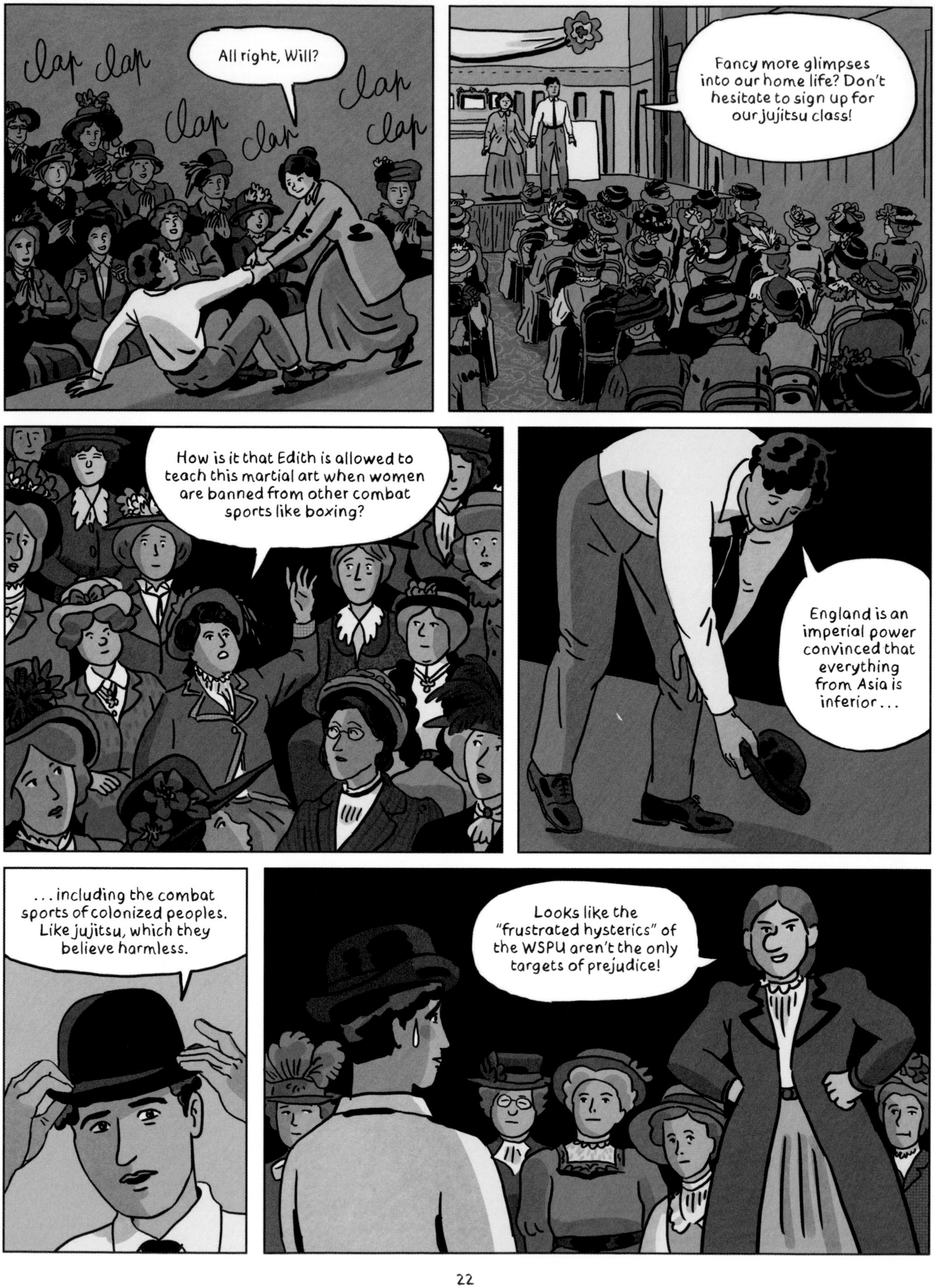
clap clap clap clap clap clap
All right, Will?
Fancy more glimpses into our home life? Don't hesitate to sign up for our jujitsu class!
How is it that Edith is allowed to teach this martial art when women are banned from other combat sports like boxing?
England is an imperial power convinced that everything from Asia is inferior...
...including the combat sports of colonized peoples. Like jujitsu, which they believe harmless.
Looks like the "frustrated hysterics" of the WSPU aren't the only targets of prejudice!

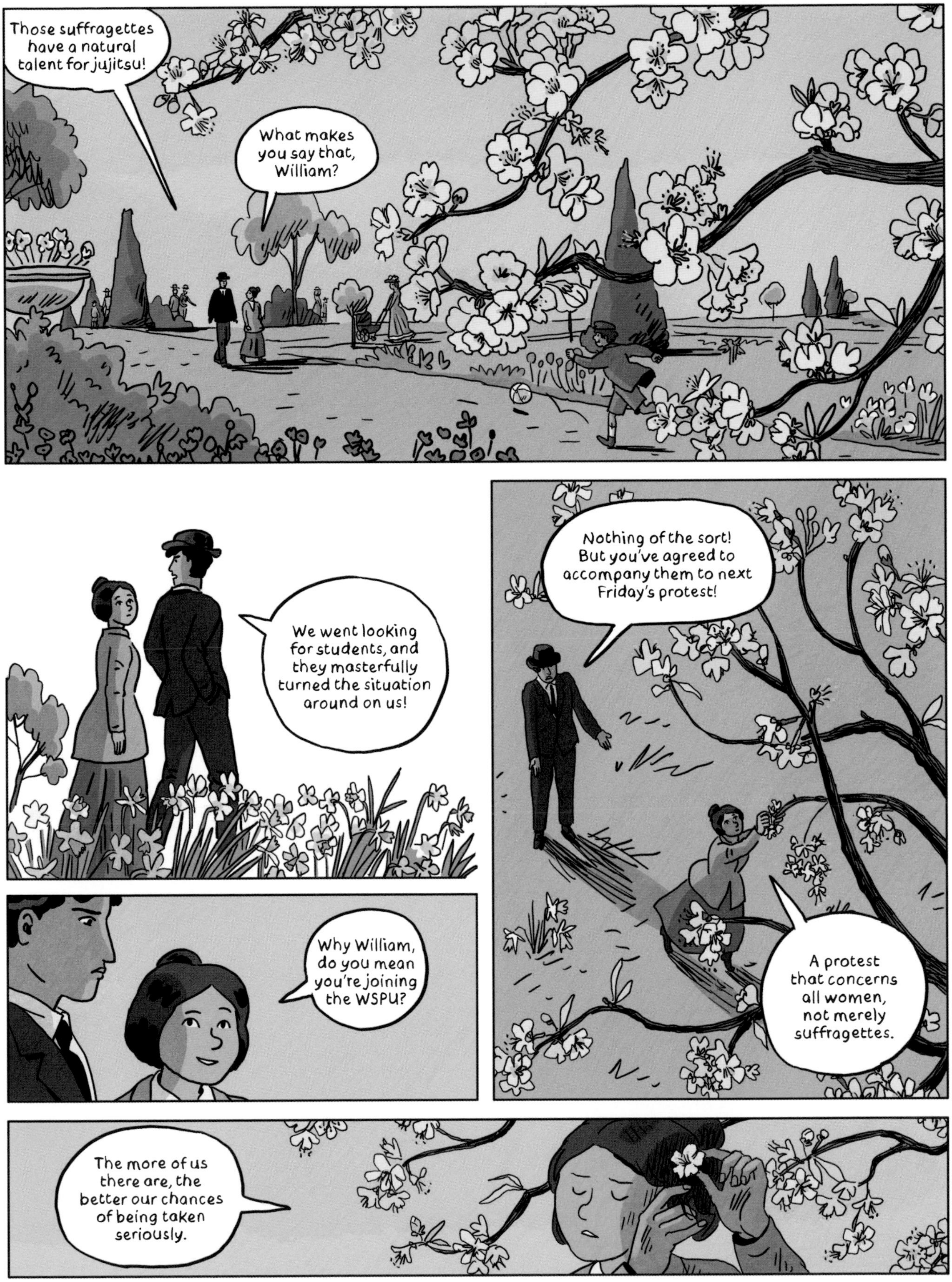
Those suffragettes have a natural talent for jujitsu!
What makes you say that, William?
We went looking for students, and they masterfully turned the situation around on us!
Nothing of the sort! But you've agreed to accompany them to next Friday's protest!
Why William, do you mean you're joining the WSPU?
A protest that concerns all women, not merely suffragettes.
The more of us there are, the better our chances of being taken seriously.

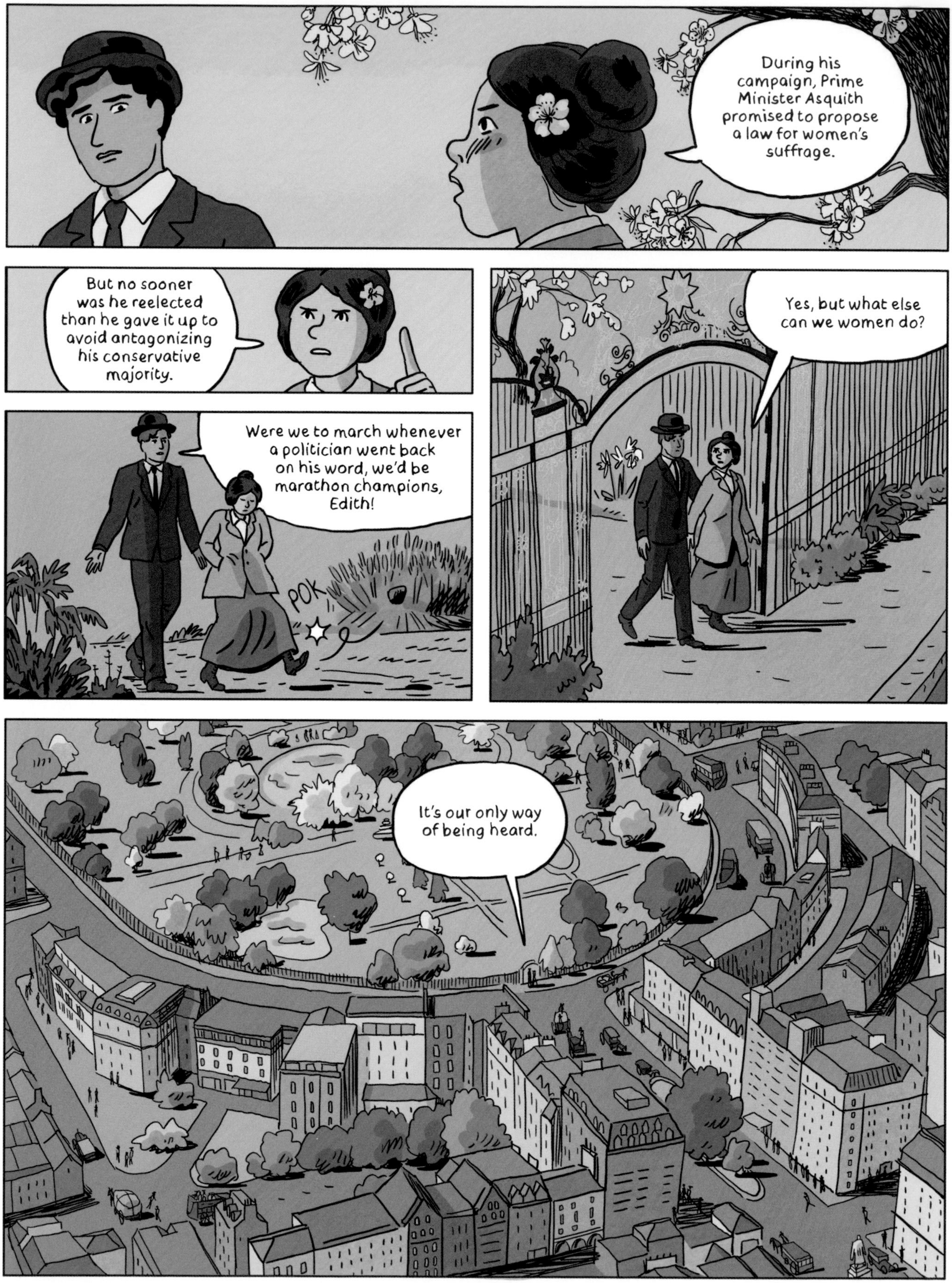
During his campaign, Prime Minister Asquith promised to propose a law for women's suffrage.
But no sooner was he reelected than he gave it up to avoid antagonizing his conservative majority.
Yes, but what else can we women do?
Were we to march whenever a politician went back on his word, we'd be marathon champions, Edith!
POK
It's our only way of being heard.

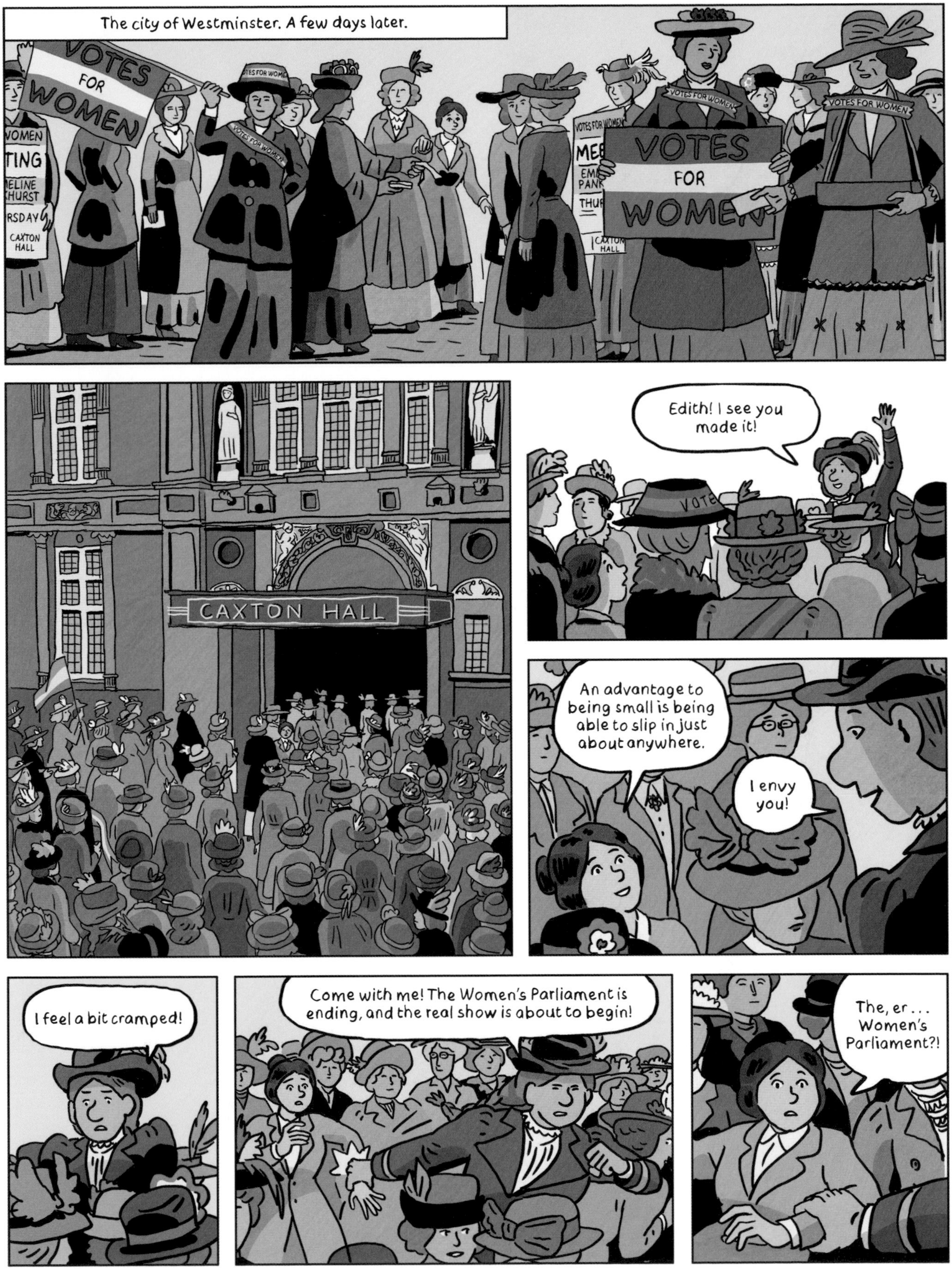
The city of Westminster. A few days later.
VOTES FOR WOMEN
VOTES FOR WOMEN
VOTES FOR WOMEN
VOTES FOR WOMEN
VOTES FOR WOMEN
CAXTON HALL
CAXTON HALL
Edith! I see you made it!
An advantage to being small is being able to slip in just about anywhere.
I envy you!
I feel a bit cramped!
Come with me! The Women's Parliament is ending, and the real show is about to begin!
The, er . . . Women's Parliament?!

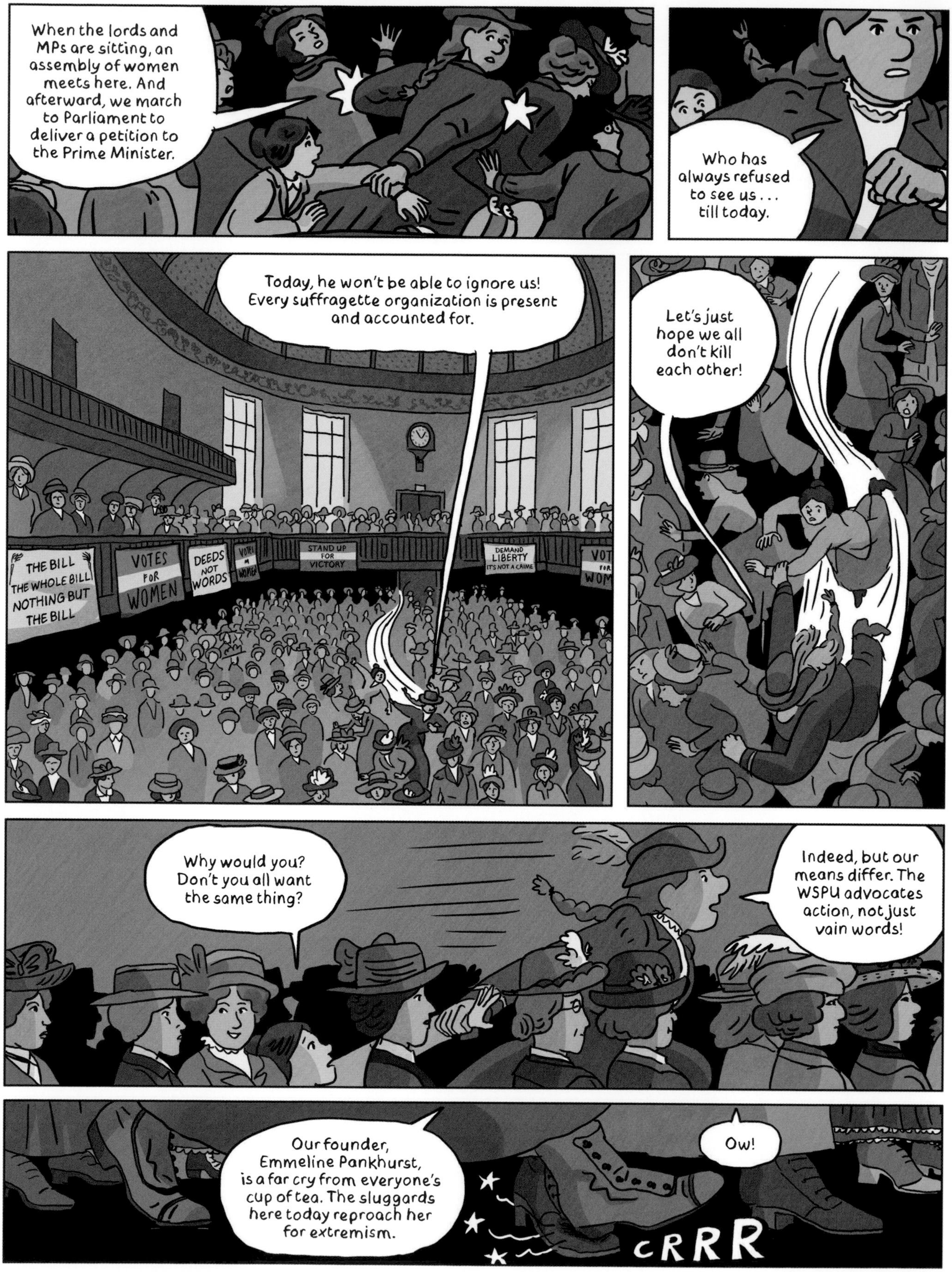
When the lords and MPs are sitting, an assembly of women meets here. And afterward, we march to Parliament to deliver a petition to the Prime Minister.
Who has always refused to see us . . . till today.
Today, he won't be able to ignore us! Every suffragette organization is present and accounted for.
THE BILL THE WHOLE BILL NOTHING BUT THE BILL
VOTES FOR WOMEN
DEEDS NOT WORDS
STAND UP FOR VICTORY
DEMAND LIBERTY IT'S NOT A CRIME
Let's just hope we all don't kill each other!
Why would you? Don't you all want the same thing?
Indeed, but our means differ. The WSPU advocates action, not just vain words!
Our founder, Emmeline Pankhurst, is a far cry from everyone's cup of tea. The sluggards here today reproach her for extremism.
Ow!
CRRR

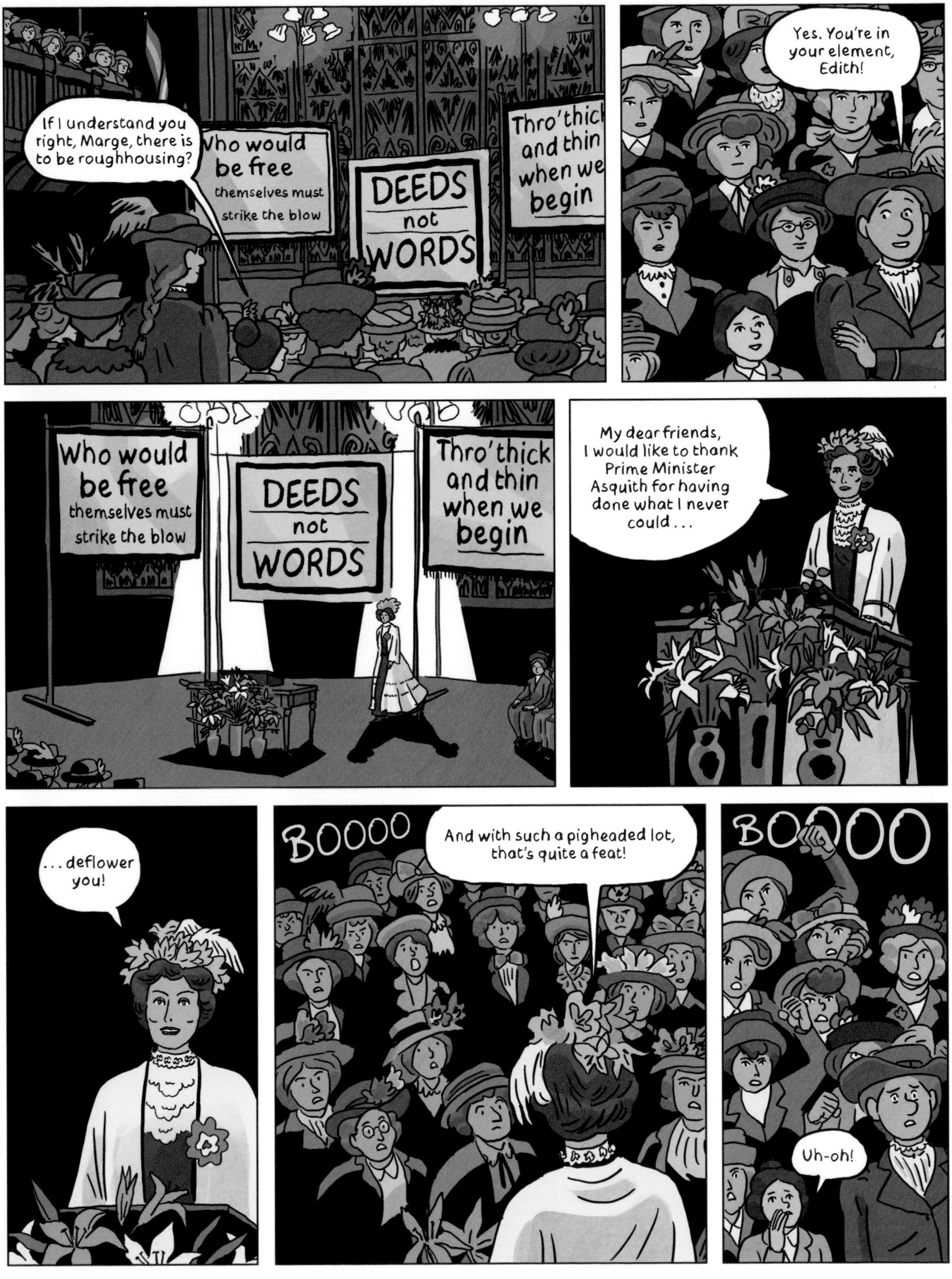
If I understand you right, Marge, there is to be roughhousing?
Who would be free themselves must strike the blow
DEEDS not WORDS
Thro' thick and thin when we begin
Yes. You're in your element, Edith!
Who would be free themselves must strike the blow
DEEDS not WORDS
Thro' thick and thin when we begin
My dear friends, I would like to thank Prime Minister Asquith for having done what I never could...
...deflower you!
BOOOO
And with such a pigheaded lot, that's quite a feat!
BOOOO
Uh-oh!

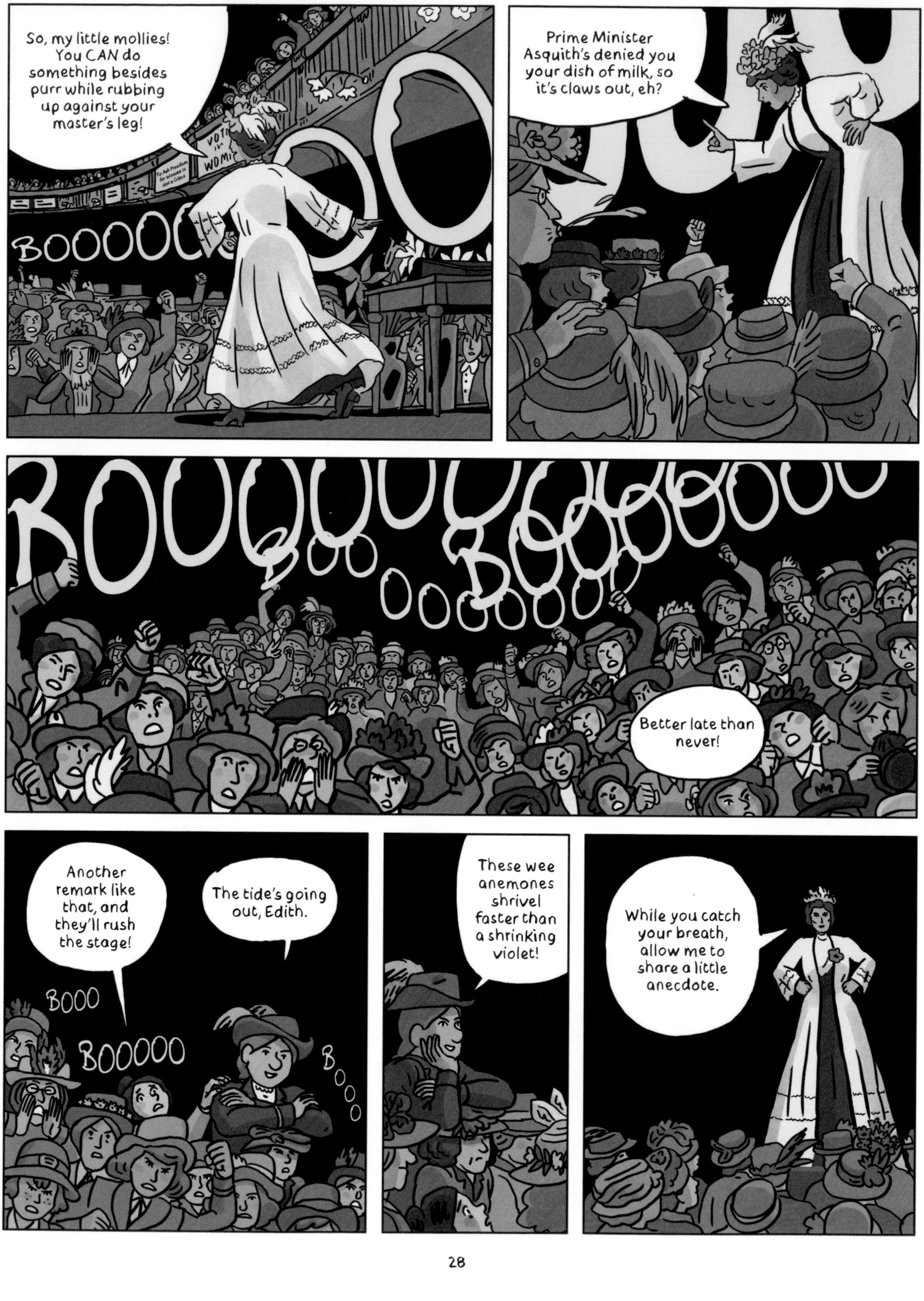
So, my little mollies! You CAN do something besides purr while rubbing up against your master's leg!
BOOOOO
Prime Minister Asquith's denied you your dish of milk, so it's claws out, eh?
BOOOOOOOOOOOOO
Better late than never!
Another remark like that, and they'll rush the stage!
The tide's going out, Edith.
BOOO
BOOOOO
BOOO
These wee anemones shrivel faster than a shrinking violet!
While you catch your breath, allow me to share a little anecdote.

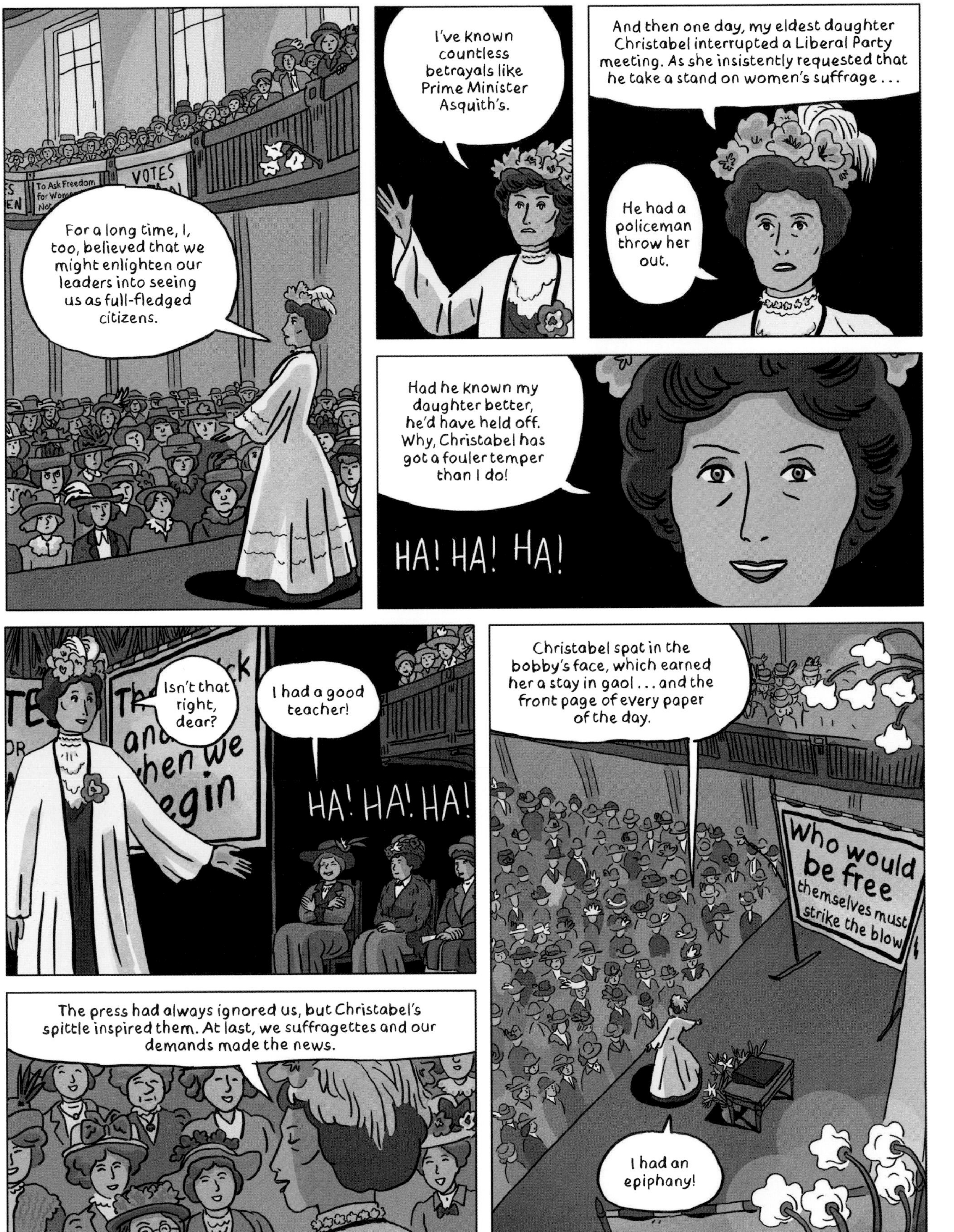
VOTES
For a long time, I, too, believed that we might enlighten our leaders into seeing us as full-fledged citizens.
I've known countless betrayals like Prime Minister Asquith's.
And then one day, my eldest daughter Christabel interrupted a Liberal Party meeting. As she insistently requested that he take a stand on women's suffrage . . .
He had a policeman throw her out.
Had he known my daughter better, he'd have held off. Why, Christabel has got a fouler temper than I do!
HA! HA! HA!
Isn't that right, dear?
I had a good teacher!
HA! HA! HA!
The press had always ignored us, but Christabel's spittle inspired them. At last, we suffragettes and our demands made the news.
Christabel spat in the bobby's face, which earned her a stay in gaol . . . and the front page of every paper of the day.
Who would be free themselves must strike the blow
I had an epiphany!

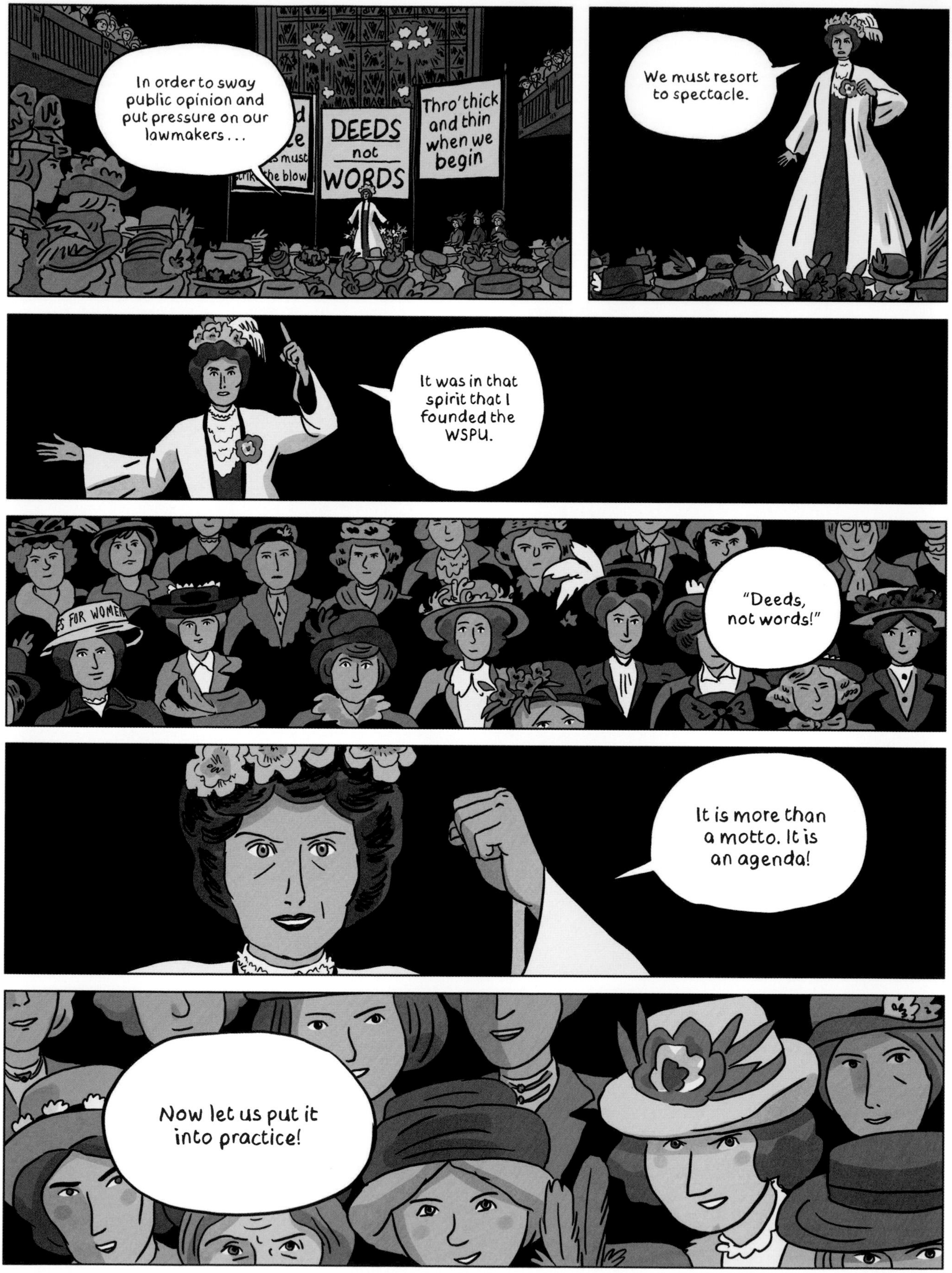
In order to sway public opinion and put pressure on our lawmakers . . .
DEEDS not WORDS
Thro' thick and thin when we begin
We must resort to spectacle.
It was in that spirit that I founded the WSPU.
"Deeds, not words!"
It is more than a motto. It is an agenda!
Now let us put it into practice!

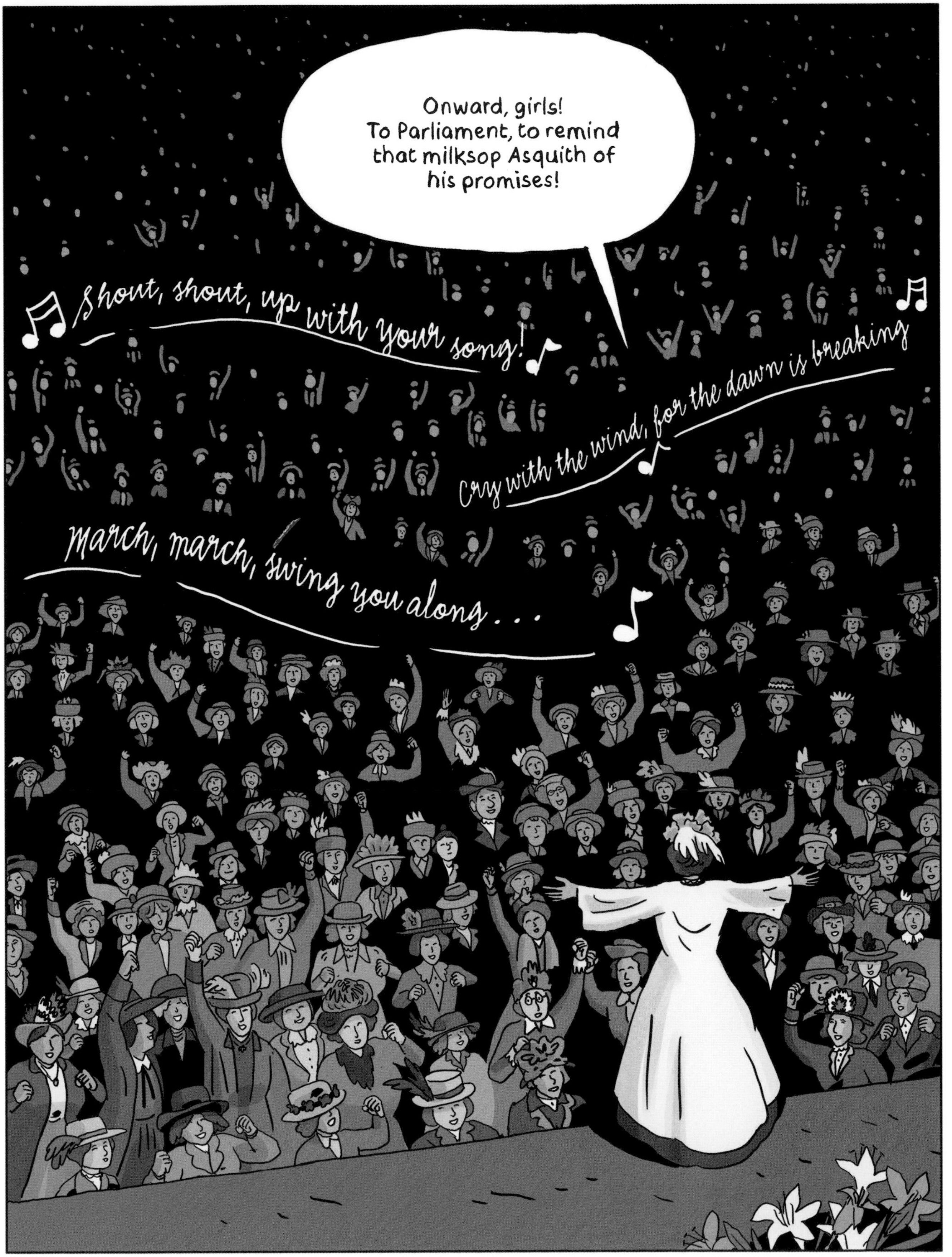
Onward, girls! To Parliament, to remind that milksop Asquith of his promises!
Shout, shout, up with your song!
Cry with the wind, for the dawn is breaking
March, march, swing you along...

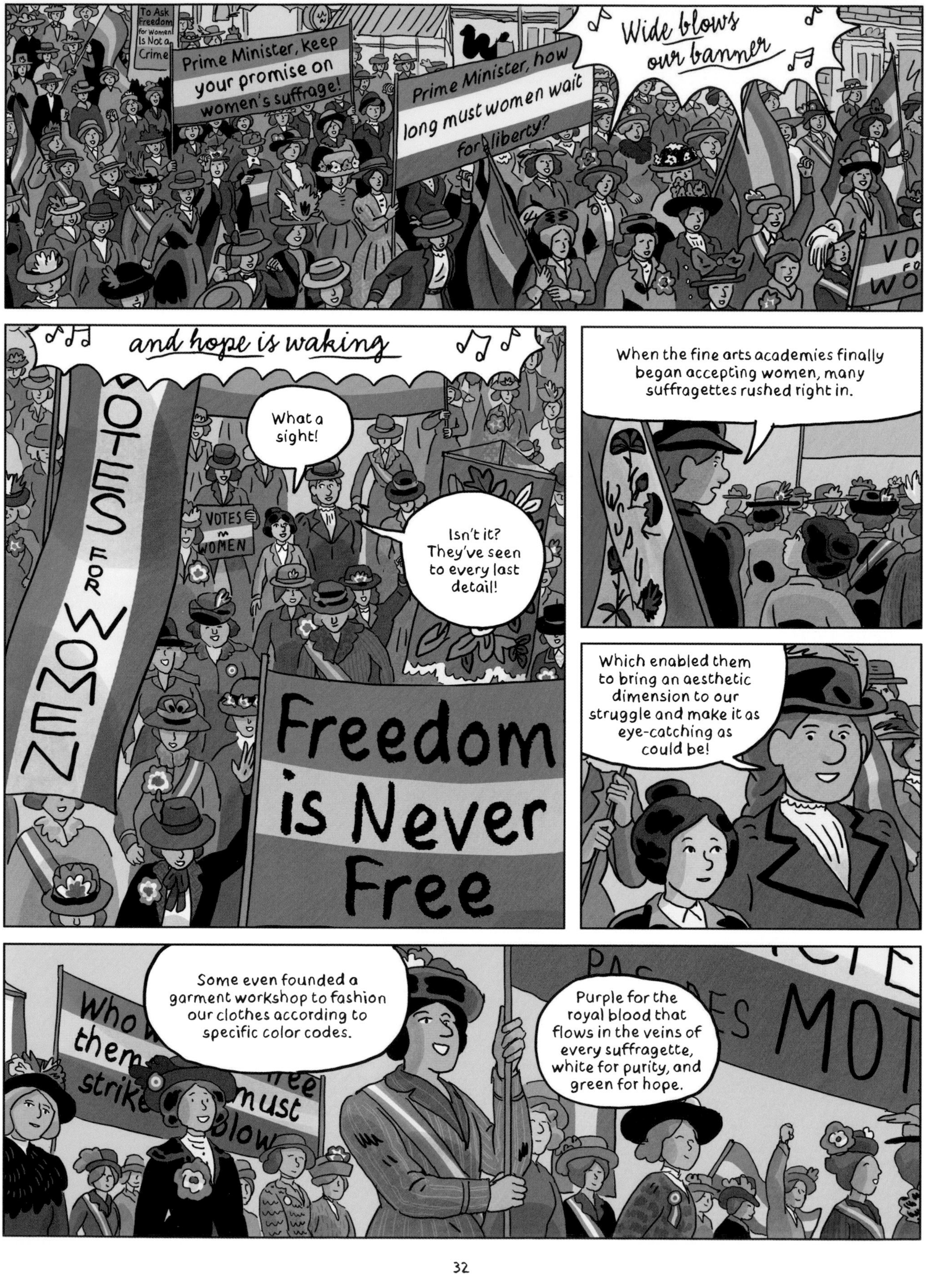

To Ask Freedom for Women Is Not a Crime
Prime Minister, keep your promise on women's suffrage!
Prime Minister, how long must women wait for liberty?
Wide blows our banner
and hope is waking
VOTES FOR WOMEN
What a sight!
VOTES for WOMEN
Isn't it? They've seen to every last detail!
Freedom is Never Free
When the fine arts academies finally began accepting women, many suffragettes rushed right in.
WSPU
Which enabled them to bring an aesthetic dimension to our struggle and make it as eye-catching as could be!
Some even founded a garment workshop to fashion our clothes according to specific color codes.
Purple for the royal blood that flows in the veins of every suffragette, white for purity, and green for hope.

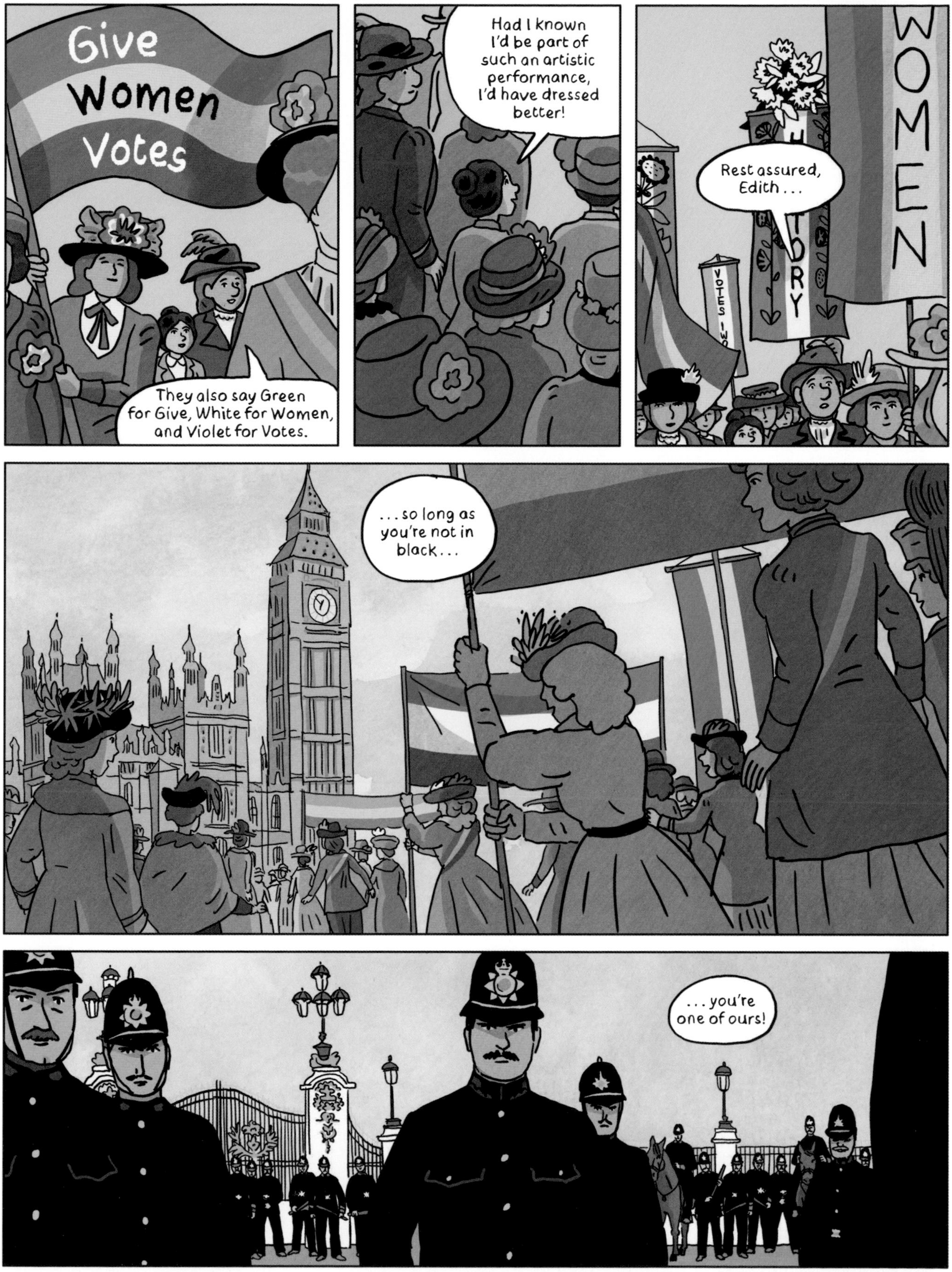
Give Women Votes
They also say Green for Give, White for Women, and Violet for Votes.
Had I known I'd be part of such an artistic performance, I'd have dressed better!
WOMEN
Rest assured, Edith . . .
. . . so long as you're not in black . . .
. . . you're one of ours!

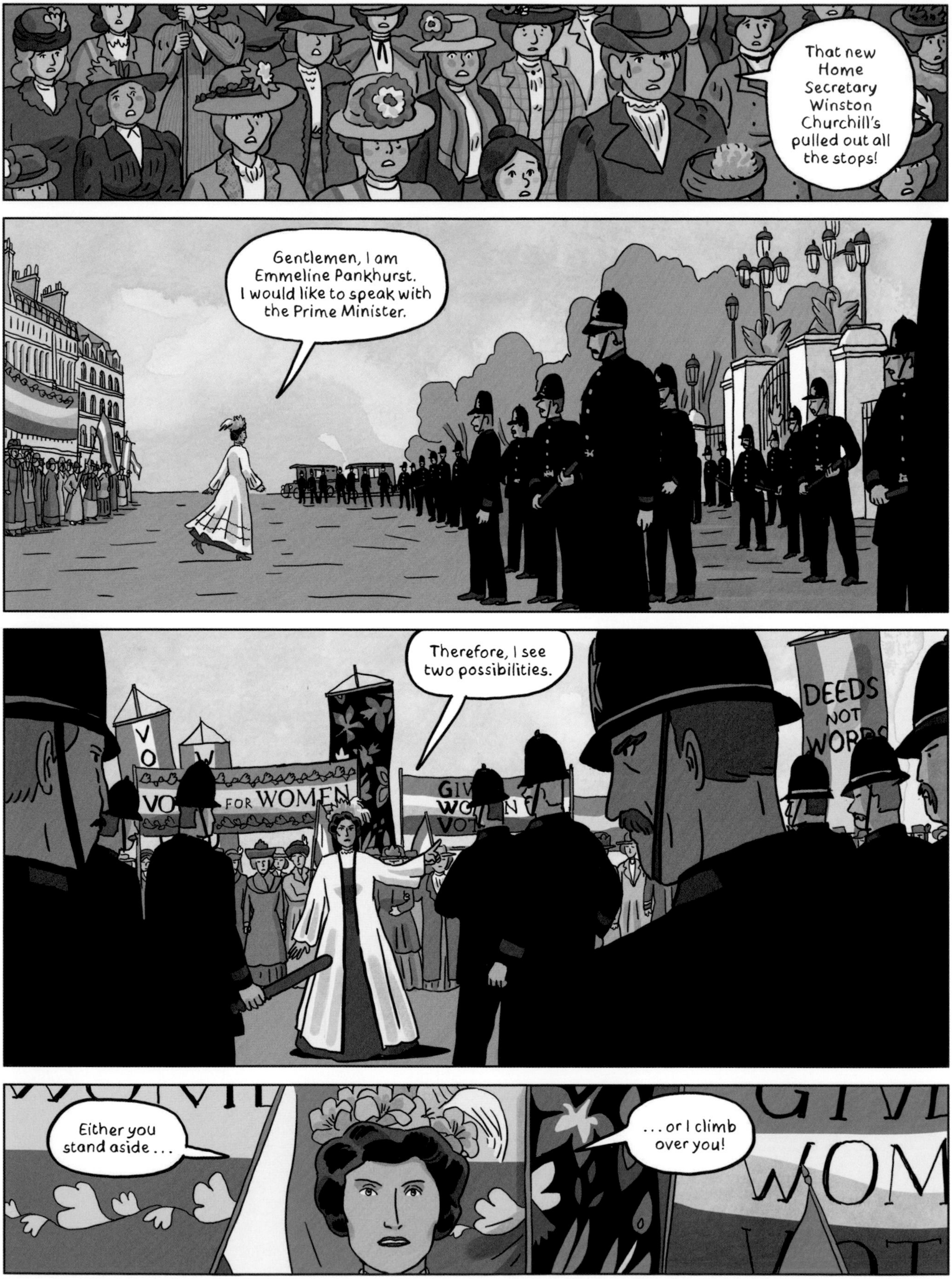
That new Home Secretary Winston Churchill's pulled out all the stops!
Gentlemen, I am Emmeline Pankhurst. I would like to speak with the Prime Minister.
Therefore, I see two possibilities.
FOR WOMEN
DEEDS NOT
Either you stand aside . . .
. . . or I climb over you!

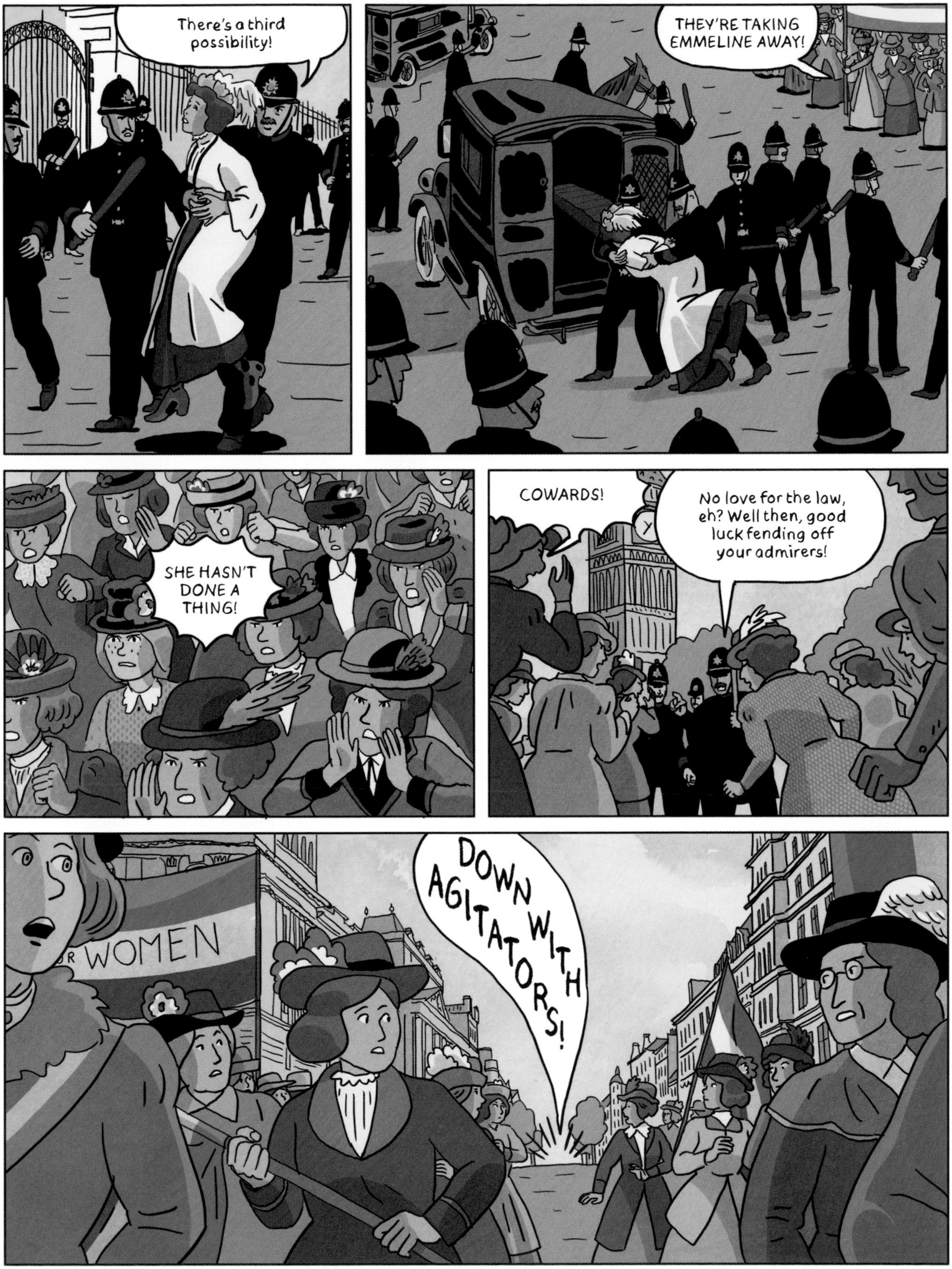
There's a third possibility!
THEY'RE TAKING EMMELINE AWAY!
SHE HASN'T DONE A THING!
COWARDS!
No love for the law, eh? Well then, good luck fending off your admirers!
WOMEN
DOWN WITH AGITATORS!

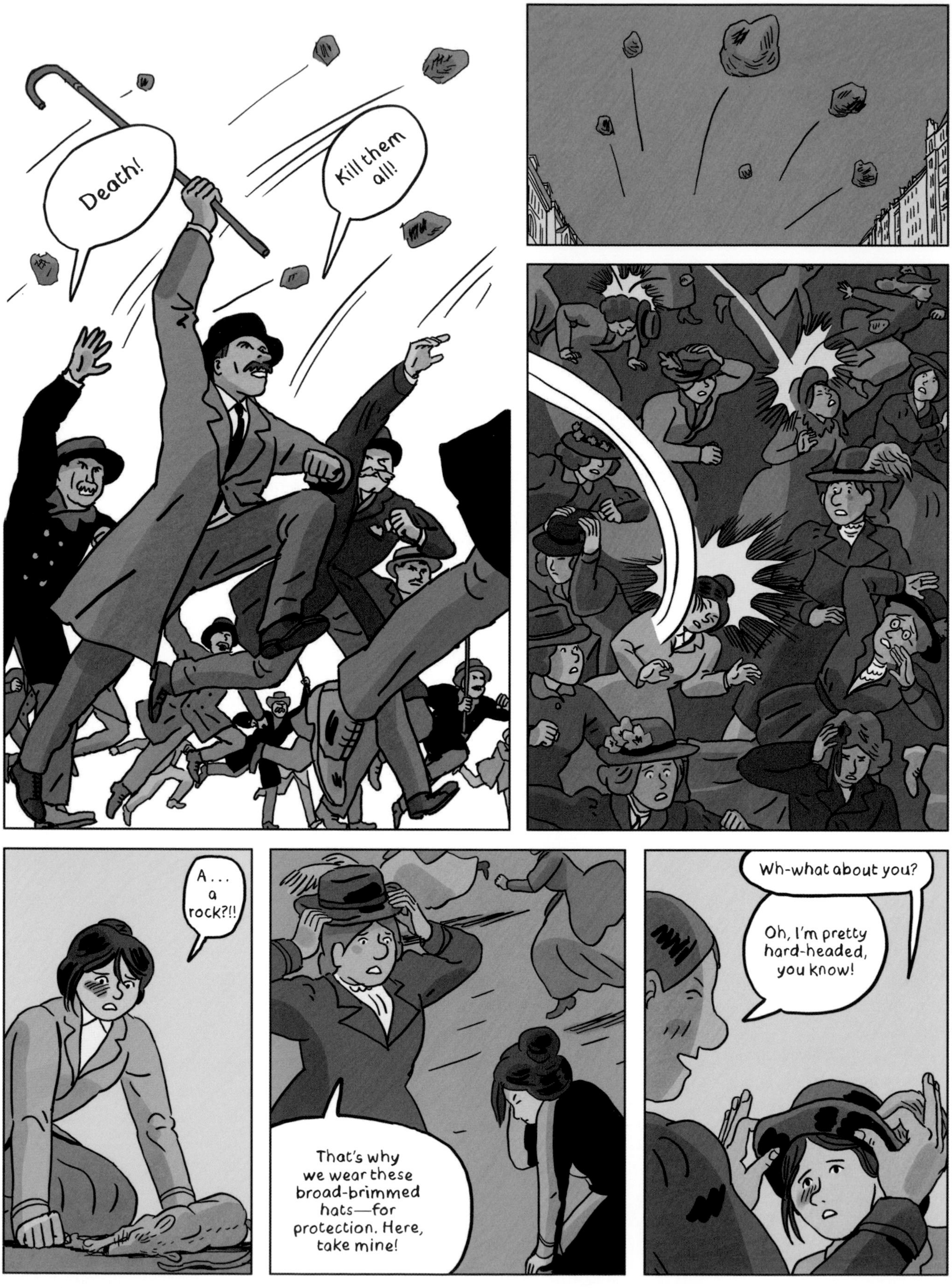
Death!
Kill them all!
A... a rock?!!
That's why we wear these broad-brimmed hats—for protection. Here, take mine!
Wh-what about you?
Oh, I'm pretty hard-headed, you know!

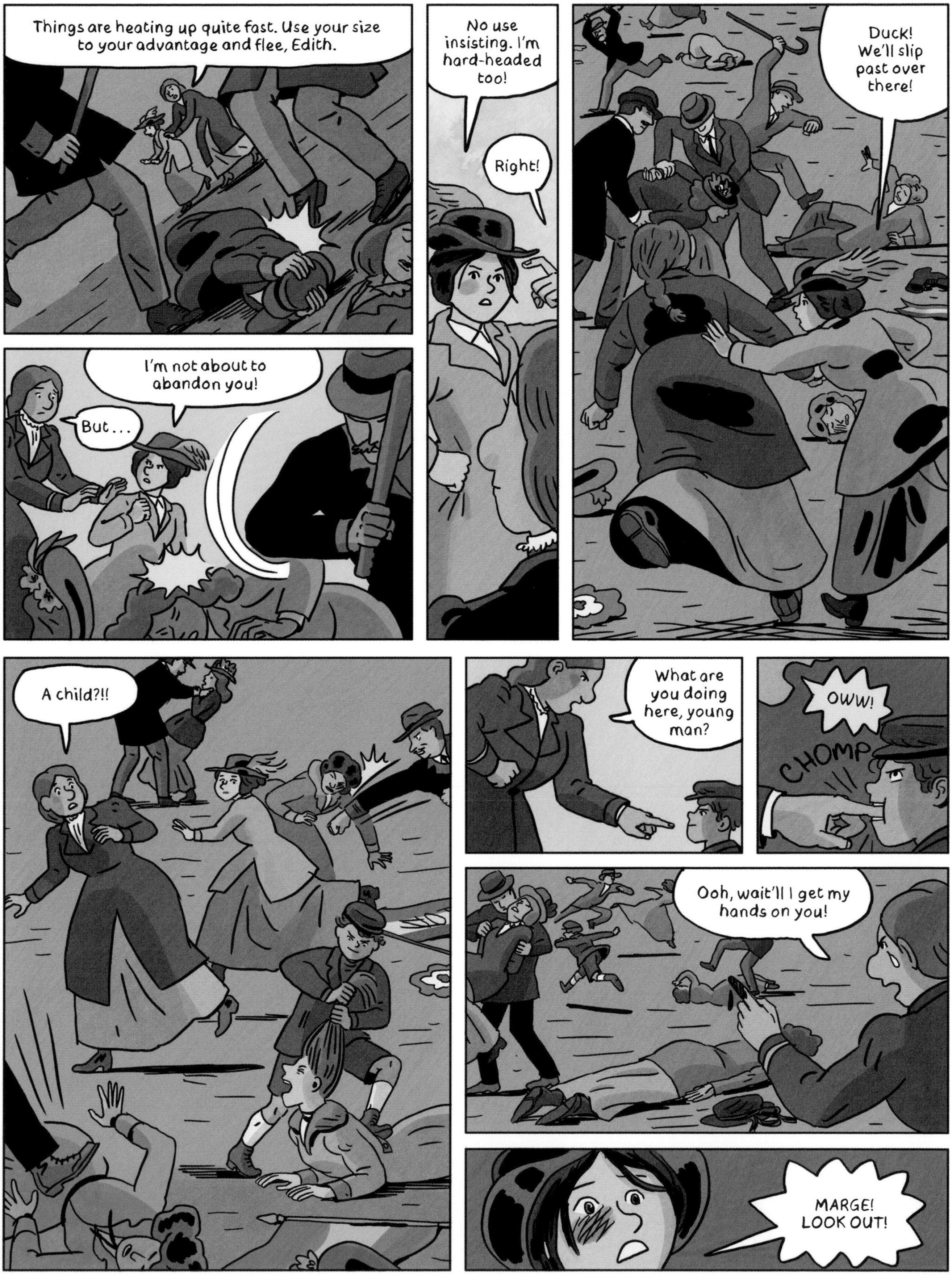
Things are heating up quite fast. Use your size to your advantage and flee, Edith.
No use insisting. I'm hard-headed too!
Right!
Duck! We'll slip past over there!
I'm not about to abandon you!
But...
A child?!!
What are you doing here, young man?
OWW!
CHOMP
Ooh, wait'll I get my hands on you!
MARGE! LOOK OUT!

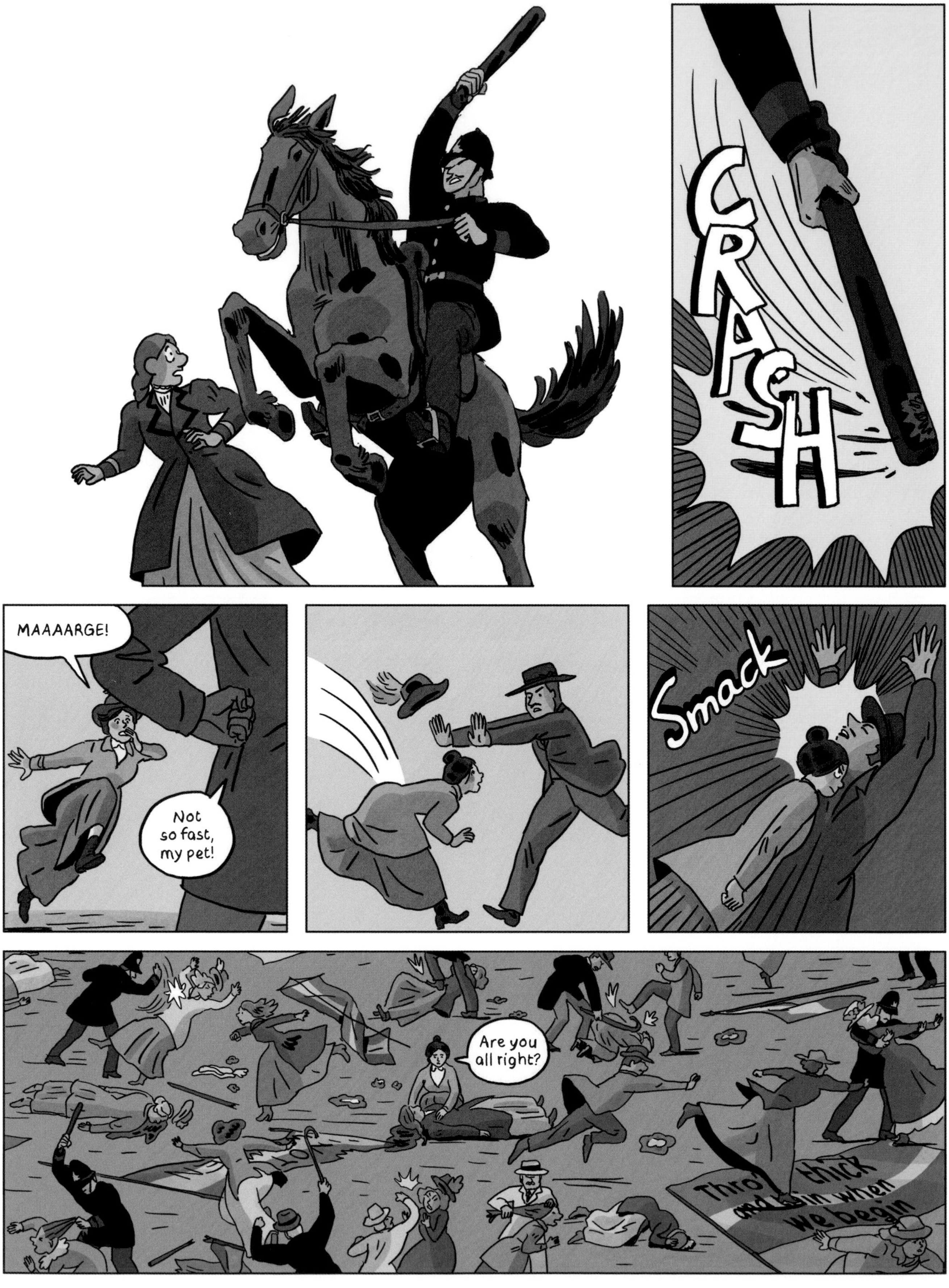
CRASH
MAAAARGE!
Not so fast, my pet!
Smack
Are you all right?
Thro' thick
we begin

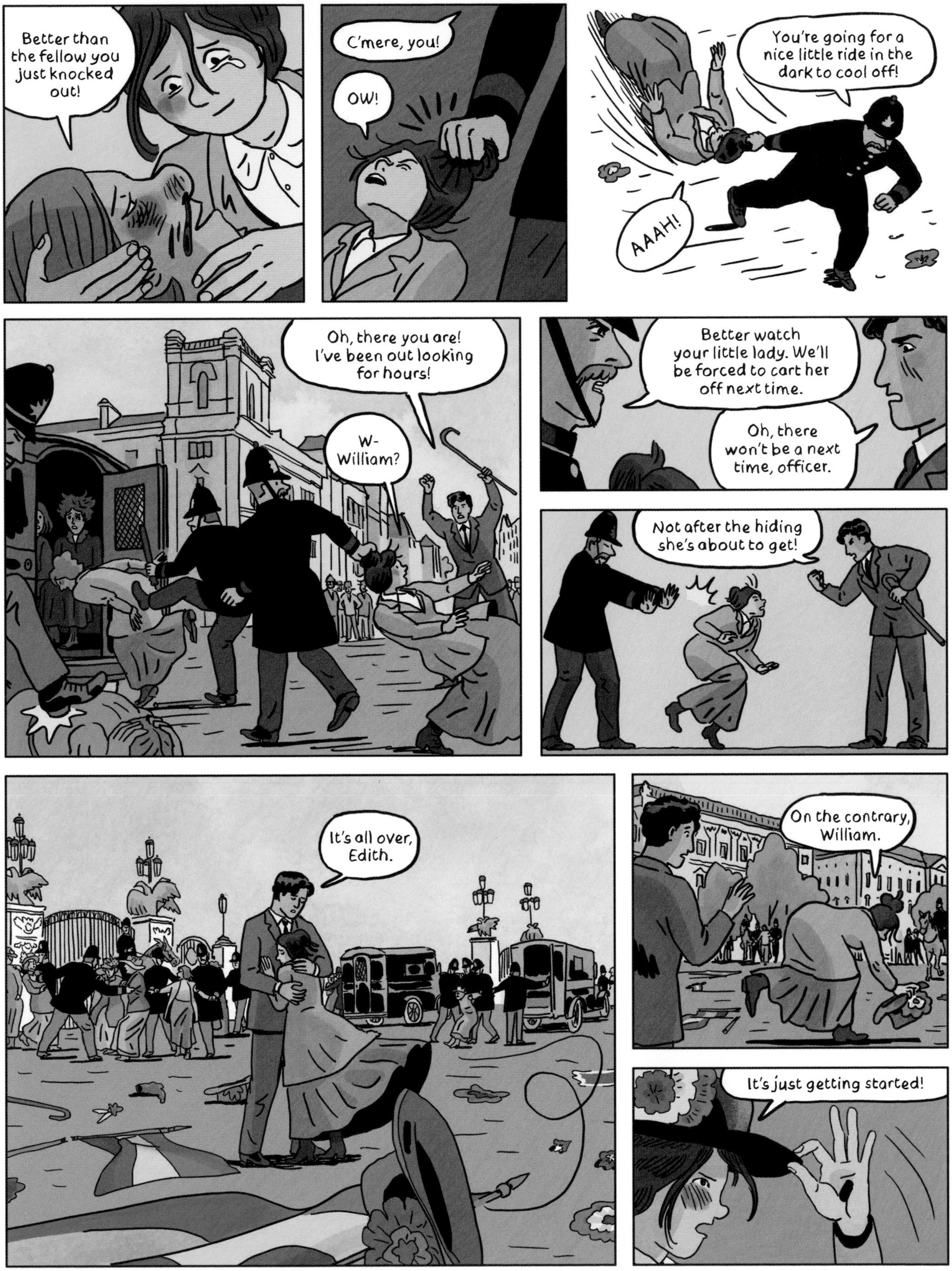
Better than the fellow you just knocked out!
C'mere, you!
OW!
You're going for a nice little ride in the dark to cool off!
AAAH!
Oh, there you are! I've been out looking for hours!
W- William?
Better watch your little lady. We'll be forced to cart her off next time.
Oh, there won't be a next time, officer.
Not after the hiding she's about to get!
It's all over, Edith.
On the contrary, William.
It's just getting started!

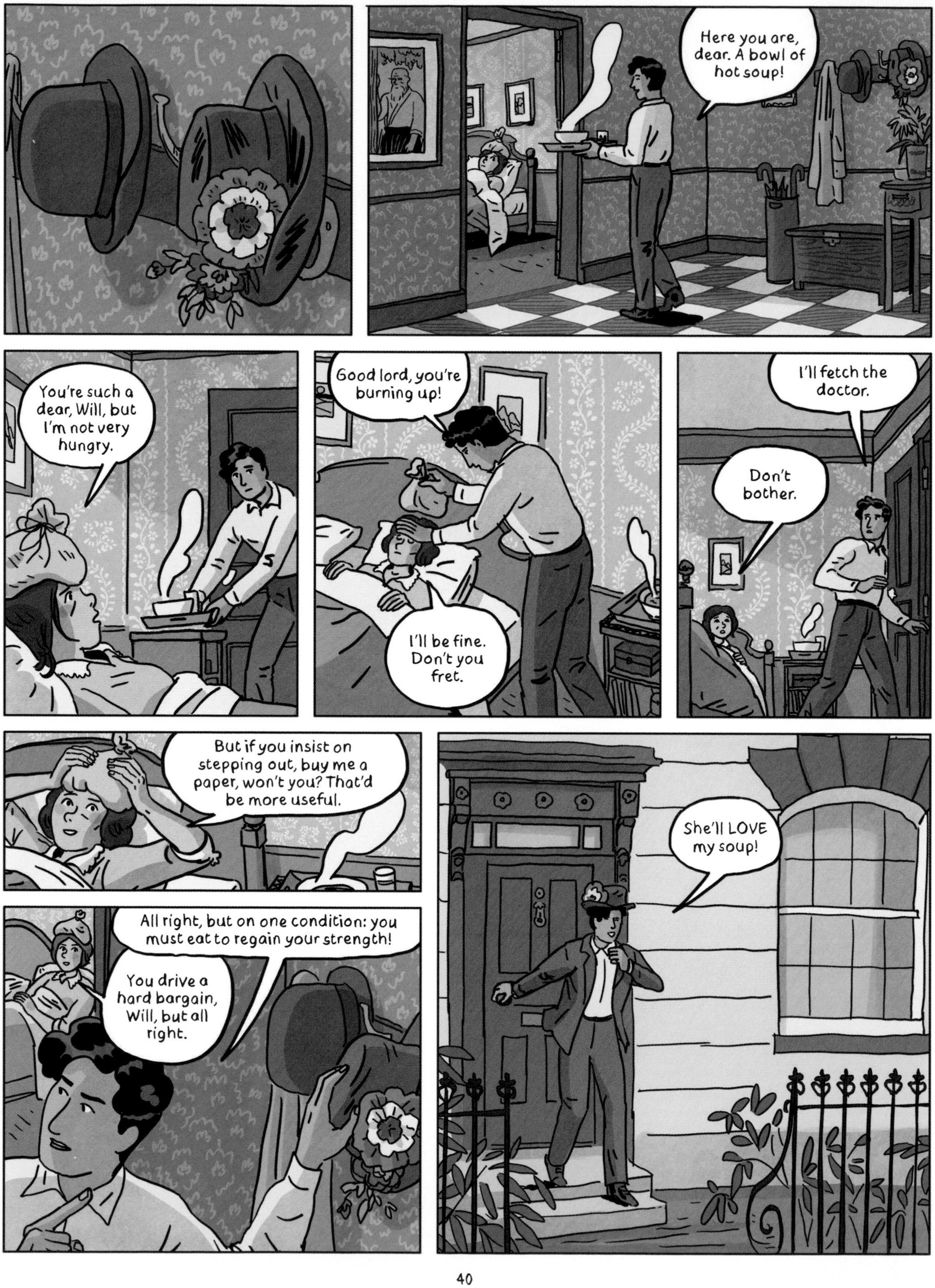
Here you are, dear. A bowl of hot soup!
You're such a dear, Will, but I'm not very hungry.
Good lord, you're burning up!
I'll be fine. Don't you fret.
I'll fetch the doctor.
Don't bother.
But if you insist on stepping out, buy me a paper, won't you? That'd be more useful.
All right, but on one condition: you must eat to regain your strength!
You drive a hard bargain, Will, but all right.
She'll LOVE my soup!

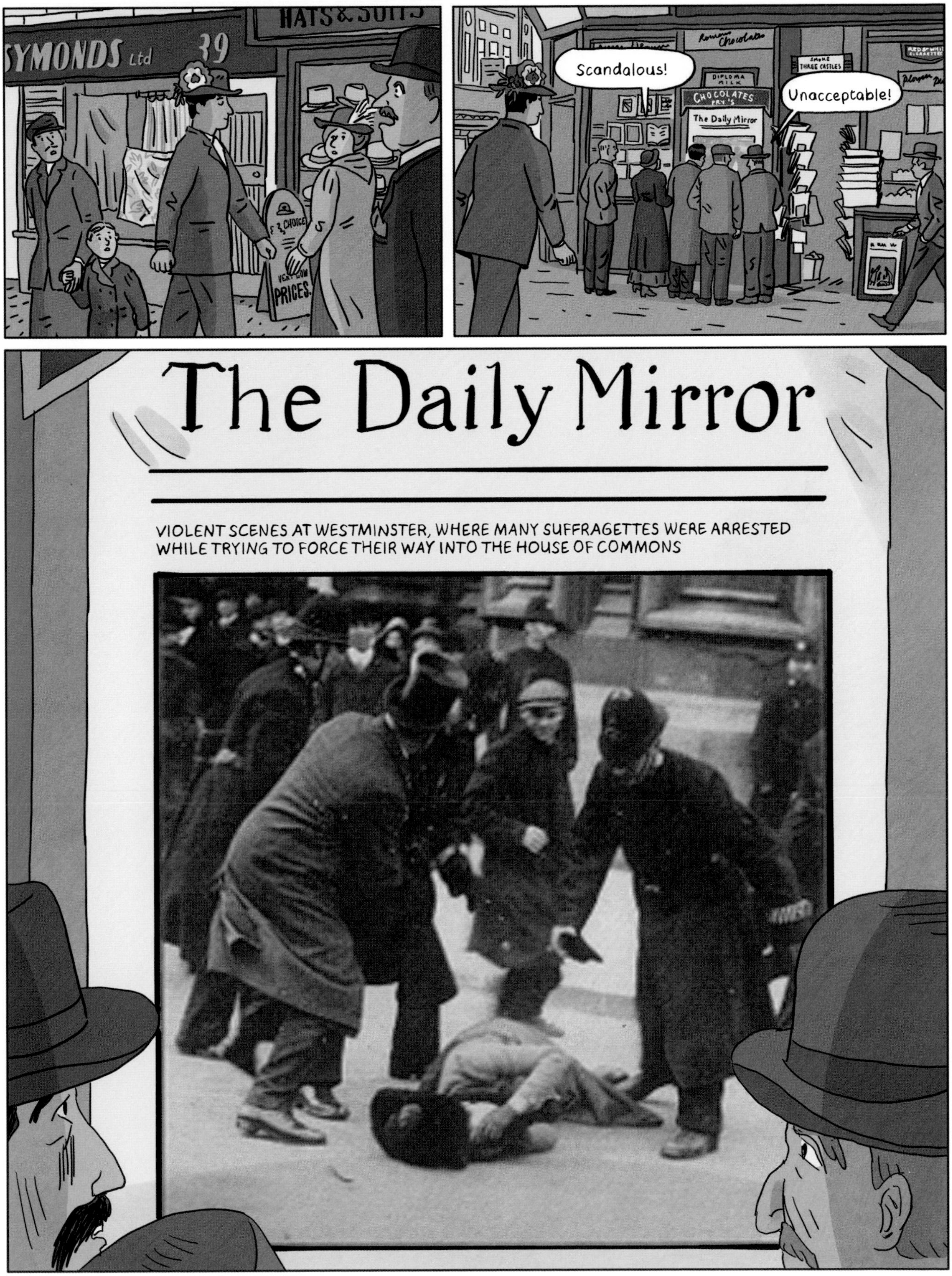
SYMONDS Ltd
39
PRICES.
Scandalous!
Unacceptable!
DIPLOMA MILK
CHOCOLATES FRY'S
The Daily Mirror
SMOKE THREE CASTLES
The Daily Mirror
VIOLENT SCENES AT WESTMINSTER, WHERE MANY SUFFRAGETTES WERE ARRESTED WHILE TRYING TO FORCE THEIR WAY INTO THE HOUSE OF COMMONS

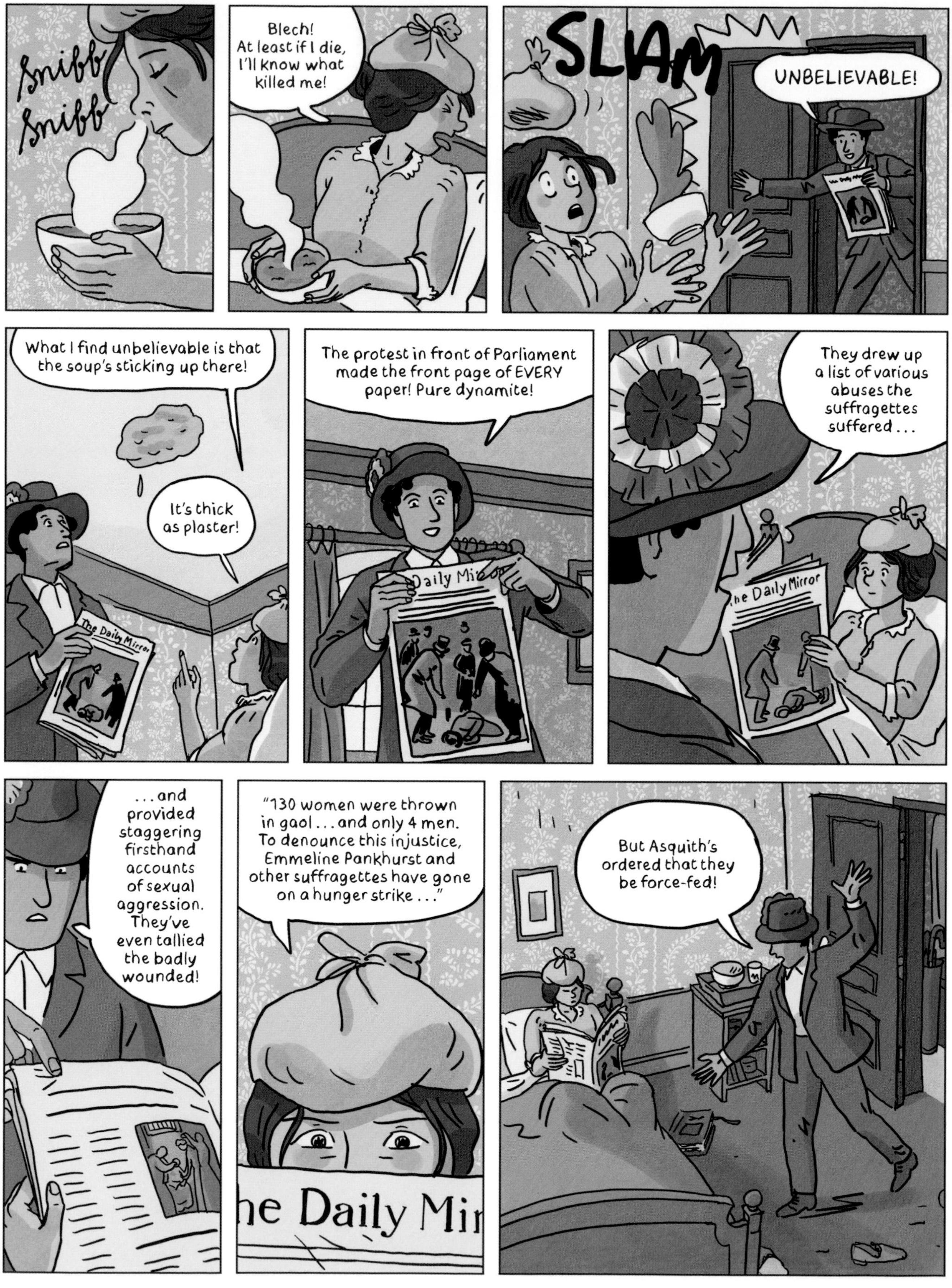
Snibb Snibb
Blech! At least if I die, I'll know what killed me!
SLAM
UNBELIEVABLE!
What I find unbelievable is that the soup's sticking up there!
It's thick as plaster!
The Daily Mirror
The protest in front of Parliament made the front page of EVERY paper! Pure dynamite!
They drew up a list of various abuses the suffragettes suffered . . .
. . . and provided staggering firsthand accounts of sexual aggression. They've even tallied the badly wounded!
"130 women were thrown in gaol . . . and only 4 men. To denounce this injustice, Emmeline Pankhurst and other suffragettes have gone on a hunger strike . . ."
he Daily Mir
But Asquith's ordered that they be force-fed!

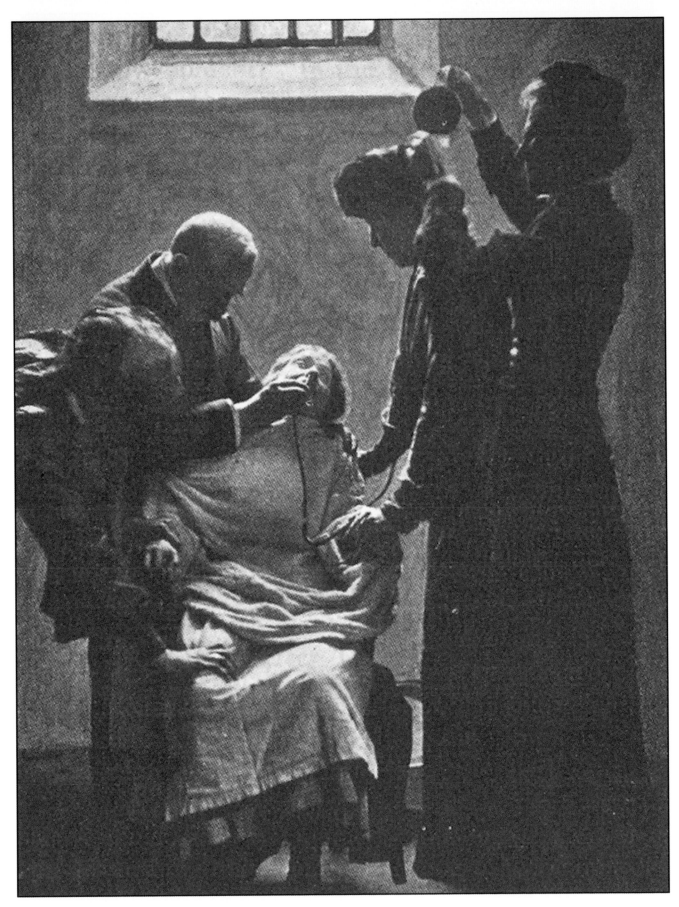

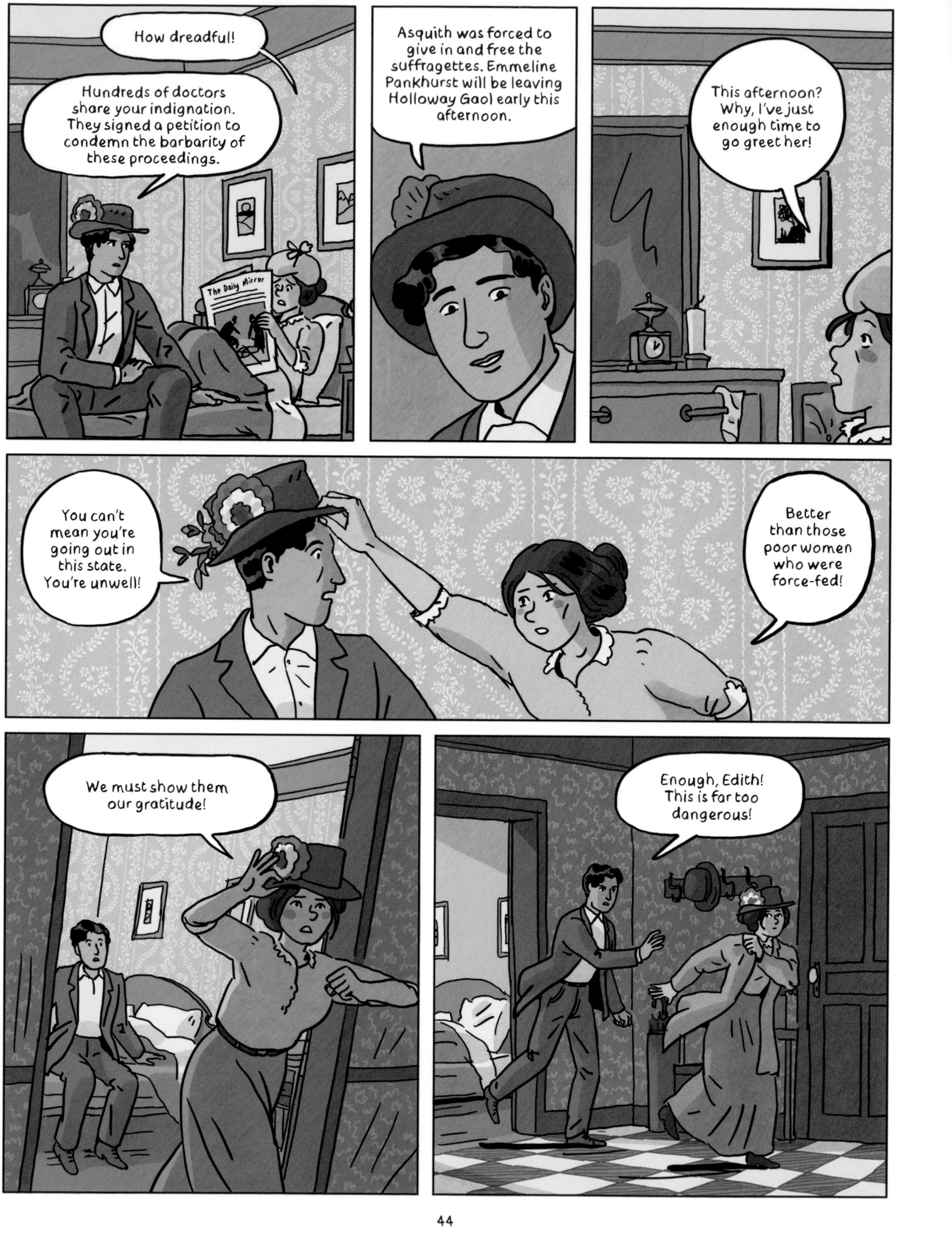
How dreadful!
Hundreds of doctors share your indignation. They signed a petition to condemn the barbarity of these proceedings.
The Daily Mirror
Asquith was forced to give in and free the suffragettes. Emmeline Pankhurst will be leaving Holloway Gaol early this afternoon.
This afternoon? Why, I've just enough time to go greet her!
You can't mean you're going out in this state. You're unwell!
Better than those poor women who were force-fed!
We must show them our gratitude!
Enough, Edith! This is far too dangerous!

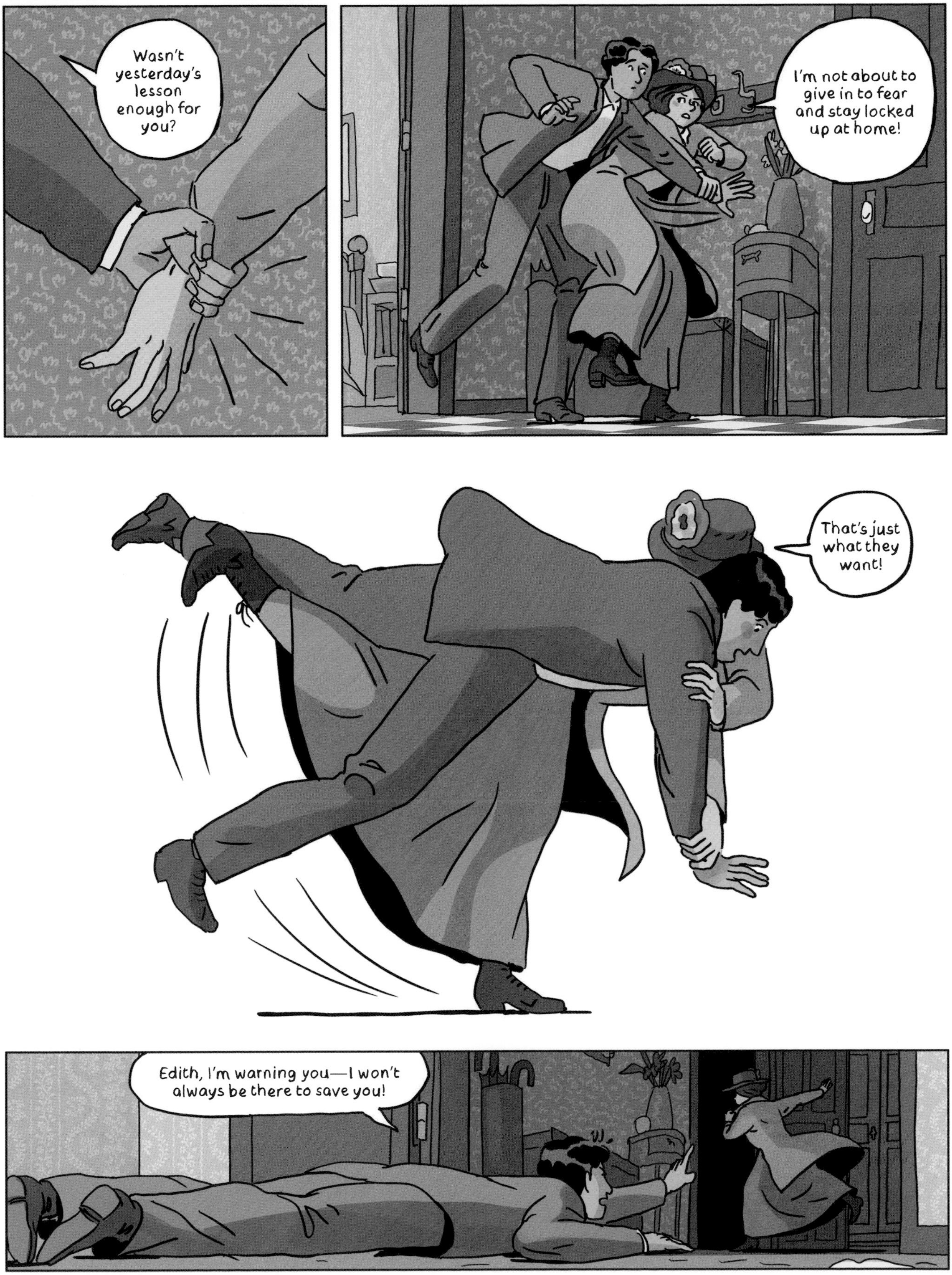
Wasn't yesterday's lesson enough for you?
I'm not about to give in to fear and stay locked up at home!
That's just what they want!
Edith, I'm warning you—I won't always be there to save you!

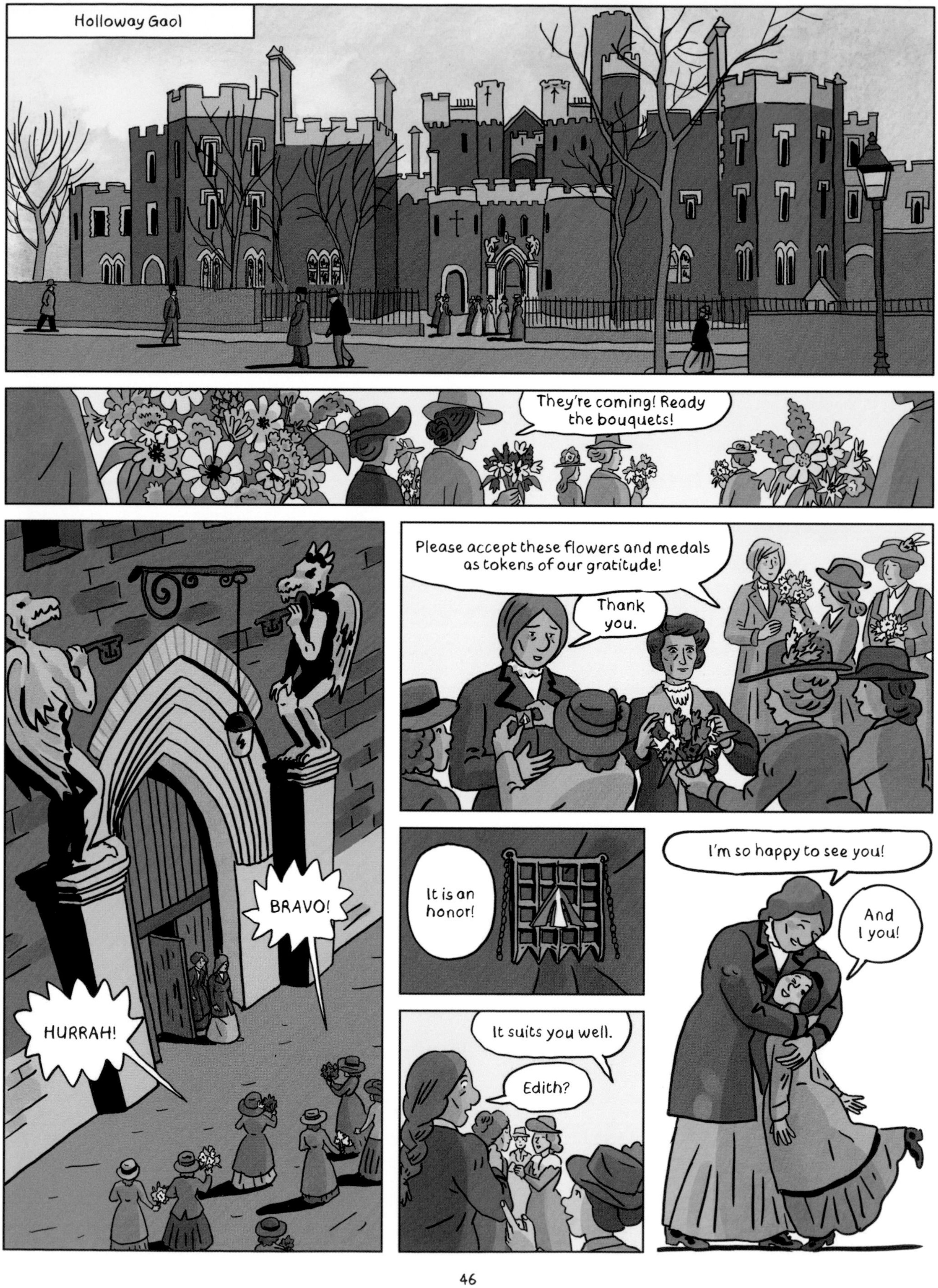
Holloway Gaol
They're coming! Ready the bouquets!
HURRAH!
BRAVO!
Please accept these flowers and medals as tokens of our gratitude!
Thank you.
It is an honor!
It suits you well.
Edith?
I'm so happy to see you!
And I you!

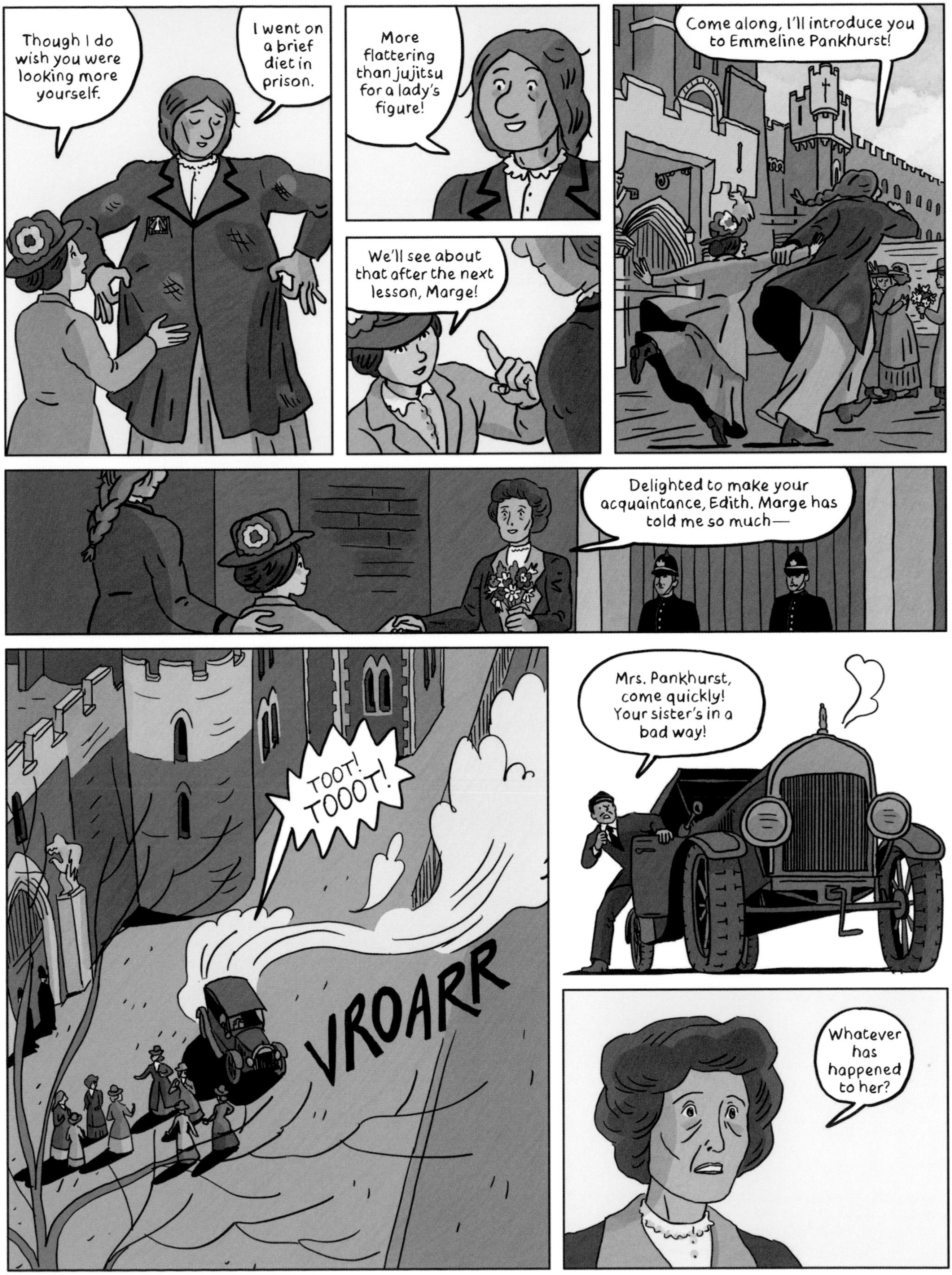
Though I do wish you were looking more yourself.
I went on a brief diet in prison.
More flattering than jujitsu for a lady's figure!
We'll see about that after the next lesson, Marge!
Come along, I'll introduce you to Emmeline Pankhurst!
Delighted to make your acquaintance, Edith. Marge has told me so much—
TOOT! TOOOT!
VROARR
Mrs. Pankhurst, come quickly! Your sister's in a bad way!
Whatever has happened to her?

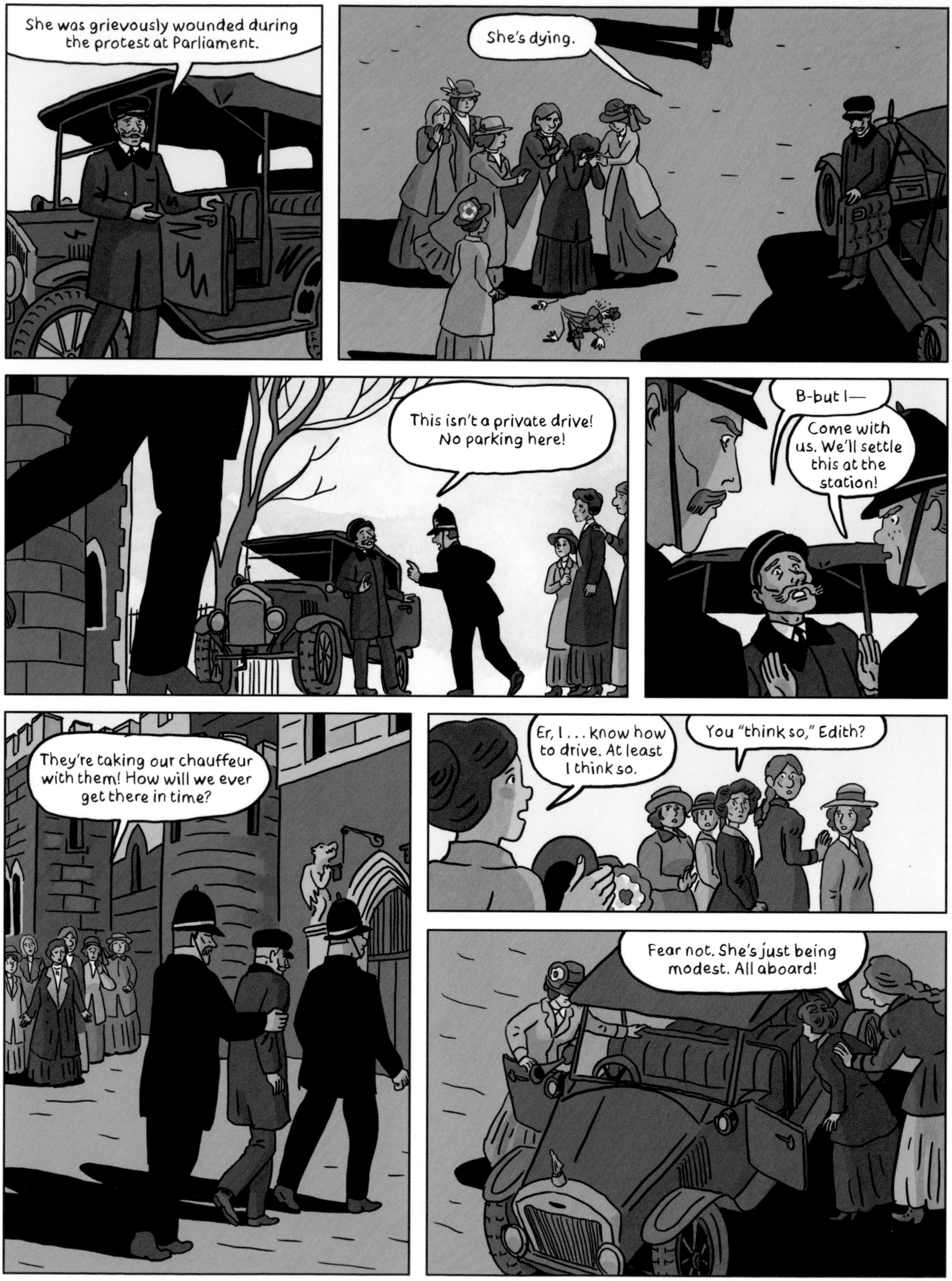
She was grievously wounded during the protest at Parliament.
She's dying.
This isn't a private drive! No parking here!
B-but I—
Come with us. We'll settle this at the station!
They're taking our chauffeur with them! How will we ever get there in time?
Er, I . . . know how to drive. At least I think so.
You "think so," Edith?
Fear not. She's just being modest. All aboard!

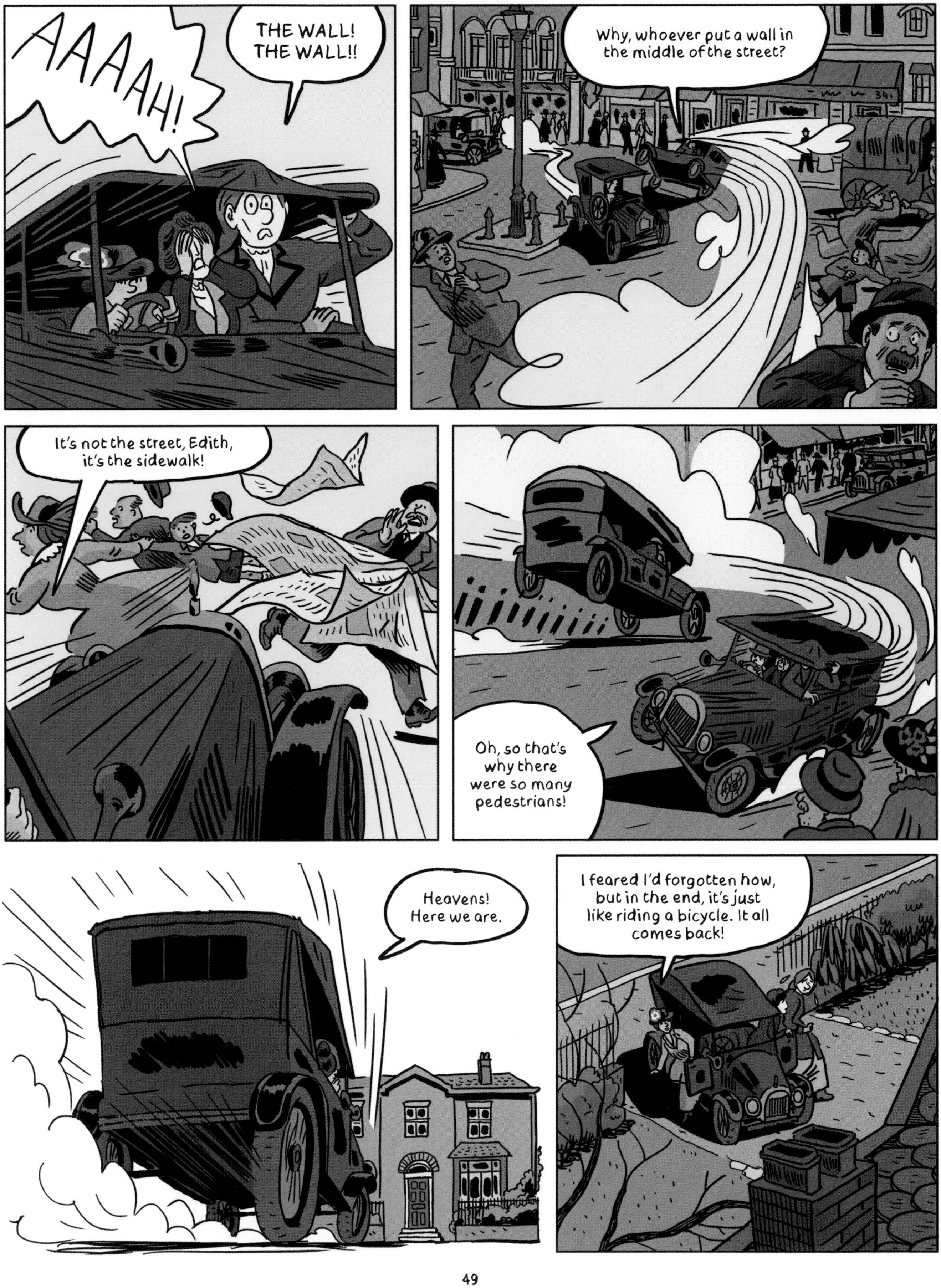
AAAAAH!
THE WALL! THE WALL!!
Why, whoever put a wall in the middle of the street?
It's not the street, Edith, it's the sidewalk!
Oh, so that's why there were so many pedestrians!
Heavens! Here we are.
I feared I'd forgotten how, but in the end, it's just like riding a bicycle. It all comes back!

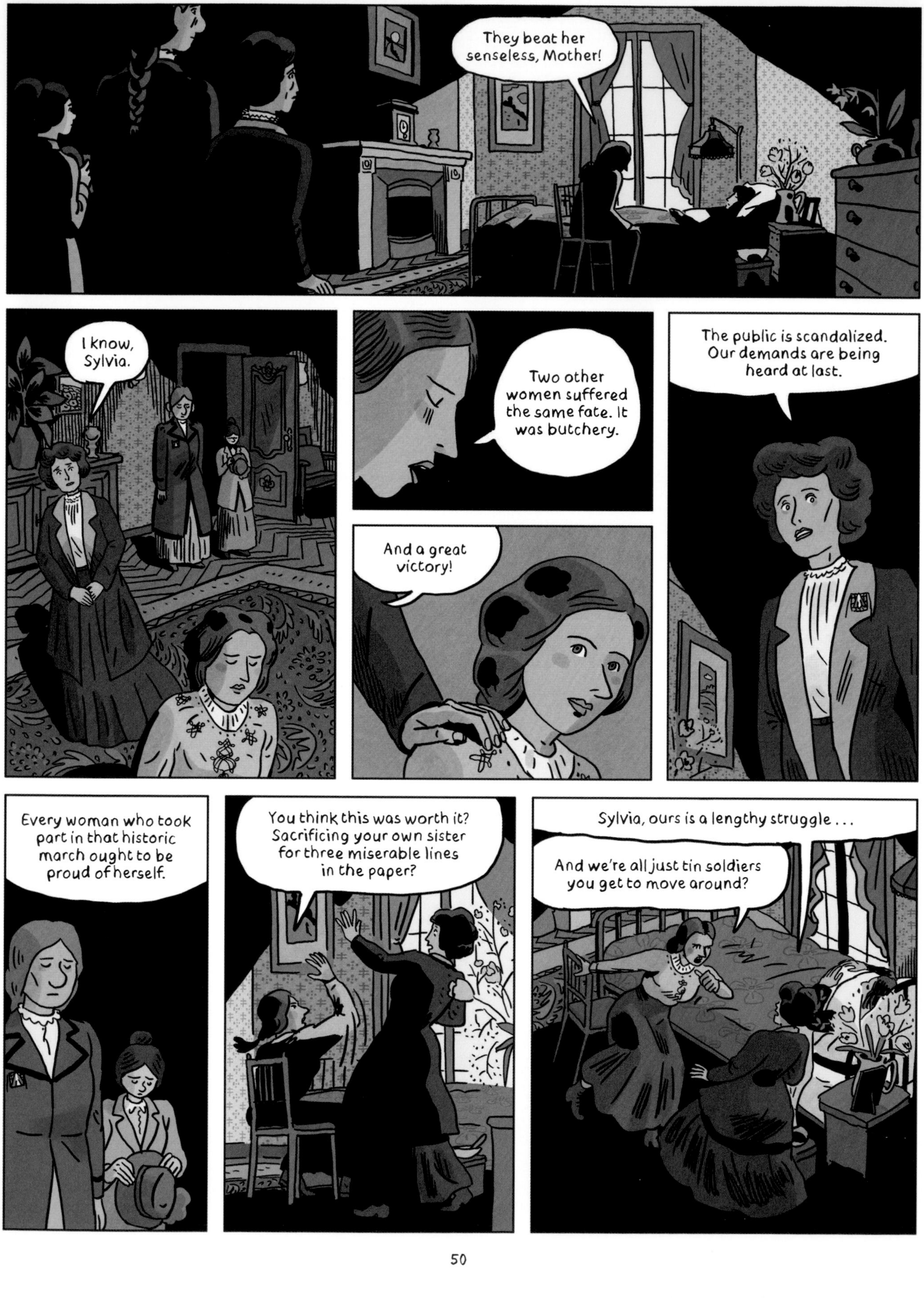
They beat her senseless, Mother!
I know, Sylvia.
Two other women suffered the same fate. It was butchery.
And a great victory!
The public is scandalized. Our demands are being heard at last.
Every woman who took part in that historic march ought to be proud of herself.
You think this was worth it? Sacrificing your own sister for three miserable lines in the paper?
Sylvia, ours is a lengthy struggle . . .
And we're all just tin soldiers you get to move around?

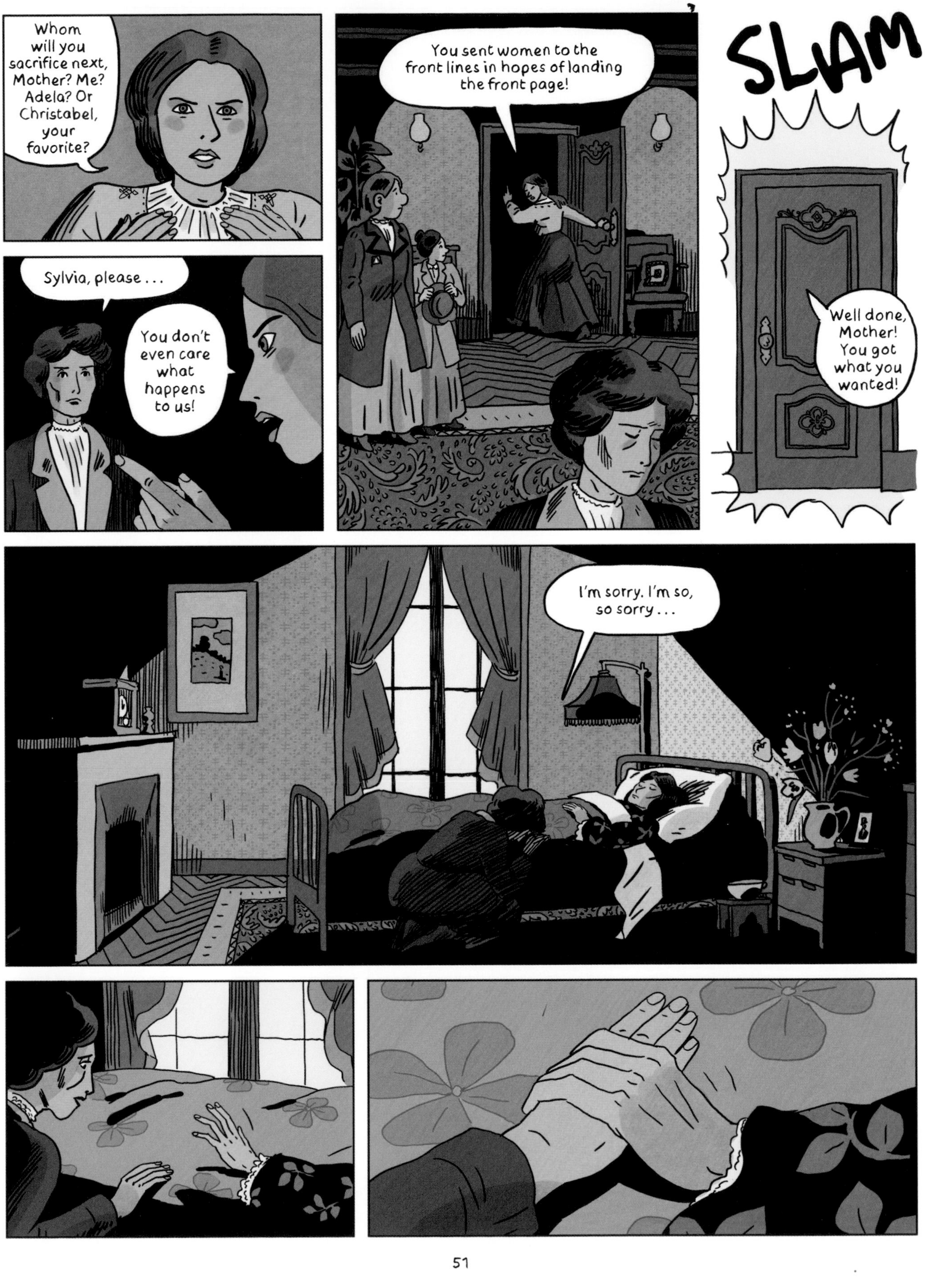
Whom will you sacrifice next, Mother? Me? Adela? Or Christabel, your favorite?
Sylvia, please . . .
You don't even care what happens to us!
You sent women to the front lines in hopes of landing the front page!
SLAM
Well done, Mother! You got what you wanted!
I'm sorry. I'm so, so sorry . . .

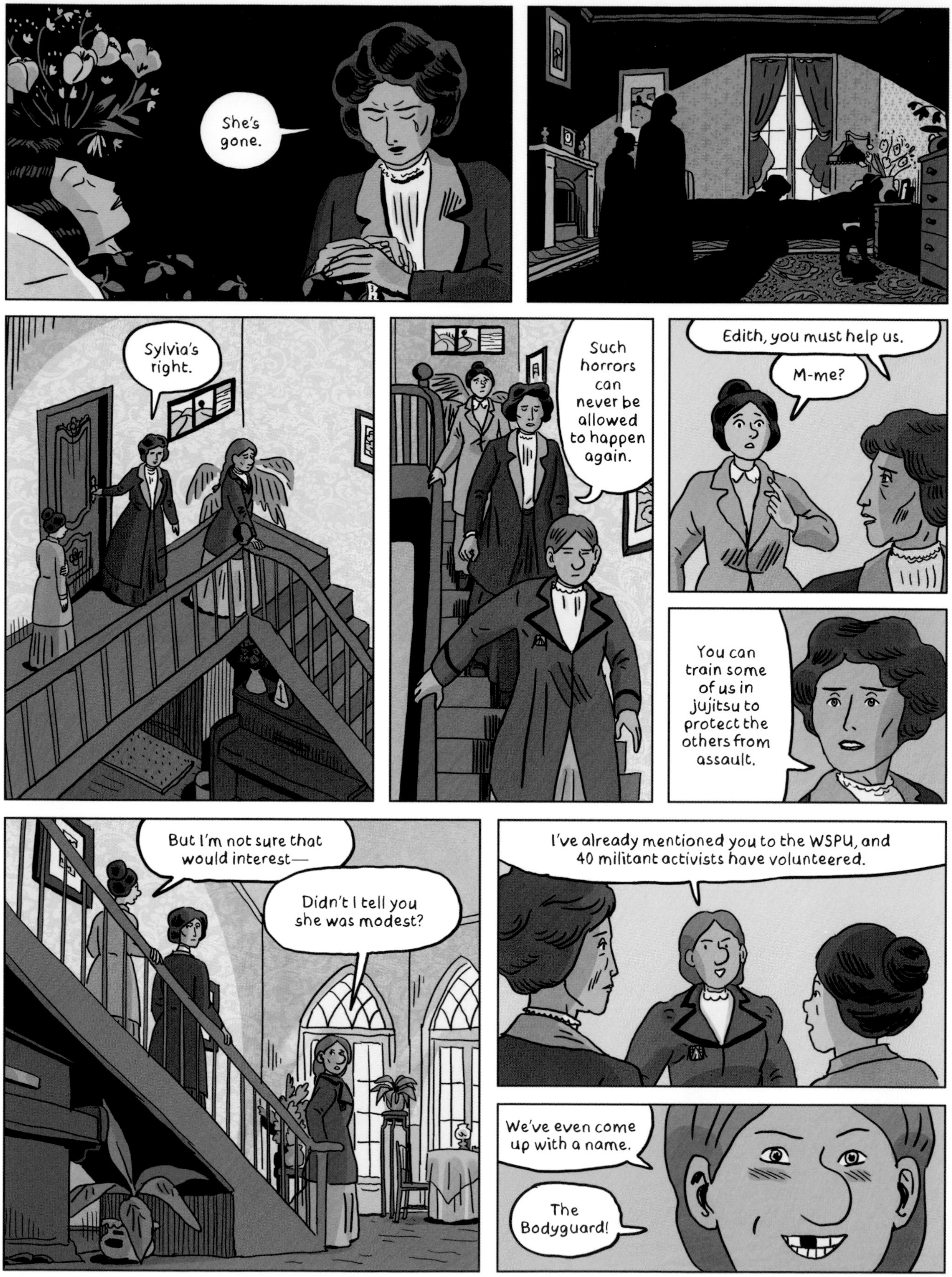
She's gone.
Sylvia's right.
Such horrors can never be allowed to happen again.
Edith, you must help us.
M-me?
You can train some of us in jujitsu to protect the others from assault.
But I'm not sure that would interest—
Didn't I tell you she was modest?
I've already mentioned you to the WSPU, and 40 militant activists have volunteered.
We've even come up with a name.
The Bodyguard!

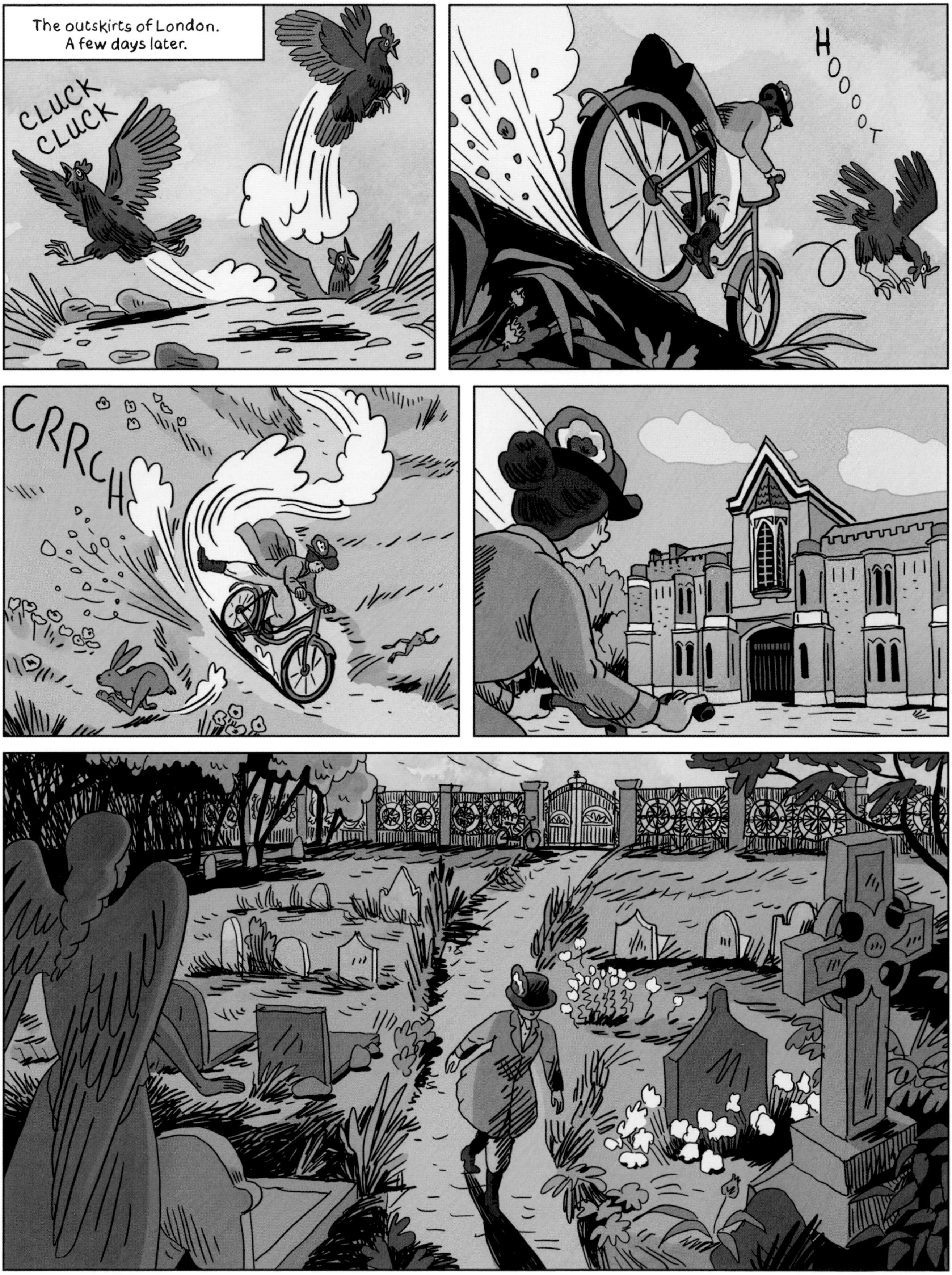
The outskirts of London.
A few days later.
CLUCK CLUCK
HOOOOOT
CRRCH

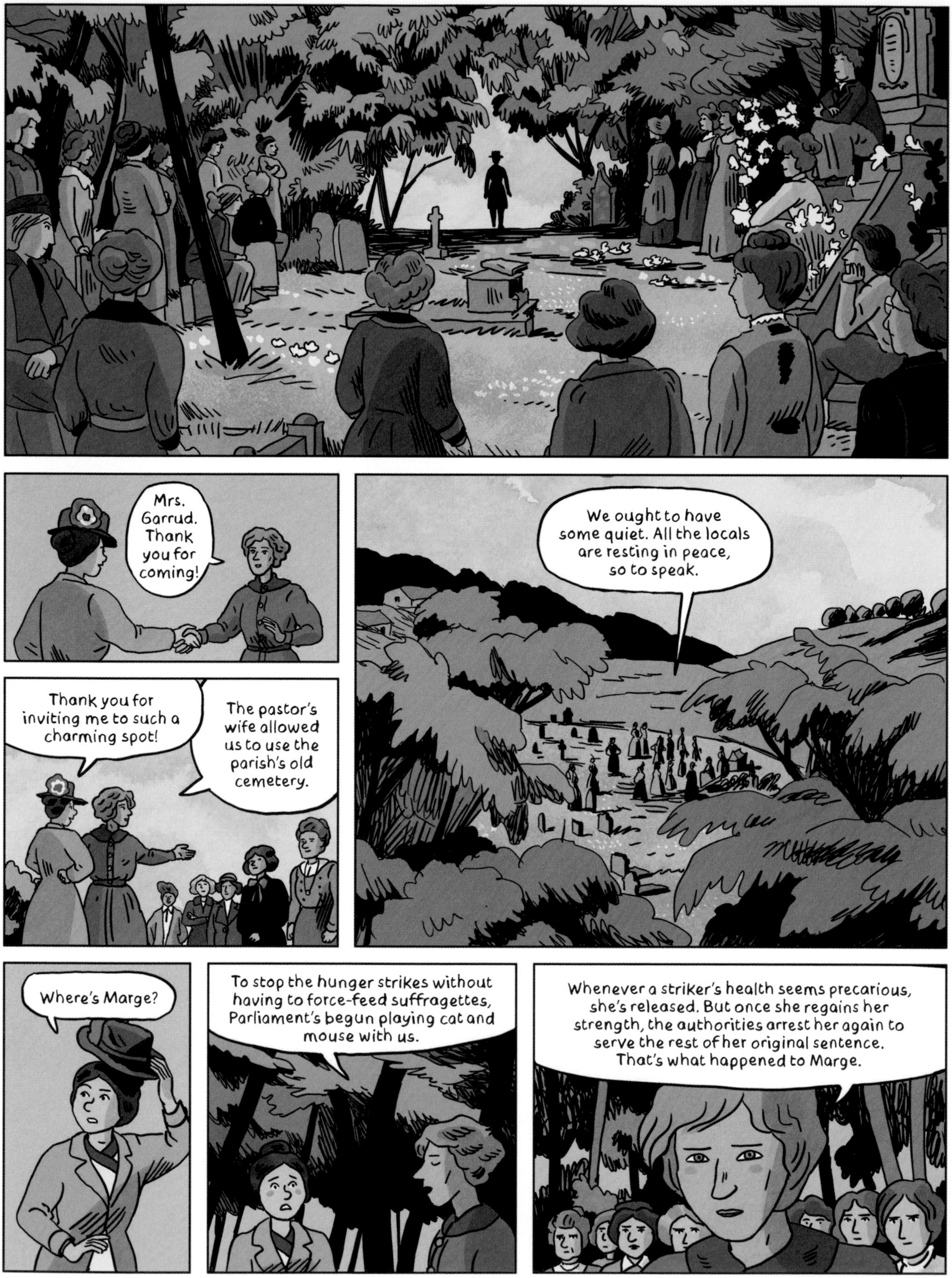
Mrs. Garrud. Thank you for coming!
We ought to have some quiet. All the locals are resting in peace, so to speak.
Thank you for inviting me to such a charming spot!
The pastor's wife allowed us to use the parish's old cemetery.
Where's Marge?
To stop the hunger strikes without having to force-feed suffragettes, Parliament's begun playing cat and mouse with us.
Whenever a striker's health seems precarious, she's released. But once she regains her strength, the authorities arrest her again to serve the rest of her original sentence. That's what happened to Marge.

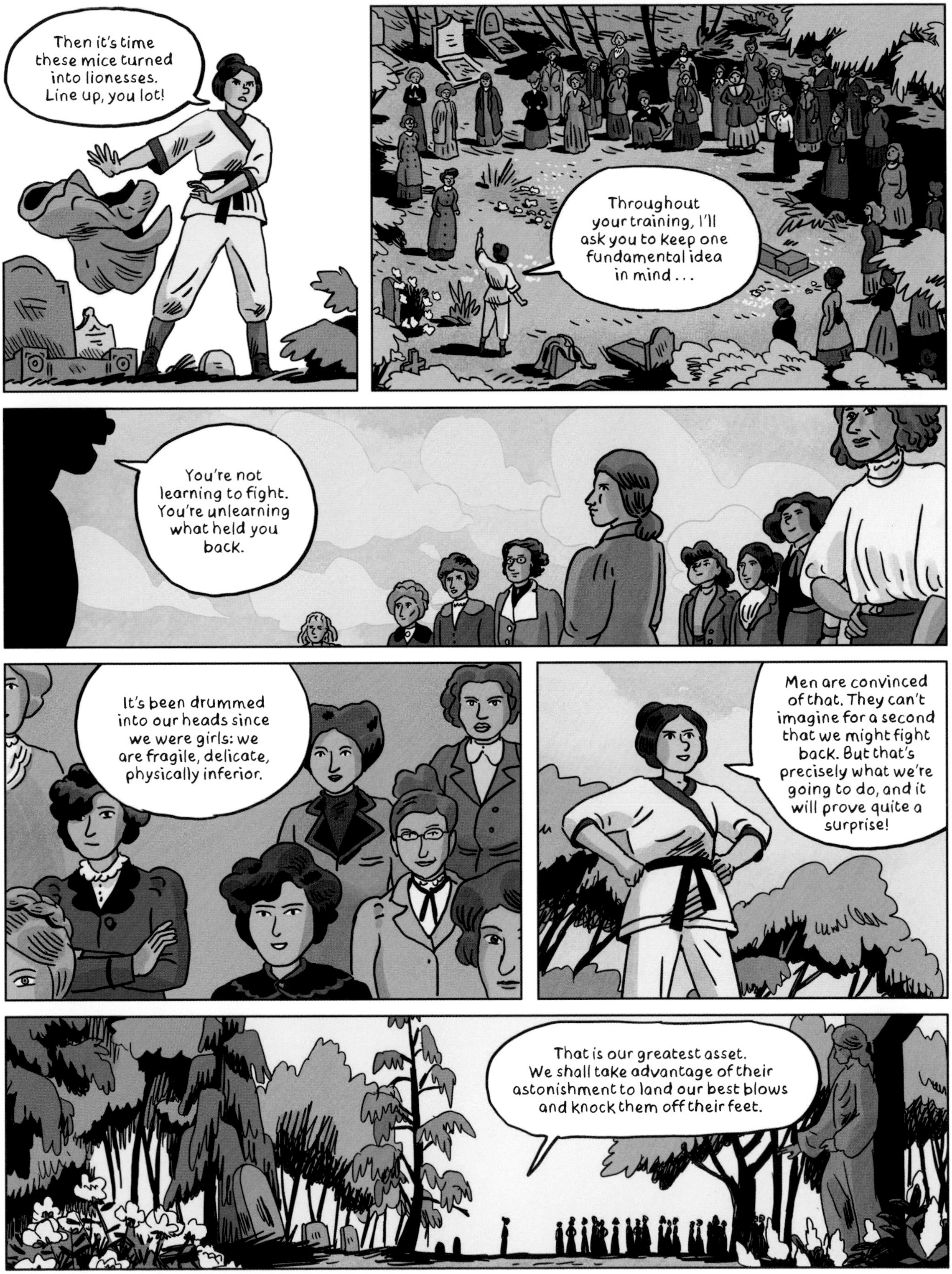
Then it's time these mice turned into lionesses. Line up, you lot!
Throughout your training, I'll ask you to keep one fundamental idea in mind . . .
You're not learning to fight. You're unlearning what held you back.
It's been drummed into our heads since we were girls: we are fragile, delicate, physically inferior.
Men are convinced of that. They can't imagine for a second that we might fight back. But that's precisely what we're going to do, and it will prove quite a surprise!
That is our greatest asset. We shall take advantage of their astonishment to land our best blows and knock them off their feet.

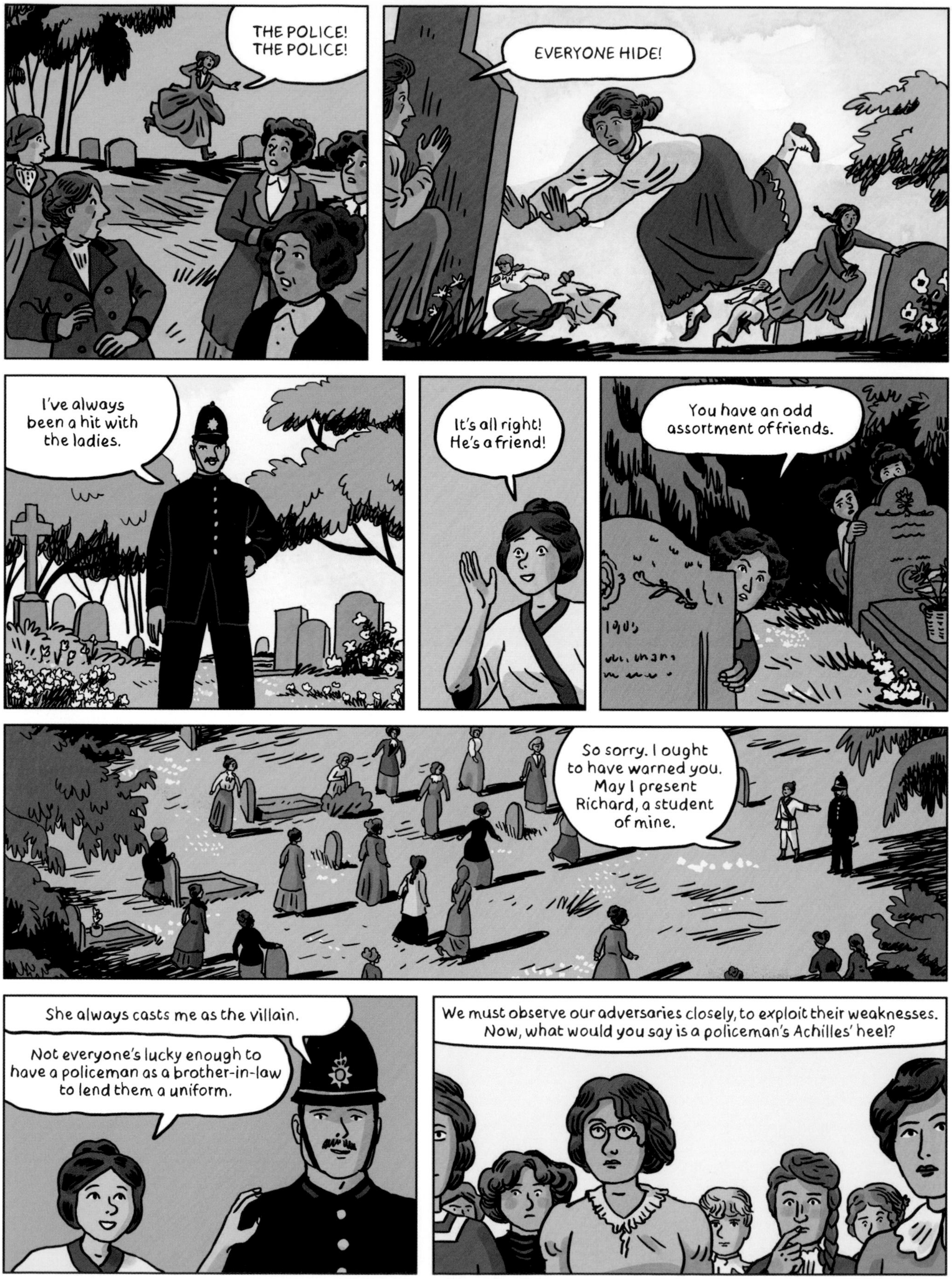
THE POLICE! THE POLICE!
EVERYONE HIDE!
I've always been a hit with the ladies.
It's all right! He's a friend!
You have an odd assortment of friends.
So sorry. I ought to have warned you. May I present Richard, a student of mine.
She always casts me as the villain.
Not everyone's lucky enough to have a policeman as a brother-in-law to lend them a uniform.
We must observe our adversaries closely, to exploit their weaknesses. Now, what would you say is a policeman's Achilles' heel?

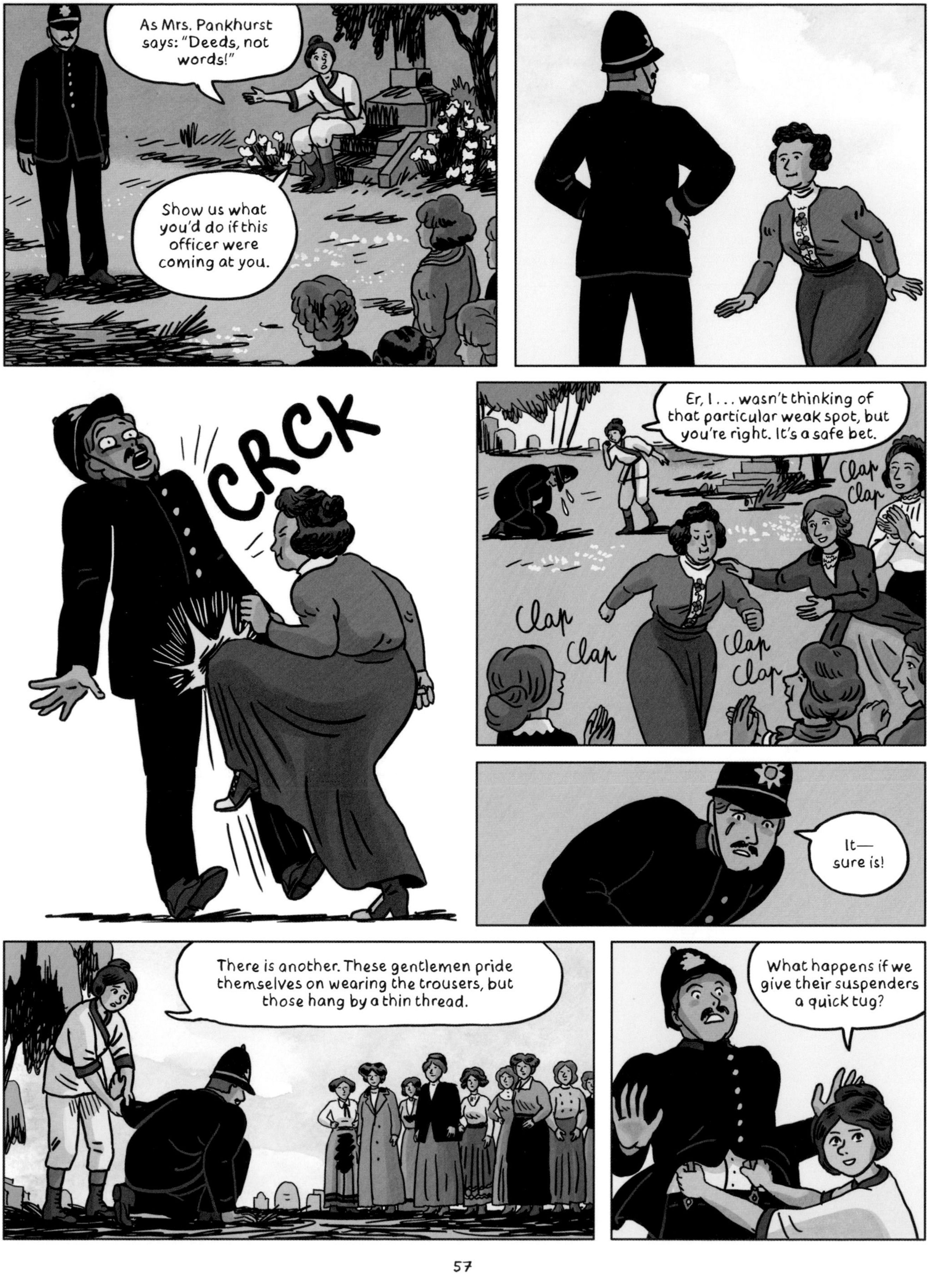
As Mrs. Pankhurst says: "Deeds, not words!"
Show us what you'd do if this officer were coming at you.
CRCK
Er, I . . . wasn't thinking of that particular weak spot, but you're right. It's a safe bet.
Clap Clap
Clap Clap
Clap Clap
It— sure is!
There is another. These gentlemen pride themselves on wearing the trousers, but those hang by a thin thread.
What happens if we give their suspenders a quick tug?

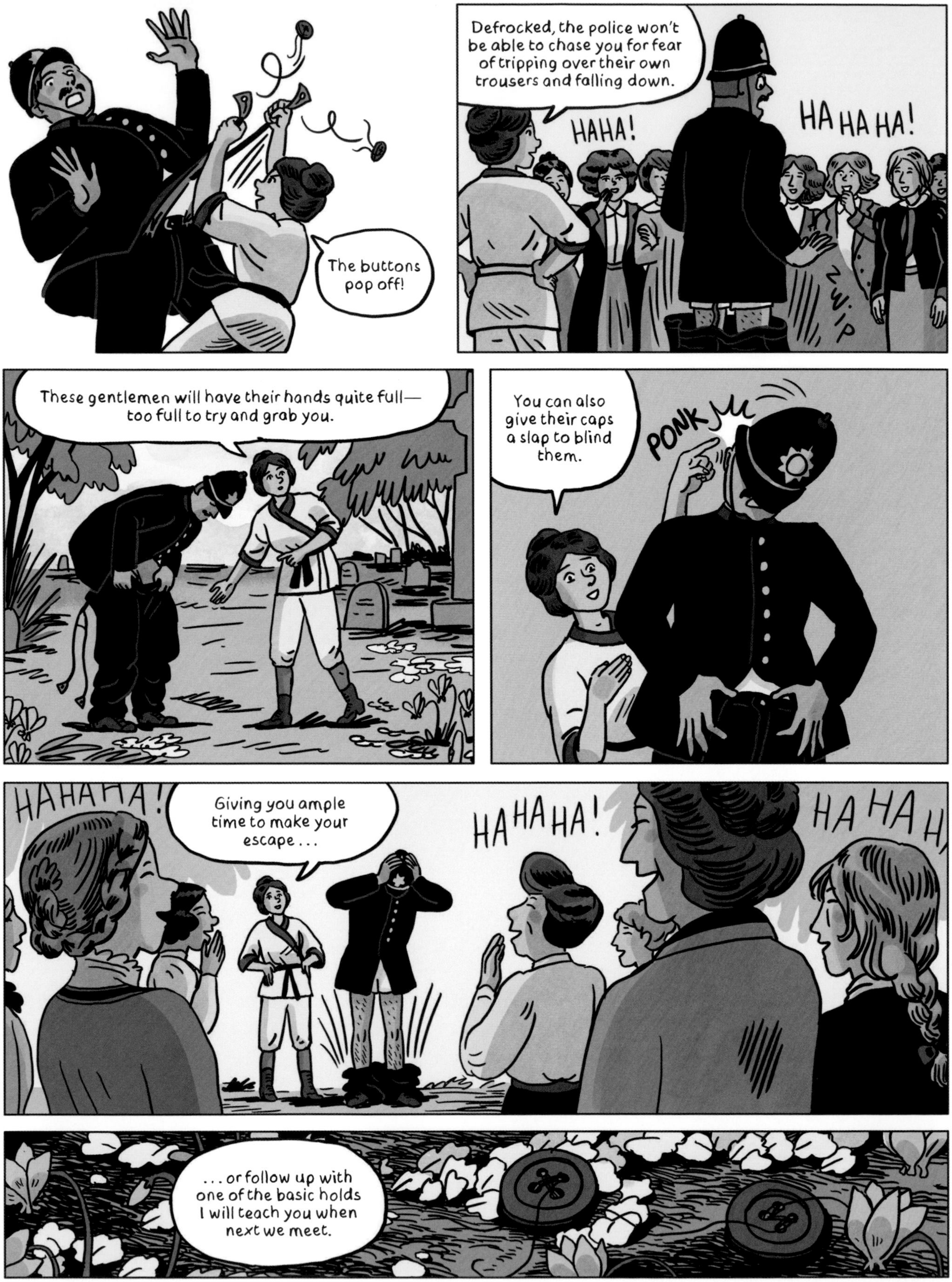
The buttons pop off!
Defrocked, the police won't be able to chase you for fear of tripping over their own trousers and falling down.
HAHA!
HA HA HA!
ZWIP
These gentlemen will have their hands quite full— too full to try and grab you.
You can also give their caps a slap to blind them.
PONK
HAHAHA!
Giving you ample time to make your escape . . .
HA HA HA!
HA HA HA
. . . or follow up with one of the basic holds I will teach you when next we meet.

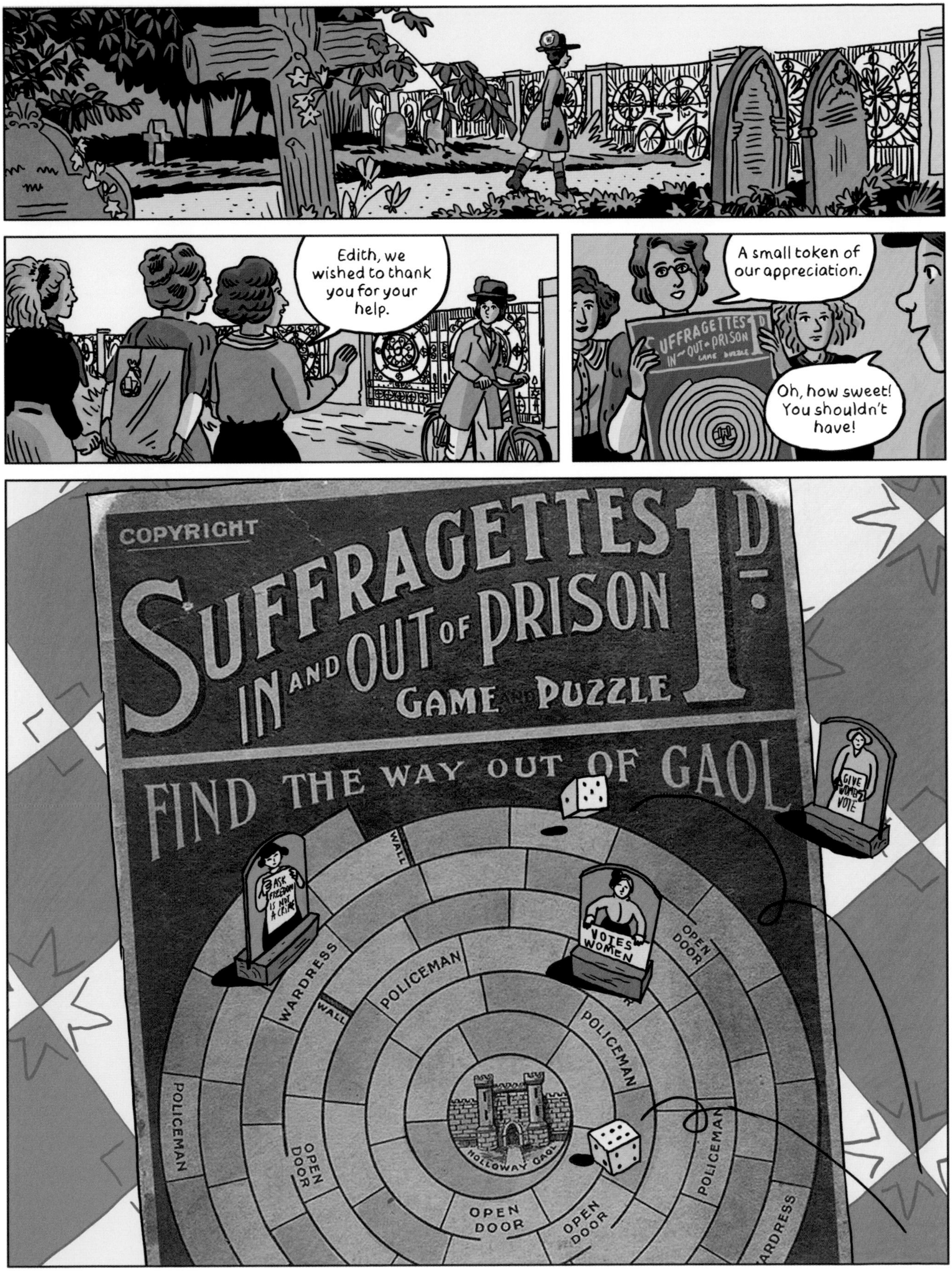
Edith, we wished to thank you for your help.
A small token of our appreciation.
Oh, how sweet! You shouldn't have!
COPYRIGHT
SUFFRAGETTES IN AND OUT OF PRISON 1D.
GAME AND PUZZLE
FIND THE WAY OUT OF GAOL
WALL
WARDRESS
POLICEMAN
OPEN DOOR
HOLLOWAY GAOL
ASK FREEDOM IS NOT A CRIME
VOTES WOMEN
GIVE WOMEN VOTE

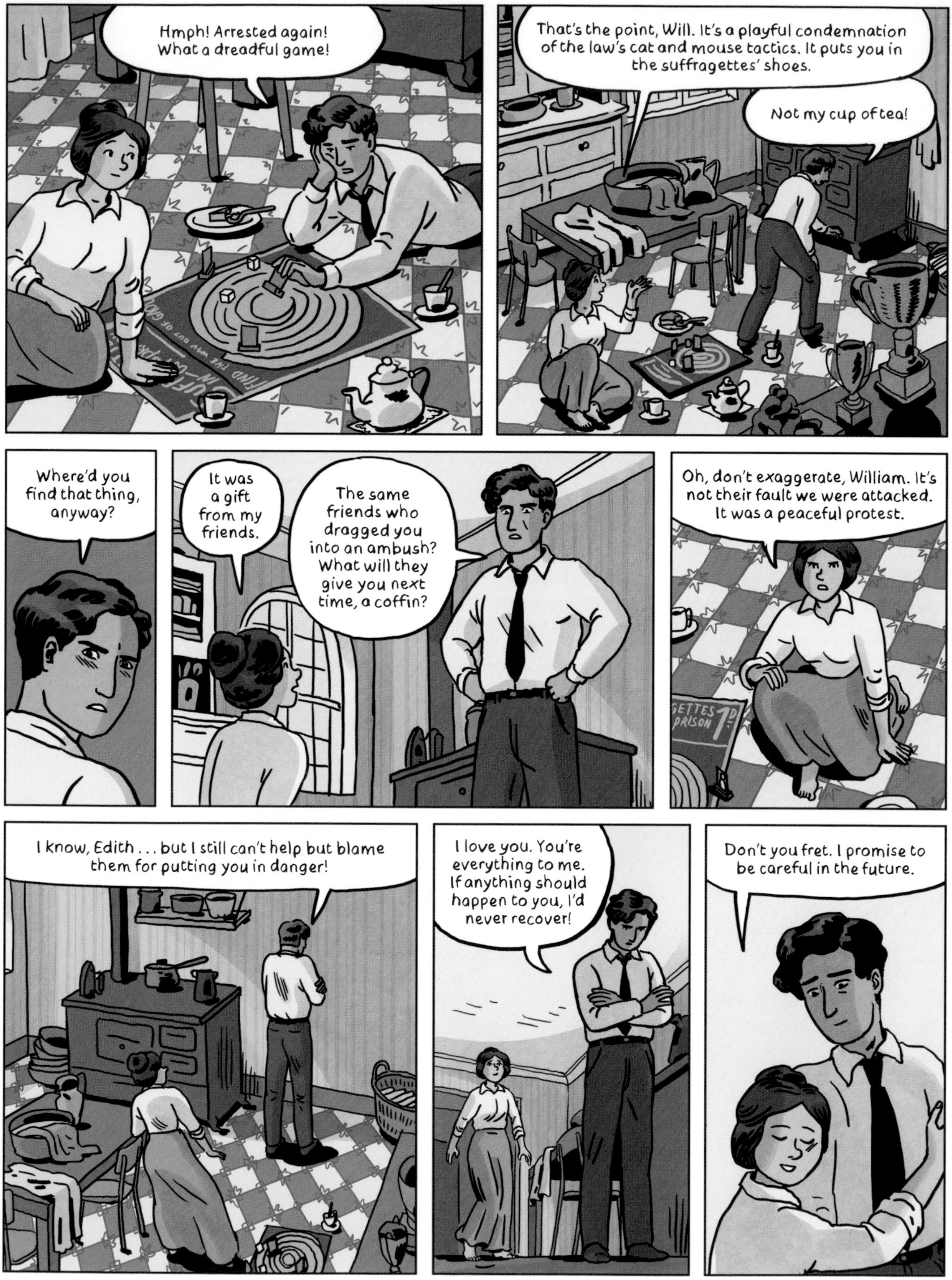
Hmph! Arrested again! What a dreadful game!
That's the point, Will. It's a playful condemnation of the law's cat and mouse tactics. It puts you in the suffragettes' shoes.
Not my cup of tea!
Where'd you find that thing, anyway?
It was a gift from my friends.
The same friends who dragged you into an ambush? What will they give you next time, a coffin?
Oh, don't exaggerate, William. It's not their fault we were attacked. It was a peaceful protest.
I know, Edith . . . but I still can't help but blame them for putting you in danger!
I love you. You're everything to me. If anything should happen to you, I'd never recover!
Don't you fret. I promise to be careful in the future.

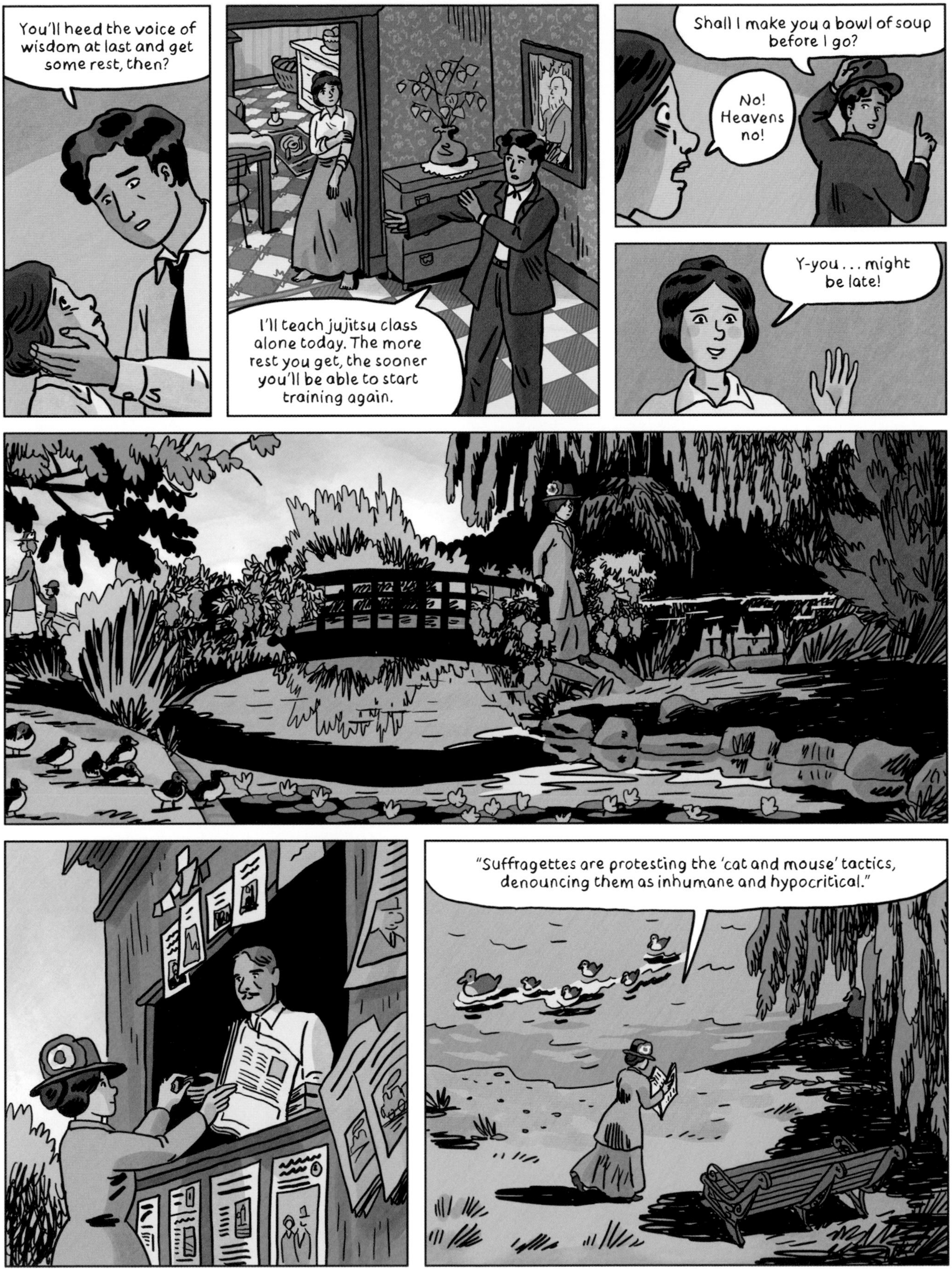
You'll heed the voice of wisdom at last and get some rest, then?
I'll teach jujitsu class alone today. The more rest you get, the sooner you'll be able to start training again.
Shall I make you a bowl of soup before I go?
No! Heavens no!
Y-you . . . might be late!
"Suffragettes are protesting the 'cat and mouse' tactics, denouncing them as inhumane and hypocritical."

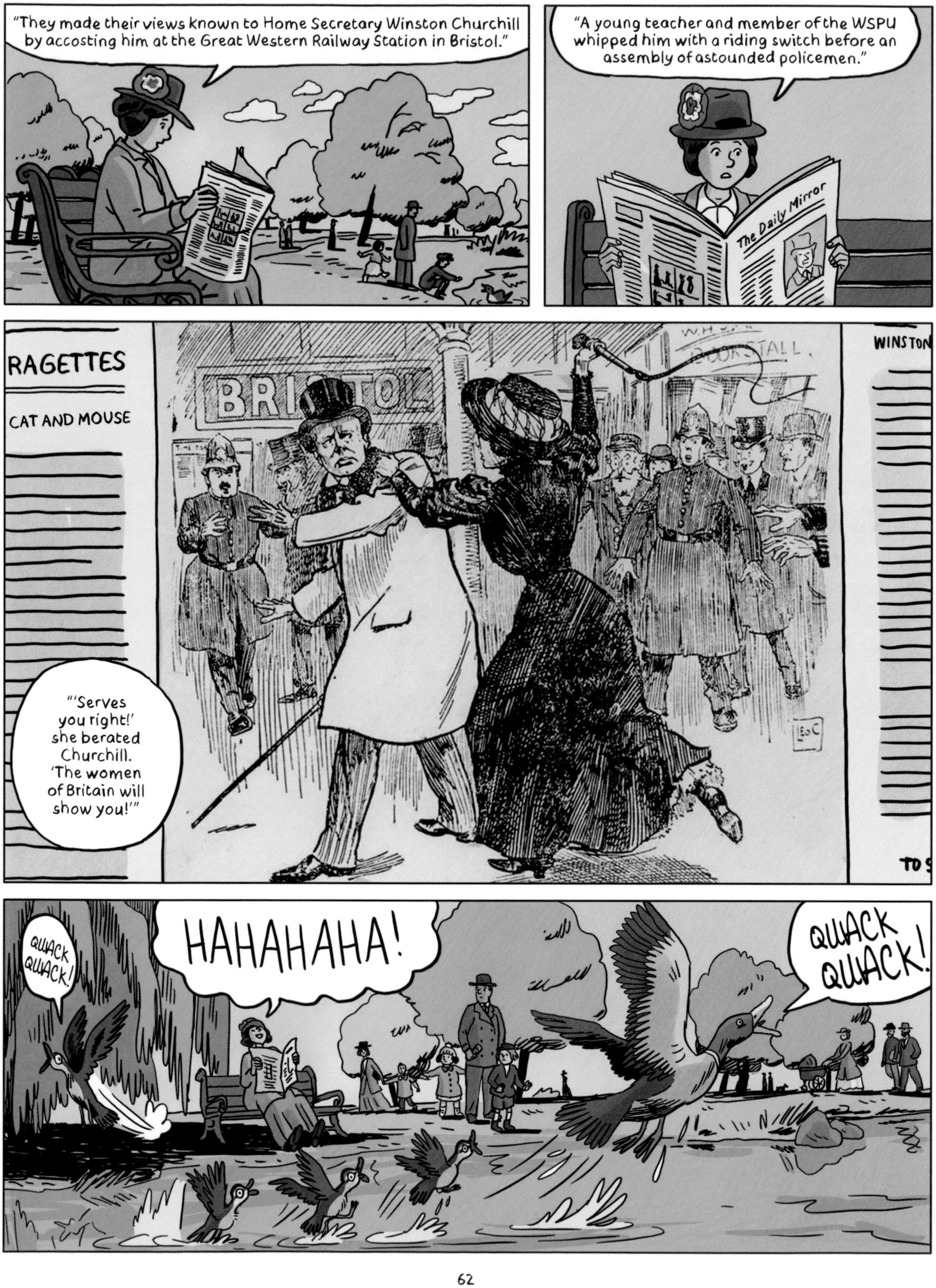
"They made their views known to Home Secretary Winston Churchill by accosting him at the Great Western Railway Station in Bristol."
"A young teacher and member of the WSPU whipped him with a riding switch before an assembly of astounded policemen."
The Daily Mirror
RAGETTES
CAT AND MOUSE
BRISTOL
W.H.S.
BOOKSTALL
WINSTON
"'Serves you right!' she berated Churchill. 'The women of Britain will show you!'"
LEOC
TO S
QUACK QUACK!
HAHAHAHA!
QUACK QUACK!

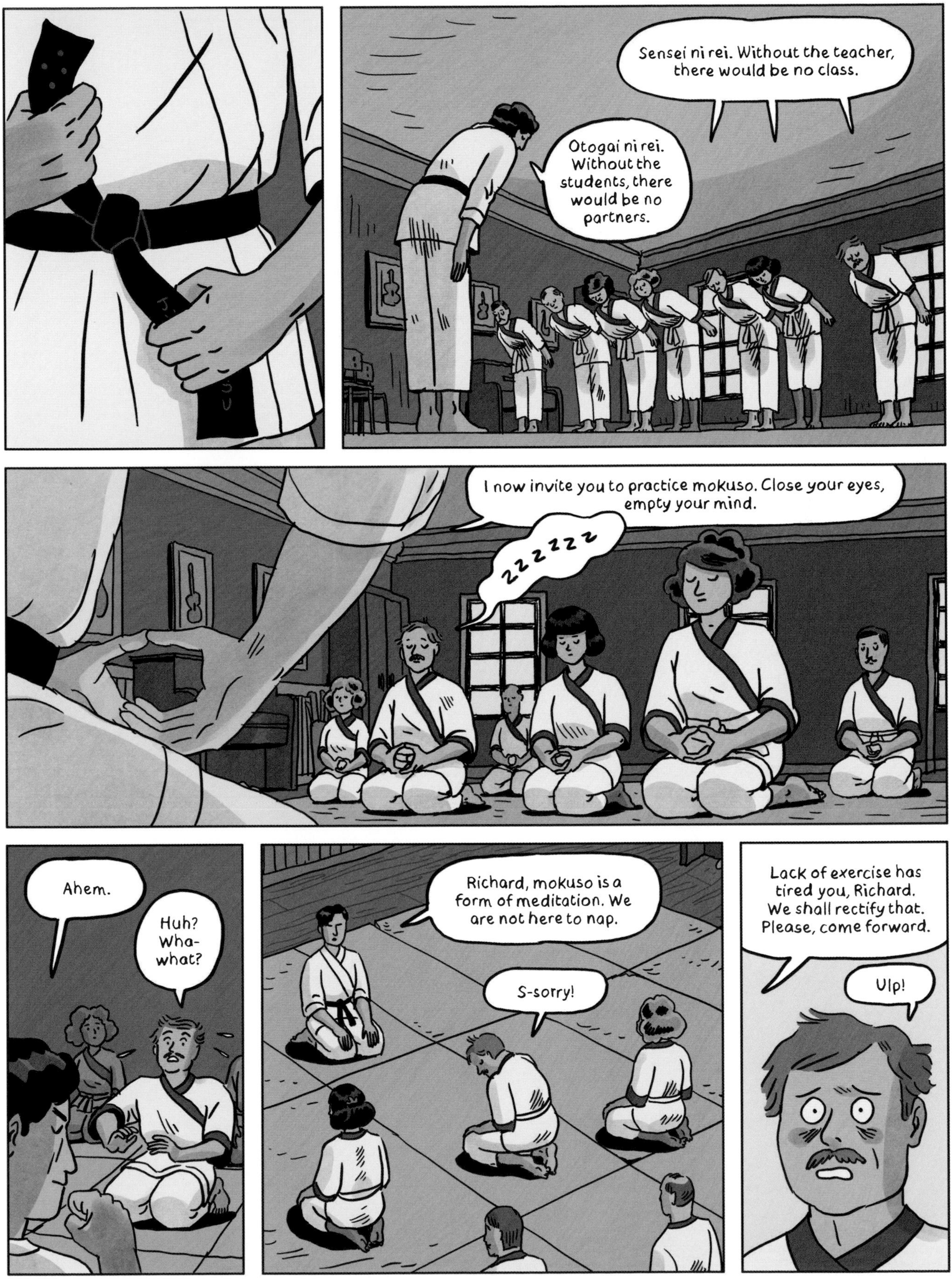

Sensei ni rei. Without the teacher, there would be no class.
Otogai ni rei. Without the students, there would be no partners.
I now invite you to practice mokuso. Close your eyes, empty your mind.
ZZZZZZ
Ahem.
Huh? Wha-what?
Richard, mokuso is a form of meditation. We are not here to nap.
S-sorry!
Lack of exercise has tired you, Richard. We shall rectify that. Please, come forward.
Ulp!

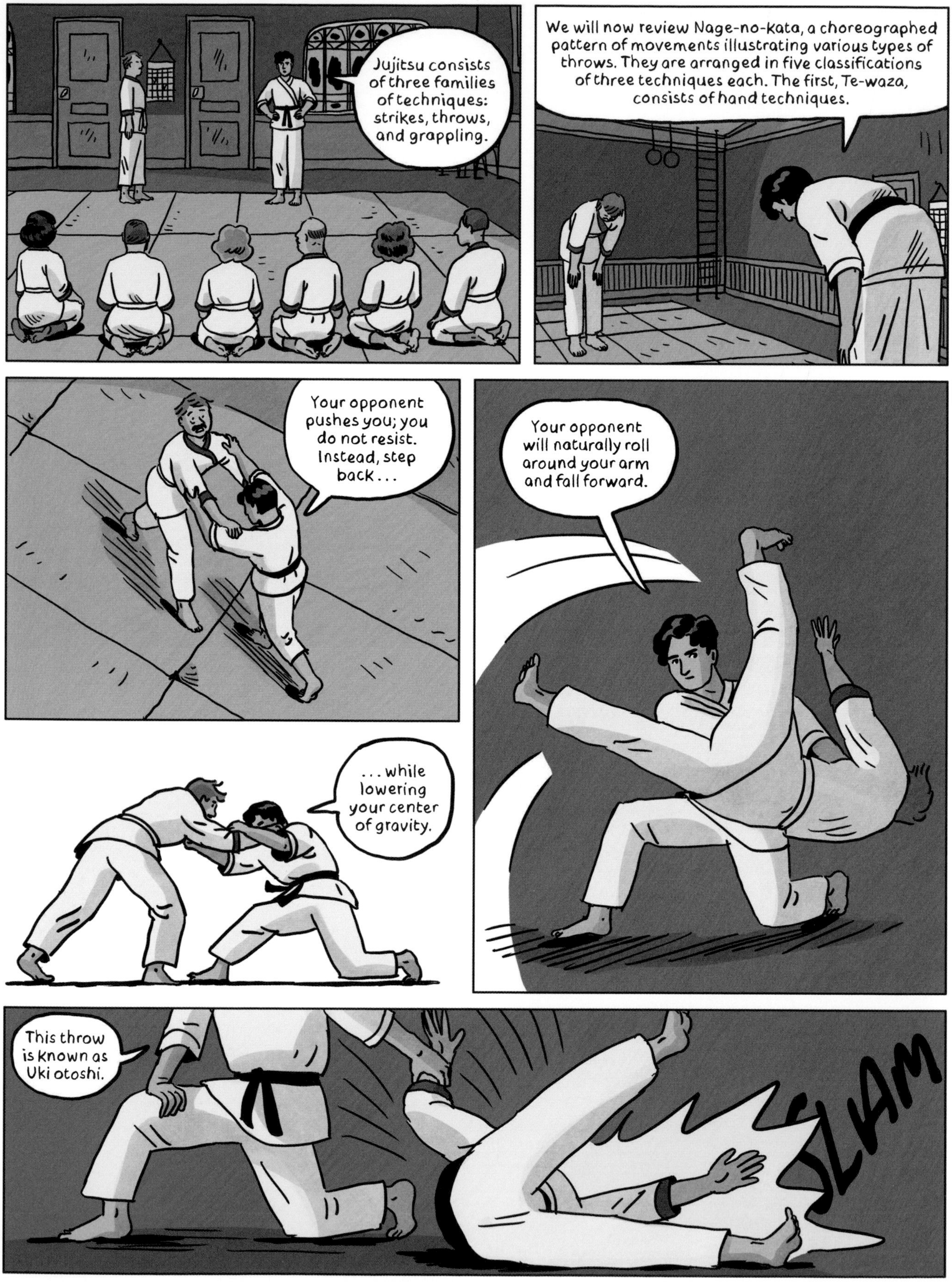
Jujitsu consists of three families of techniques: strikes, throws, and grappling.
We will now review Nage-no-kata, a choreographed pattern of movements illustrating various types of throws. They are arranged in five classifications of three techniques each. The first, Te-waza, consists of hand techniques.
Your opponent pushes you; you do not resist. Instead, step back . . .
. . . while lowering your center of gravity.
Your opponent will naturally roll around your arm and fall forward.
This throw is known as Uki otoshi.
SLAM

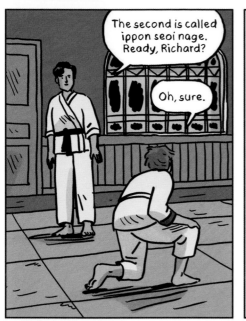

The second is called ippon seoi nage. Ready, Richard?

Oh, sure.

Your opponent attacks.

RAAARGH!

You block.

BLOKK

Seize the forearm...

...pivot...

...and lean forward.

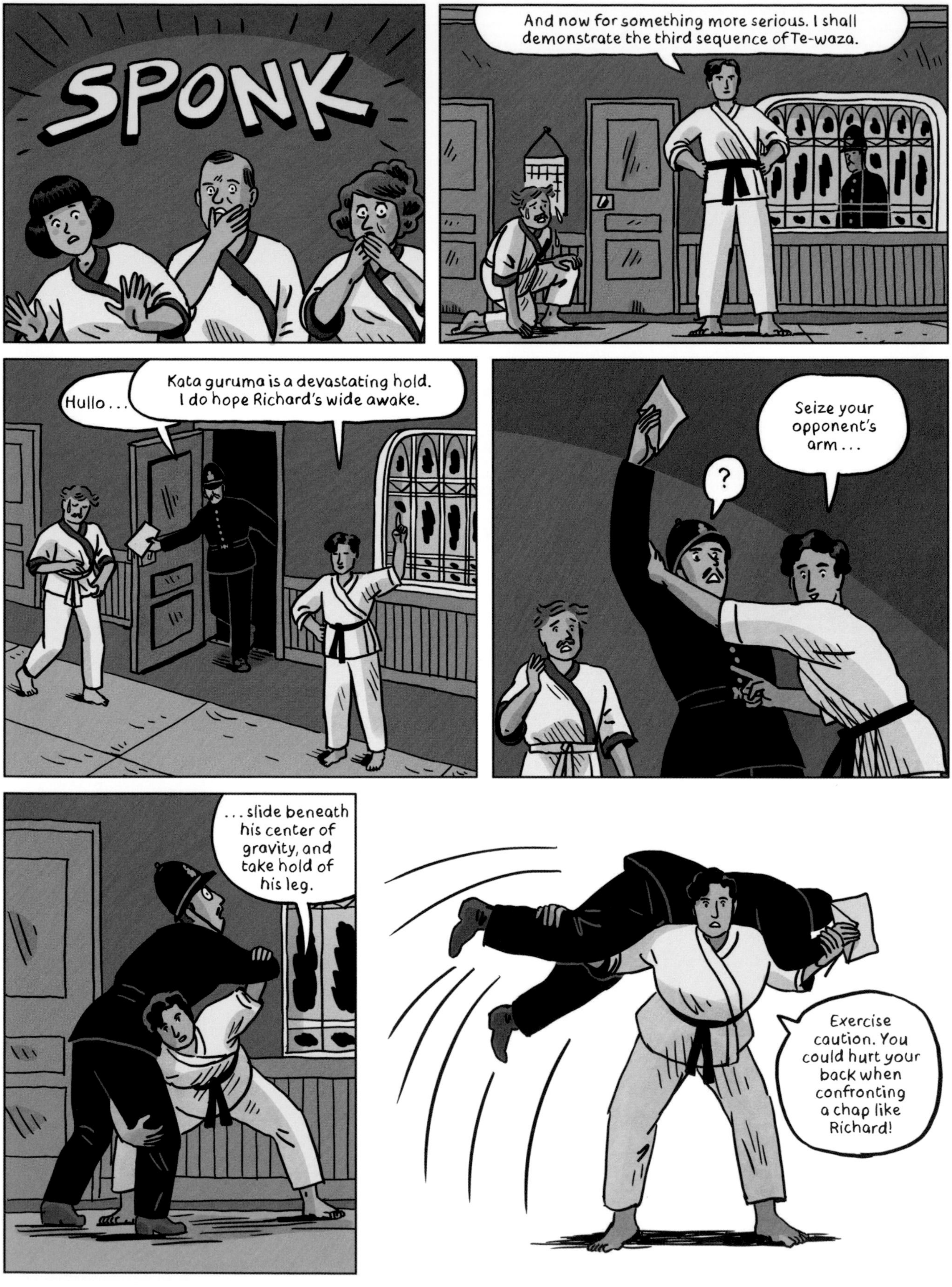
SPONK
And now for something more serious. I shall demonstrate the third sequence of Te-waza.
Hullo...
Kata guruma is a devastating hold. I do hope Richard's wide awake.
?
Seize your opponent's arm...
...slide beneath his center of gravity, and take hold of his leg.
Exercise caution. You could hurt your back when confronting a chap like Richard!

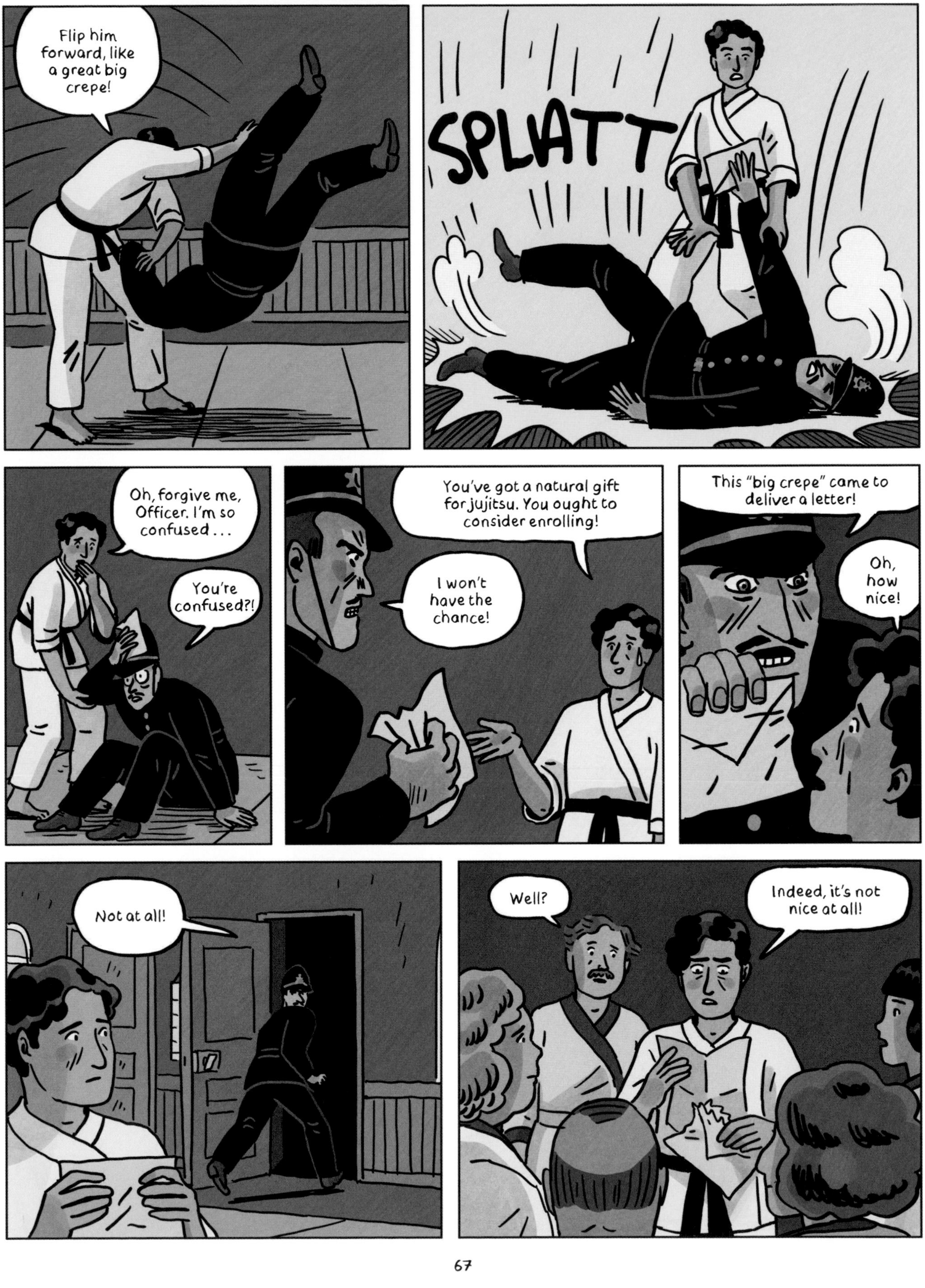
Flip him forward, like a great big crepe!
SPLATT
Oh, forgive me, Officer. I'm so confused . . .
You're confused?!
You've got a natural gift for jujitsu. You ought to consider enrolling!
I won't have the chance!
This "big crepe" came to deliver a letter!
Oh, how nice!
Not at all!
Well?
Indeed, it's not nice at all!

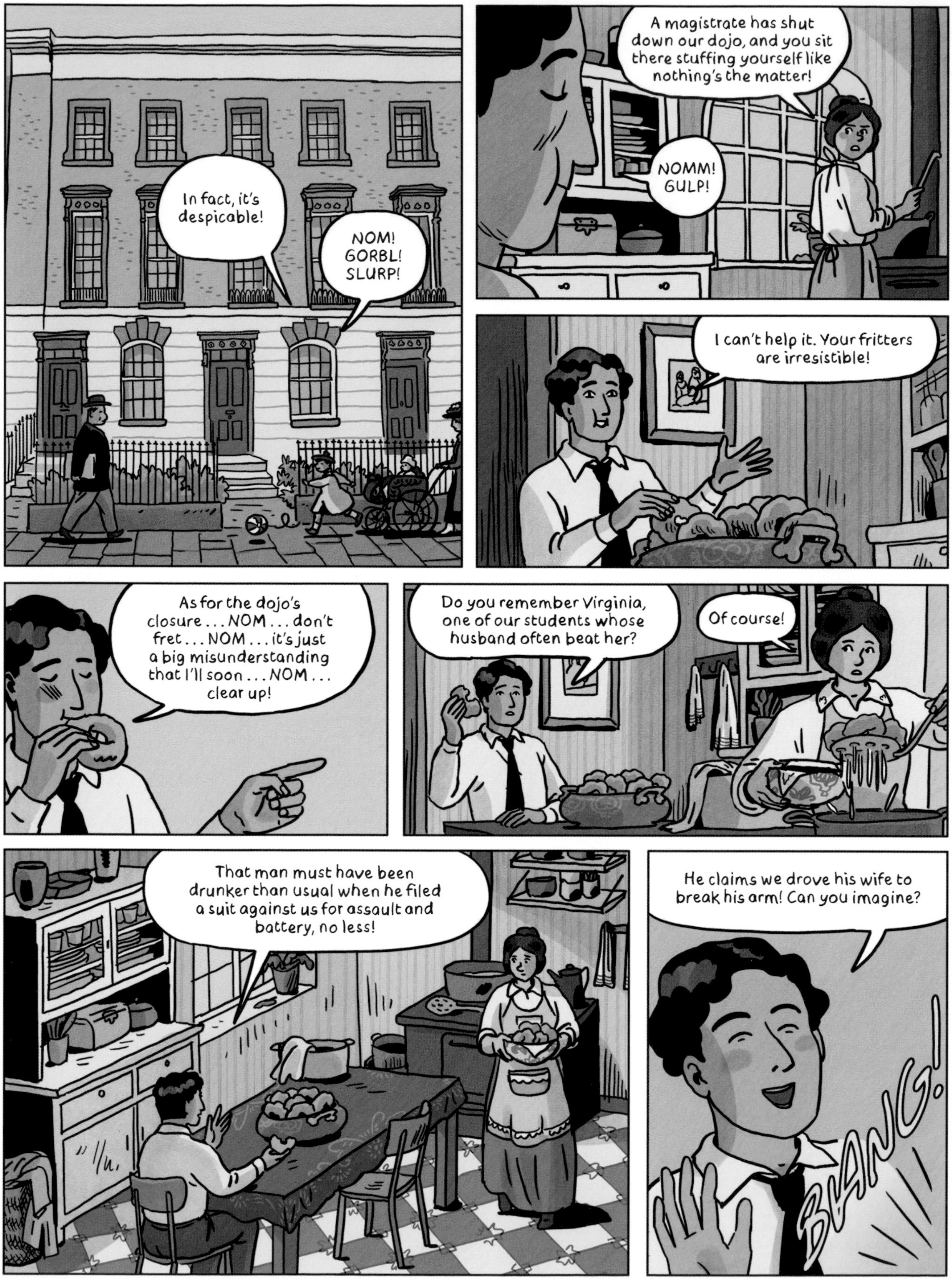
In fact, it's despicable!
NOM! GORBL! SLURP!
A magistrate has shut down our dojo, and you sit there stuffing yourself like nothing's the matter!
NOMM! GULP!
I can't help it. Your fritters are irresistible!
As for the dojo's closure . . . NOM . . . don't fret . . . NOM . . . it's just a big misunderstanding that I'll soon . . . NOM . . . clear up!
Do you remember Virginia, one of our students whose husband often beat her?
Of course!
That man must have been drunker than usual when he filed a suit against us for assault and battery, no less!
He claims we drove his wife to break his arm! Can you imagine?
BLANG!

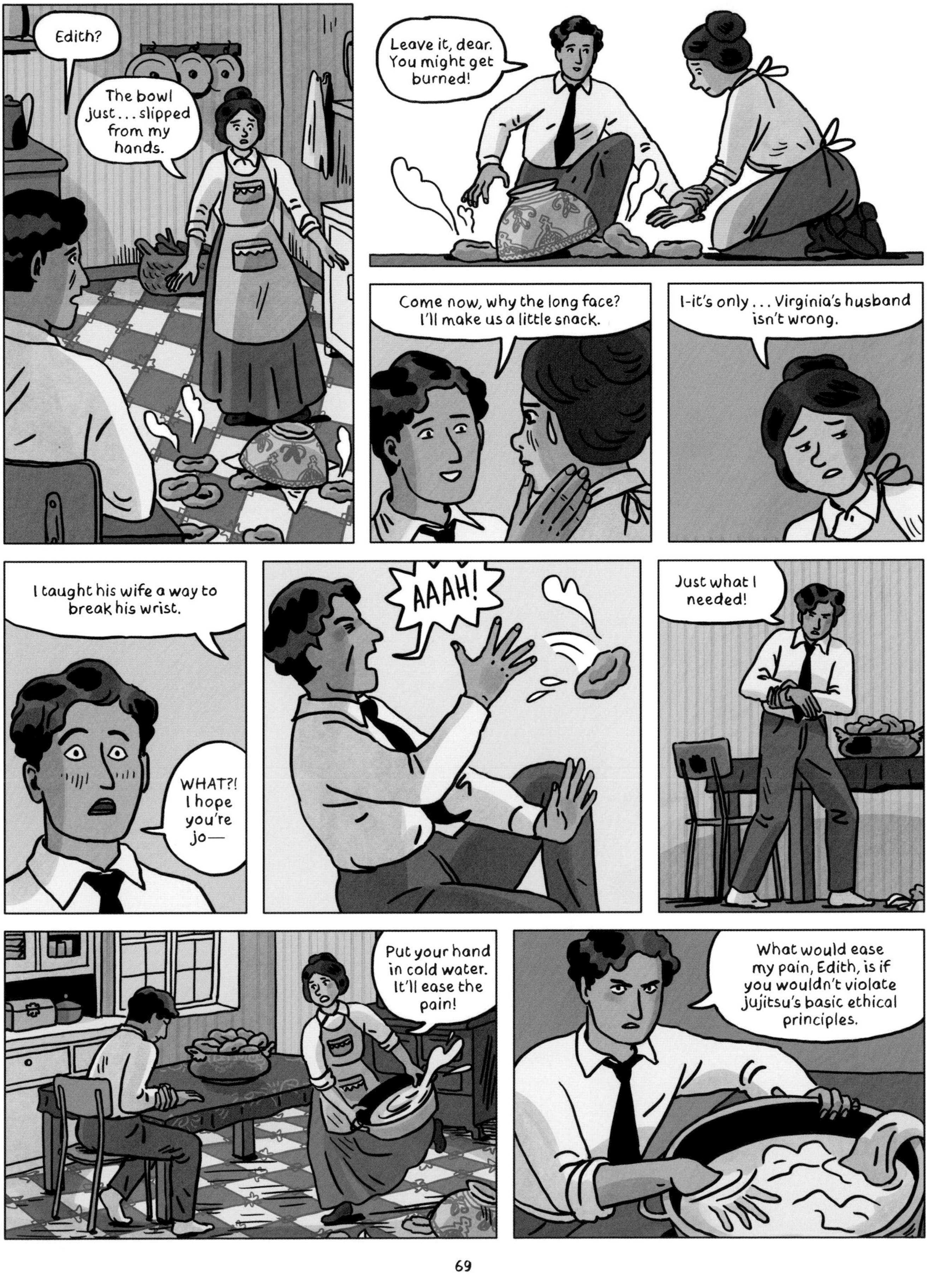
Edith?
The bowl just . . . slipped from my hands.
Leave it, dear. You might get burned!
Come now, why the long face? I'll make us a little snack.
I-it's only . . . Virginia's husband isn't wrong.
I taught his wife a way to break his wrist.
WHAT?! I hope you're jo—
AAAH!
Just what I needed!
Put your hand in cold water. It'll ease the pain!
What would ease my pain, Edith, is if you wouldn't violate jujitsu's basic ethical principles.

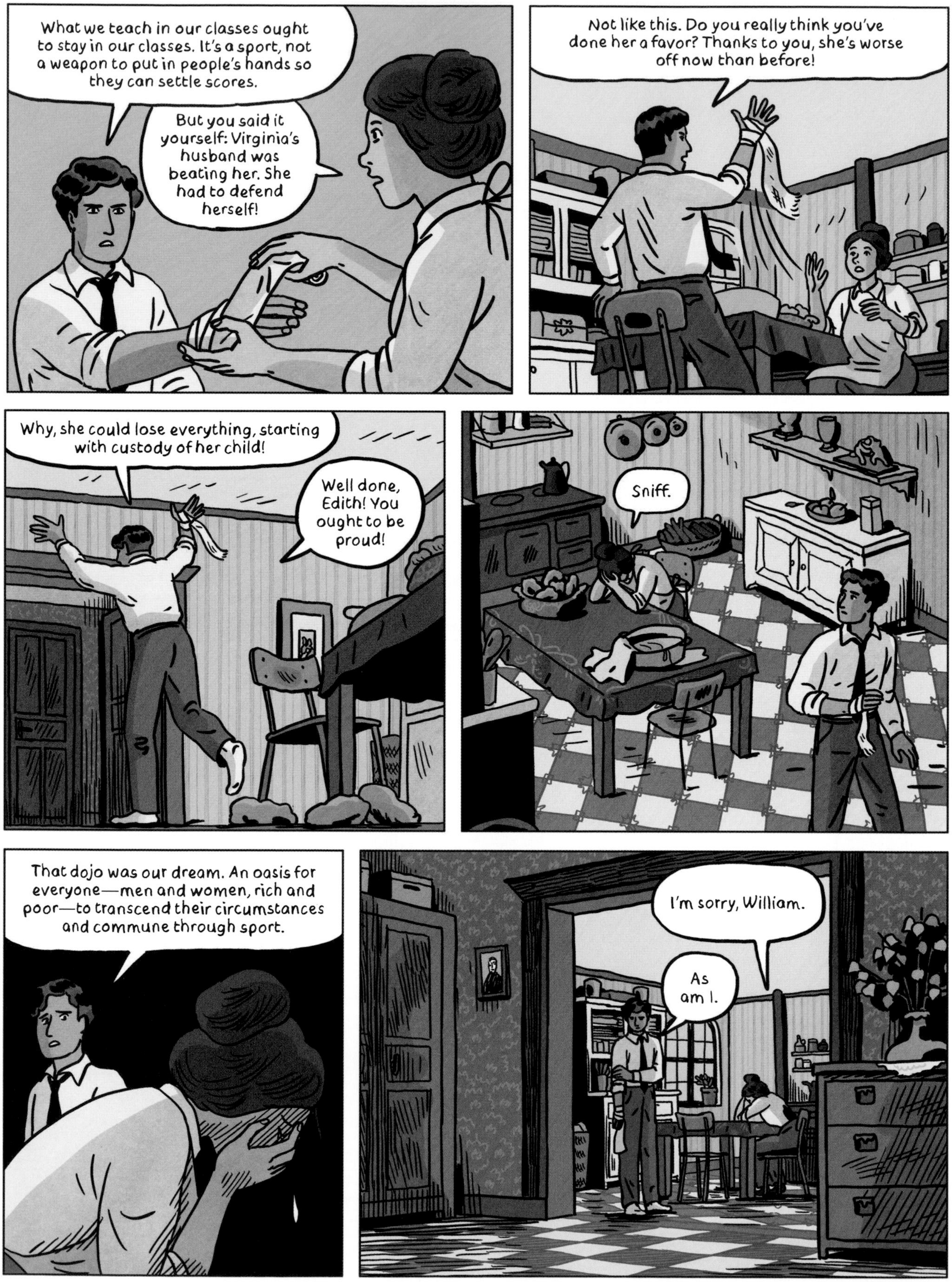
What we teach in our classes ought to stay in our classes. It's a sport, not a weapon to put in people's hands so they can settle scores.
But you said it yourself: Virginia's husband was beating her. She had to defend herself!
Not like this. Do you really think you've done her a favor? Thanks to you, she's worse off now than before!
Why, she could lose everything, starting with custody of her child!
Well done, Edith! You ought to be proud!
Sniff.
That dojo was our dream. An oasis for everyone—men and women, rich and poor—to transcend their circumstances and commune through sport.
I'm sorry, William.
As am I.

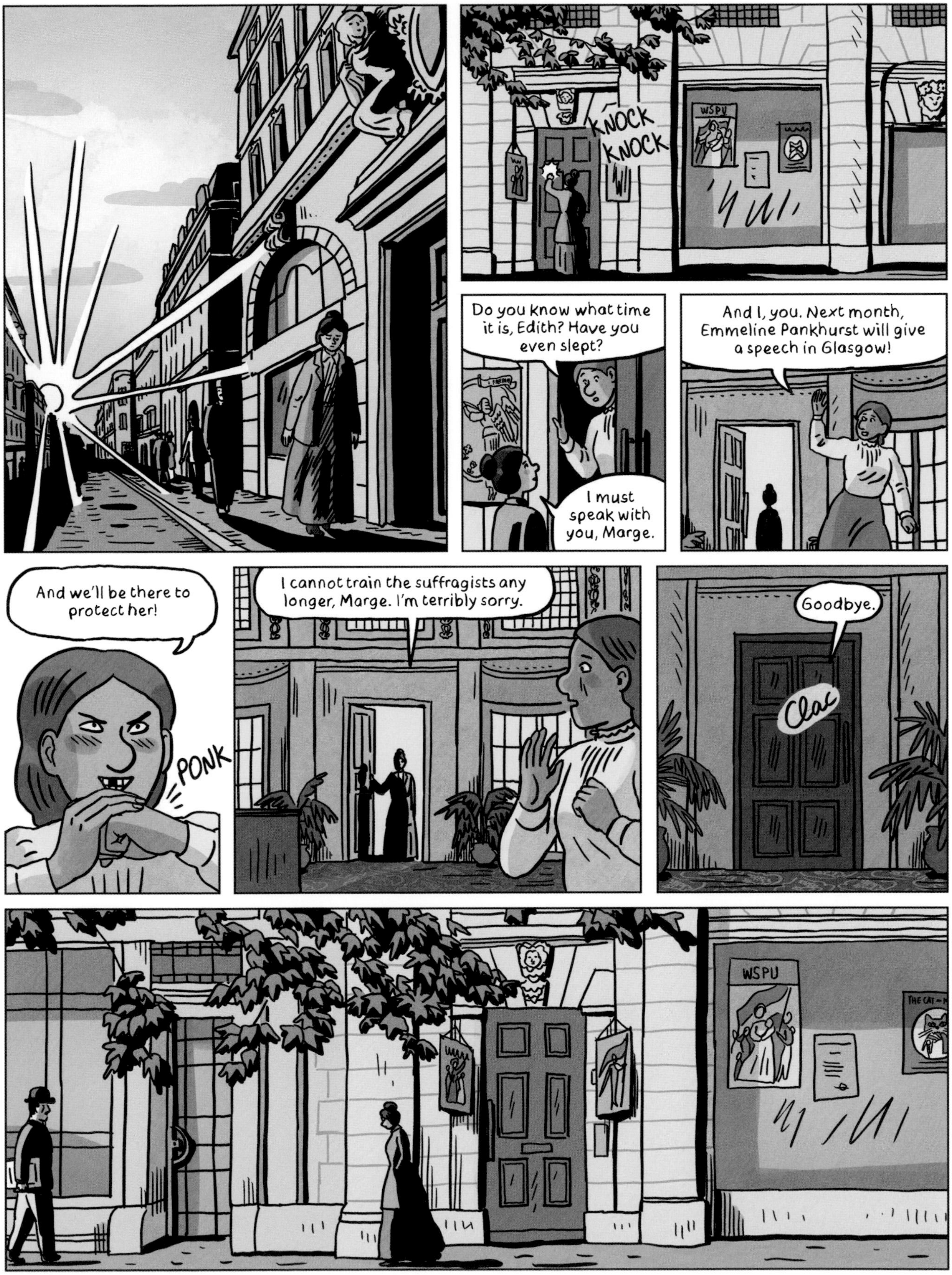
KNOCK
KNOCK
WSPU
Do you know what time it is, Edith? Have you even slept?
I must speak with you, Marge.
And I, you. Next month, Emmeline Pankhurst will give a speech in Glasgow!
And we'll be there to protect her!
PONK
I cannot train the suffragists any longer, Marge. I'm terribly sorry.
Goodbye.
Clac
WSPU

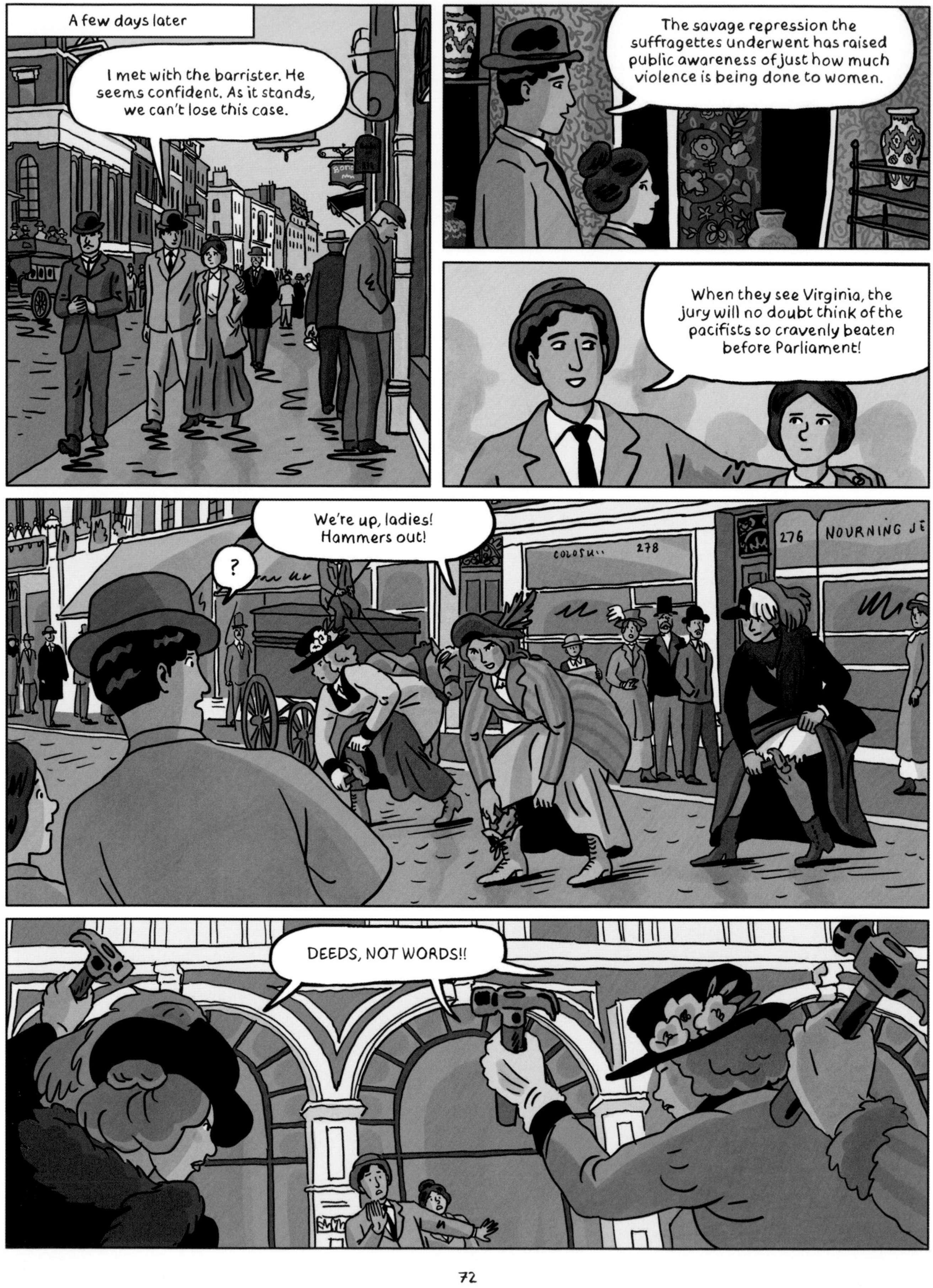
A few days later
I met with the barrister. He seems confident. As it stands, we can't lose this case.
The savage repression the suffragettes underwent has raised public awareness of just how much violence is being done to women.
When they see Virginia, the jury will no doubt think of the pacifists so cravenly beaten before Parliament!
We're up, ladies! Hammers out!
?
278
276
DEEDS, NOT WORDS!!

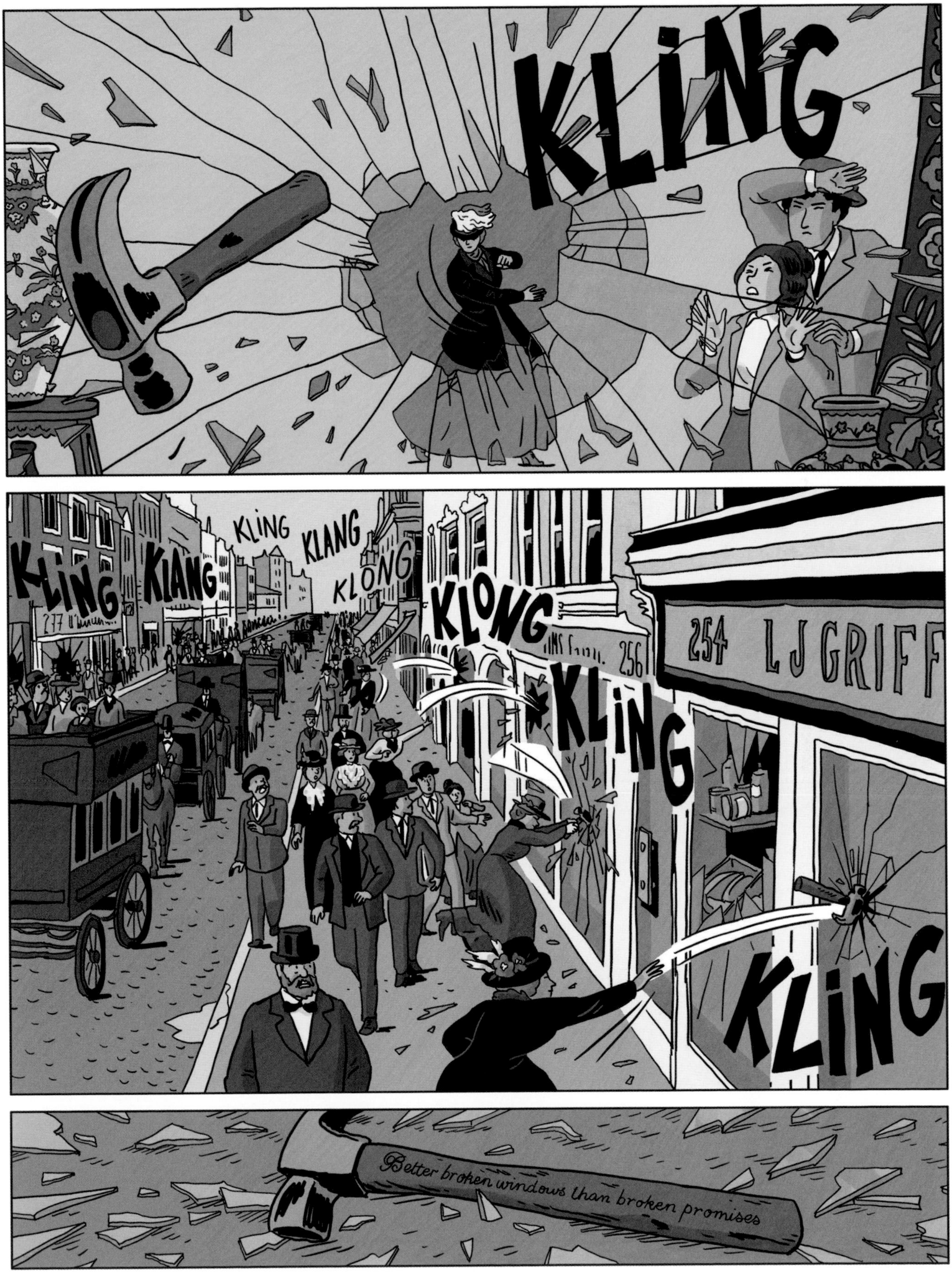
KLING
KLING
KLANG
KLING
KLANG
KLONG
KLONG
277
254 LJ GRIFF
256
KLING
KLING
Better broken windows than broken promises

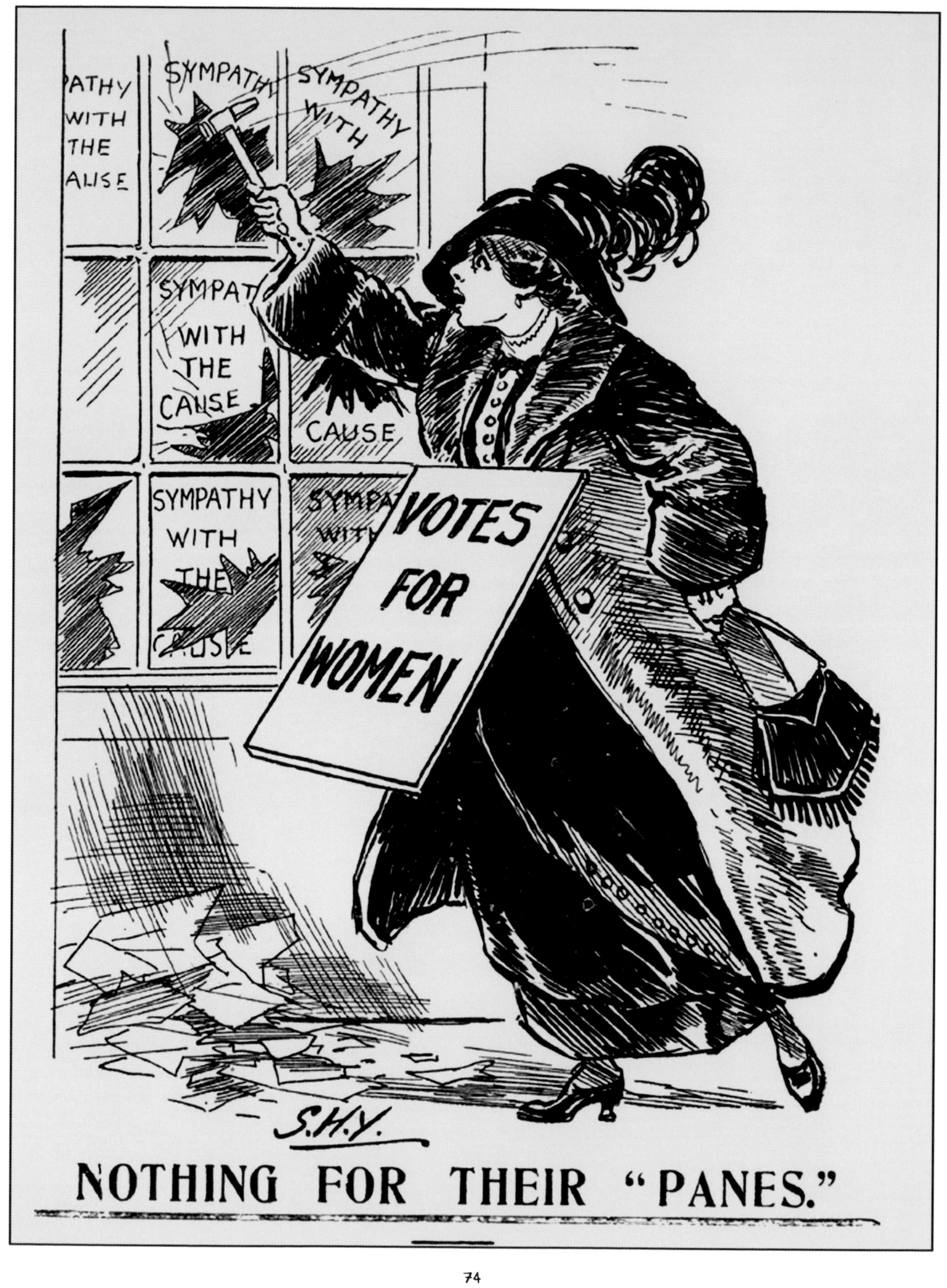
SYMPATHY
SYMPATHY WITH
SYMPAT
WITH
THE
CAUSE
CAUSE
SYMPATHY
WITH
VOTES FOR WOMEN
S.H.Y.

NOTHING FOR THEIR "PANES."

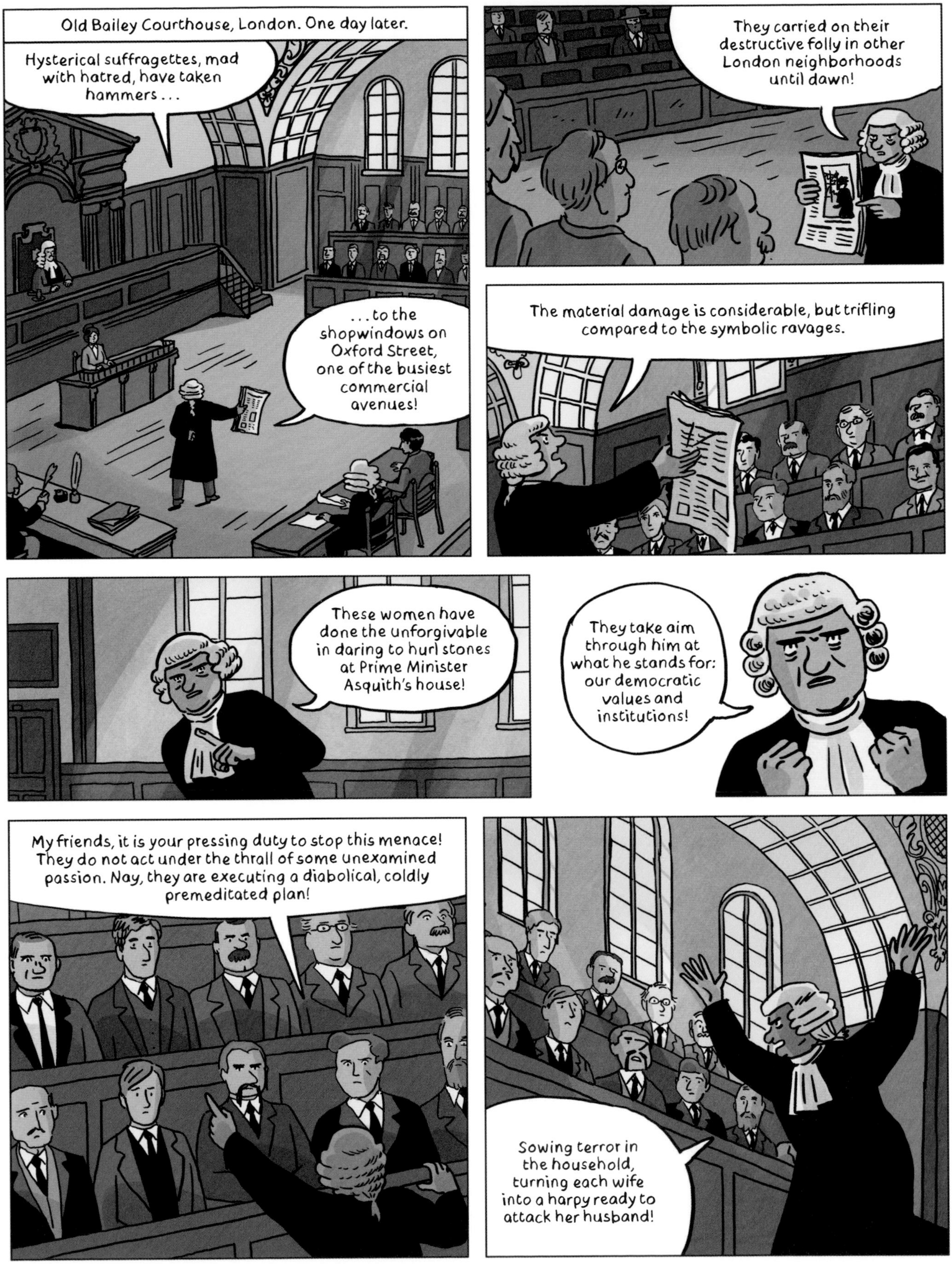
Old Bailey Courthouse, London. One day later.
Hysterical suffragettes, mad with hatred, have taken hammers . . .
. . . to the shopwindows on Oxford Street, one of the busiest commercial avenues!
They carried on their destructive folly in other London neighborhoods until dawn!
The material damage is considerable, but trifling compared to the symbolic ravages.
These women have done the unforgivable in daring to hurl stones at Prime Minister Asquith's house!
They take aim through him at what he stands for: our democratic values and institutions!
My friends, it is your pressing duty to stop this menace! They do not act under the thrall of some unexamined passion. Nay, they are executing a diabolical, coldly premeditated plan!
Sowing terror in the household, turning each wife into a harpy ready to attack her husband!

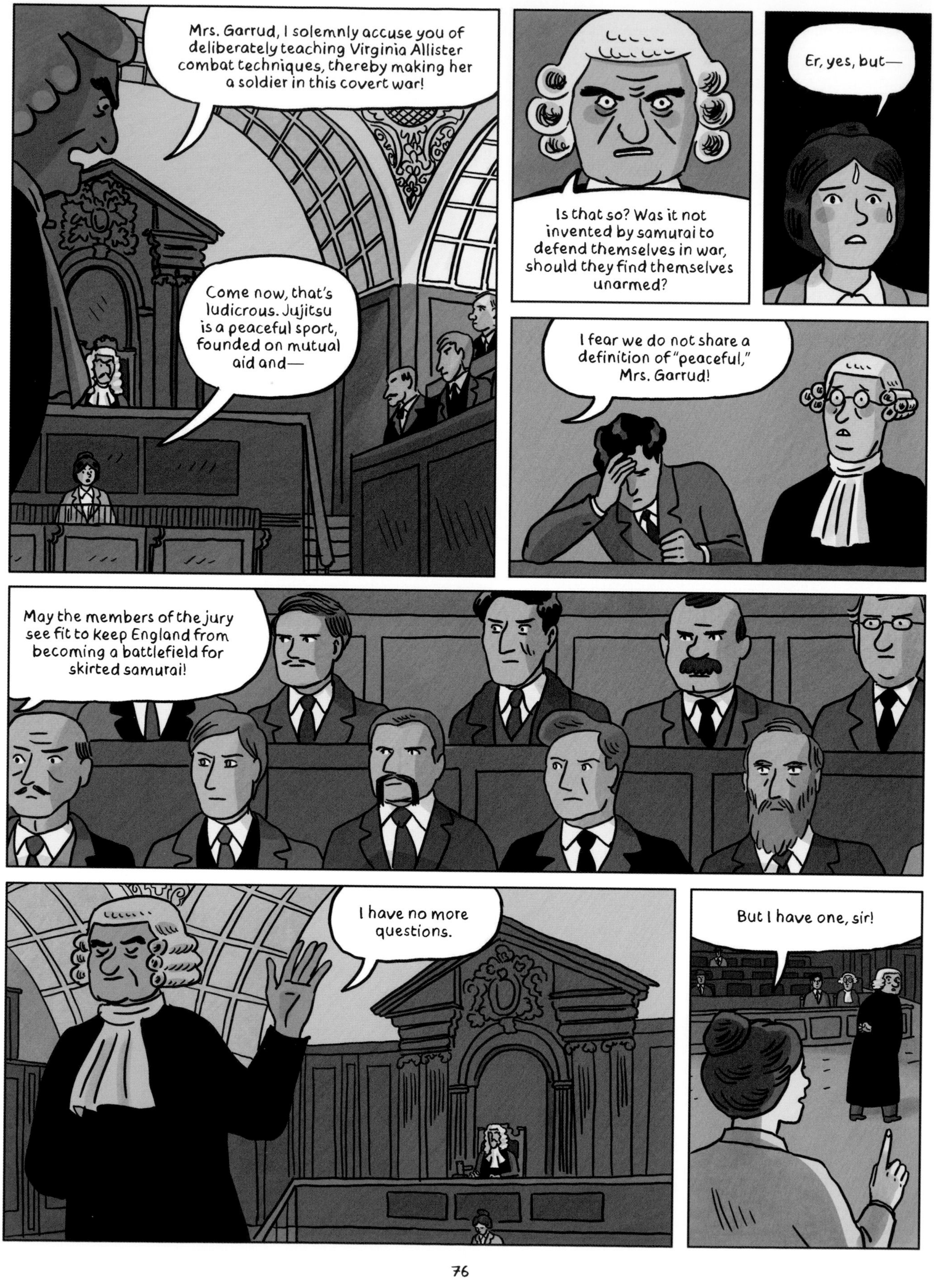
Mrs. Garrud, I solemnly accuse you of deliberately teaching Virginia Allister combat techniques, thereby making her a soldier in this covert war!
Come now, that's ludicrous. Jujitsu is a peaceful sport, founded on mutual aid and—
Is that so? Was it not invented by samurai to defend themselves in war, should they find themselves unarmed?
Er, yes, but—
I fear we do not share a definition of "peaceful," Mrs. Garrud!
May the members of the jury see fit to keep England from becoming a battlefield for skirted samurai!
I have no more questions.
But I have one, sir!

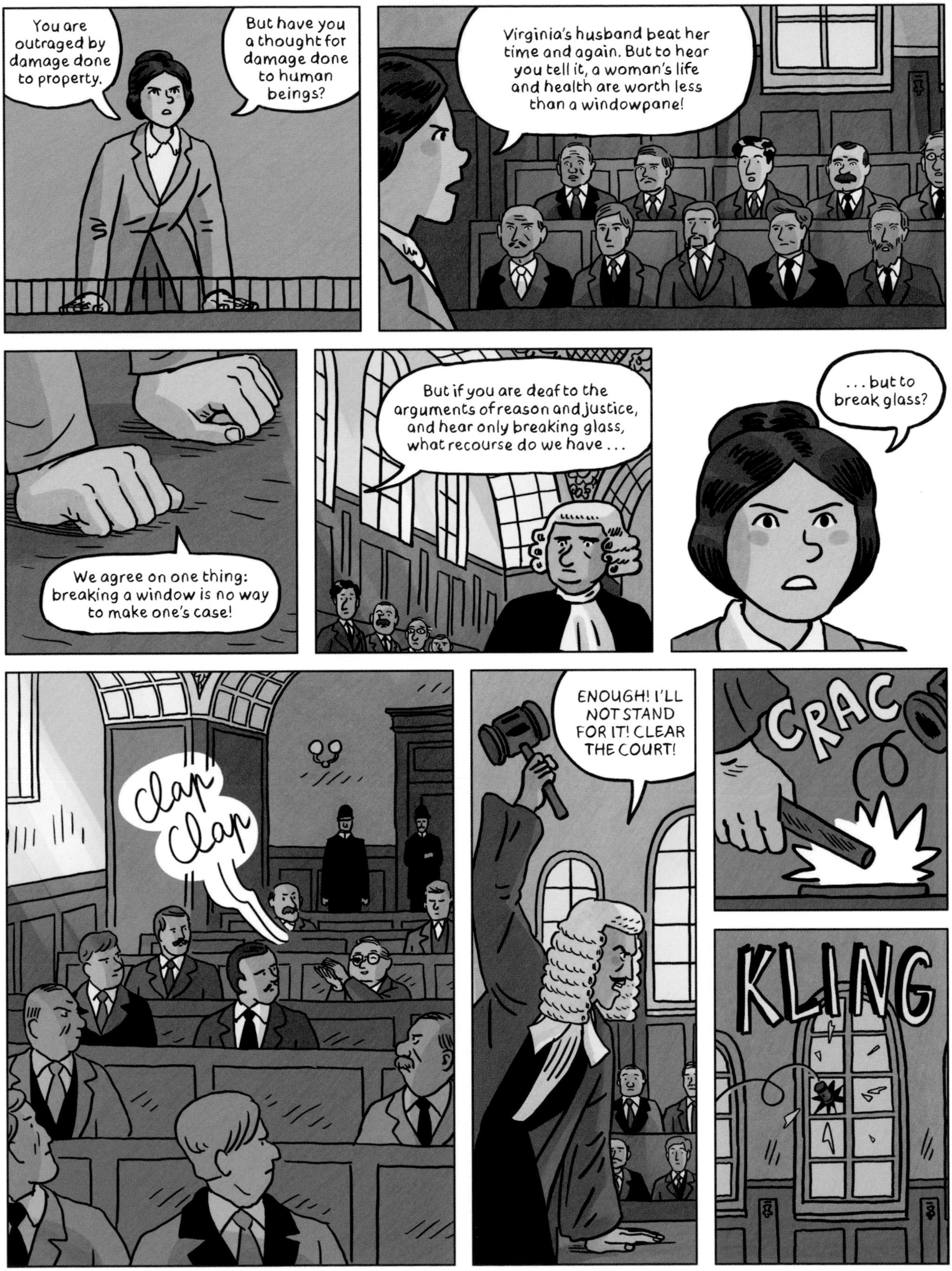
You are outraged by damage done to property.
But have you a thought for damage done to human beings?
Virginia's husband beat her time and again. But to hear you tell it, a woman's life and health are worth less than a windowpane!
We agree on one thing: breaking a window is no way to make one's case!
But if you are deaf to the arguments of reason and justice, and hear only breaking glass, what recourse do we have . . .
. . . but to break glass?
Clap
Clap
ENOUGH! I'LL NOT STAND FOR IT! CLEAR THE COURT!
CRAC
KLING

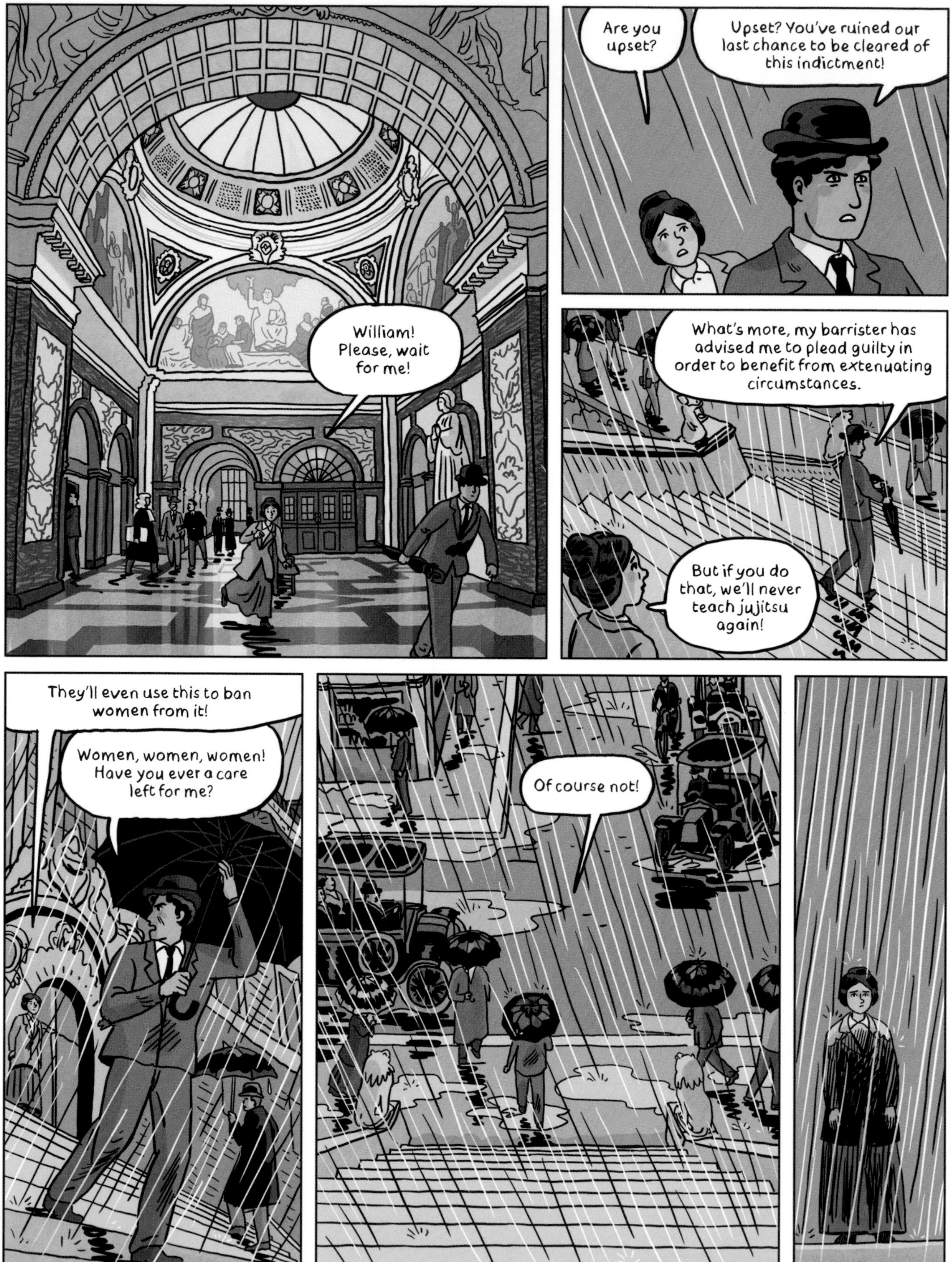
William!
Please, wait for me!
Are you upset?
Upset? You've ruined our last chance to be cleared of this indictment!
What's more, my barrister has advised me to plead guilty in order to benefit from extenuating circumstances.
But if you do that, we'll never teach jujitsu again!
They'll even use this to ban women from it!
Women, women, women! Have you ever a care left for me?
Of course not!

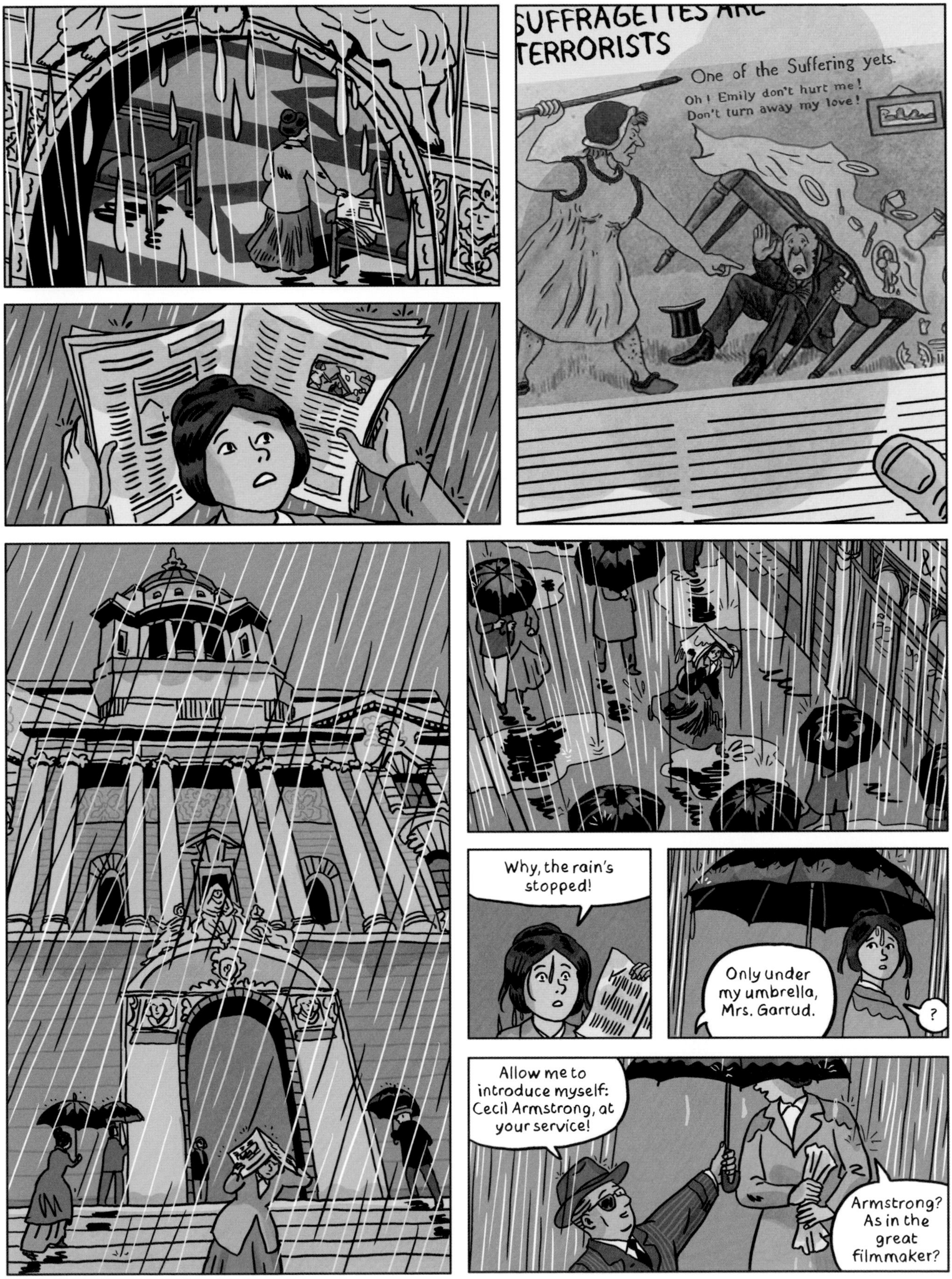
SUFFRAGETTES ARE TERRORISTS
One of the Suffering yets.
Oh! Emily don't hurt me! Don't turn away my love!
Why, the rain's stopped!
Only under my umbrella, Mrs. Garrud.
?
Allow me to introduce myself: Cecil Armstrong, at your service!
Armstrong? As in the great filmmaker?

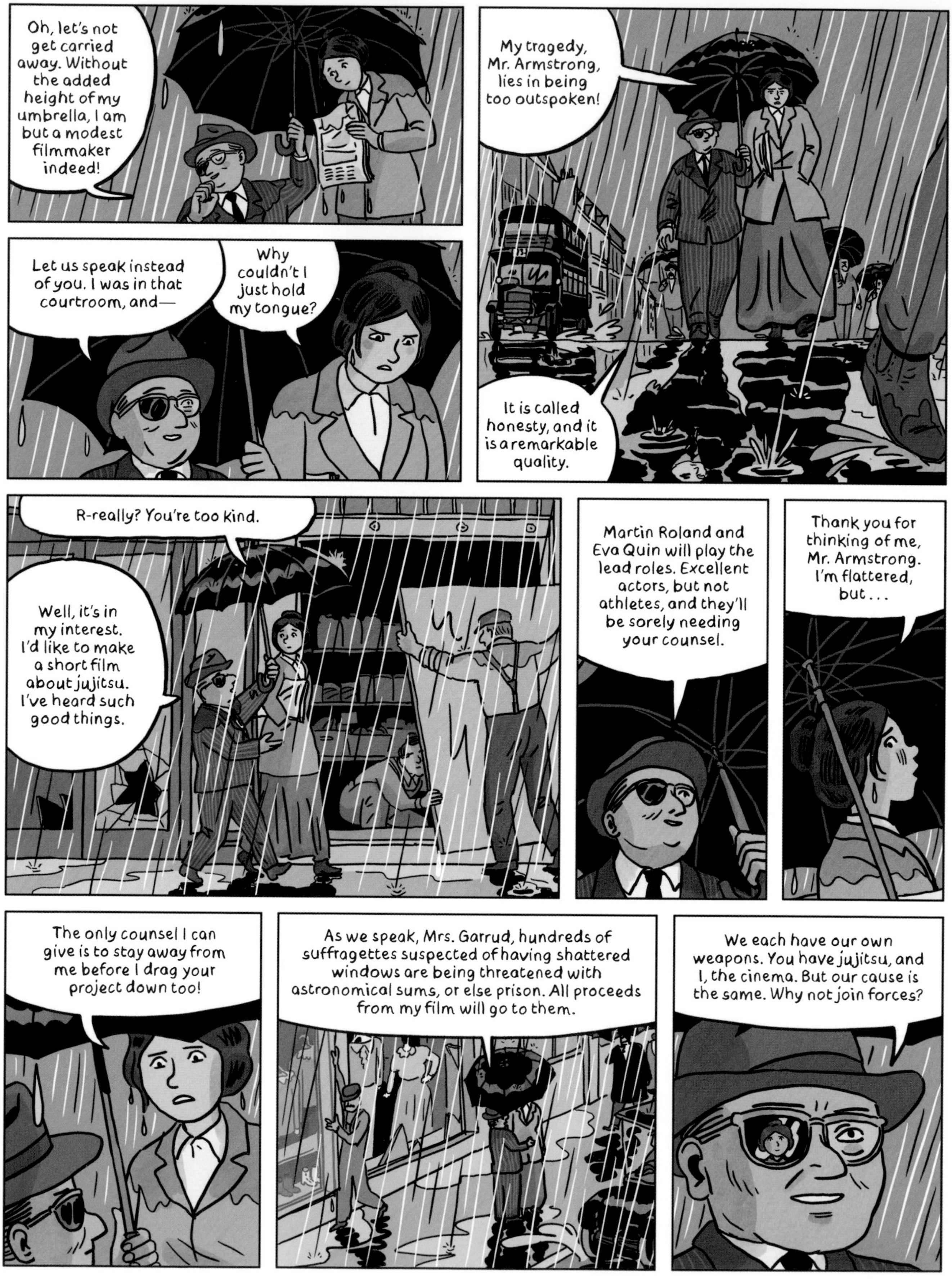
Oh, let's not get carried away. Without the added height of my umbrella, I am but a modest filmmaker indeed!
My tragedy, Mr. Armstrong, lies in being too outspoken!
Let us speak instead of you. I was in that courtroom, and—
Why couldn't I just hold my tongue?
It is called honesty, and it is a remarkable quality.
R-really? You're too kind.
Well, it's in my interest. I'd like to make a short film about jujitsu. I've heard such good things.
Martin Roland and Eva Quin will play the lead roles. Excellent actors, but not athletes, and they'll be sorely needing your counsel.
Thank you for thinking of me, Mr. Armstrong. I'm flattered, but . . .
The only counsel I can give is to stay away from me before I drag your project down too!
As we speak, Mrs. Garrud, hundreds of suffragettes suspected of having shattered windows are being threatened with astronomical sums, or else prison. All proceeds from my film will go to them.
We each have our own weapons. You have jujitsu, and I, the cinema. But our cause is the same. Why not join forces?

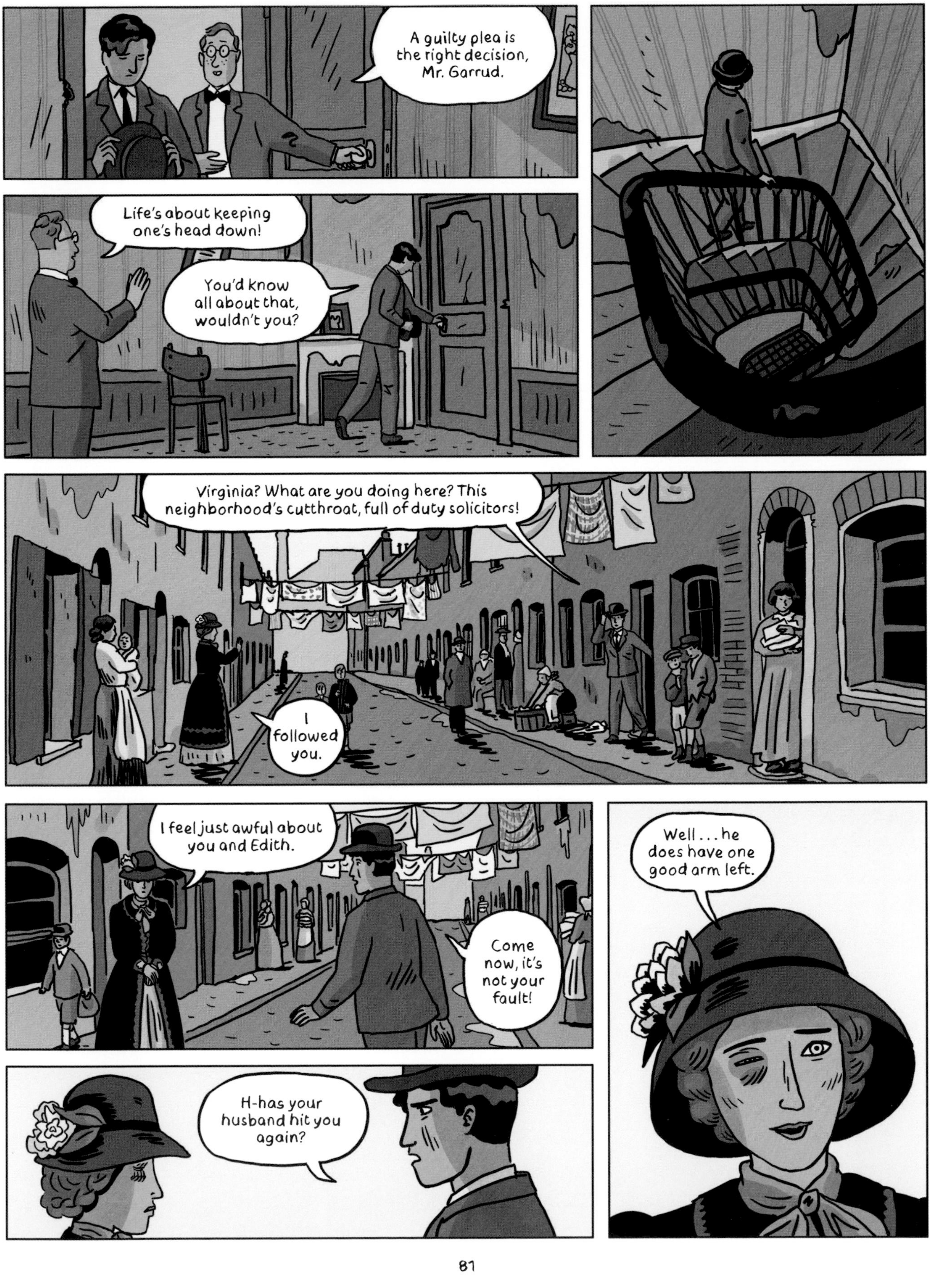

A guilty plea is the right decision, Mr. Garrud.
Life's about keeping one's head down!
You'd know all about that, wouldn't you?
Virginia? What are you doing here? This neighborhood's cutthroat, full of duty solicitors!
I followed you.
I feel just awful about you and Edith.
Come now, it's not your fault!
H-has your husband hit you again?
Well . . . he does have one good arm left.

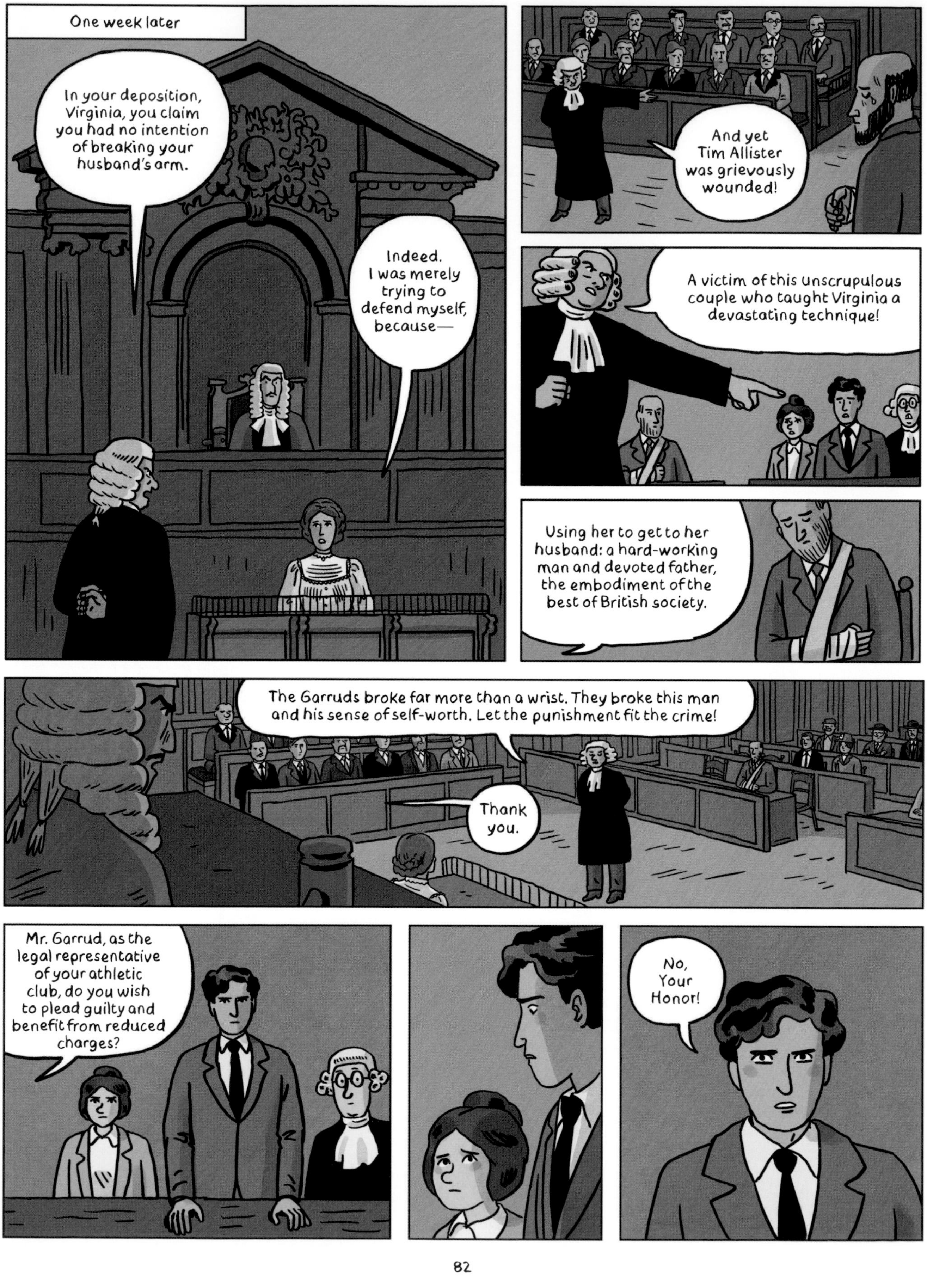
One week later
In your deposition, Virginia, you claim you had no intention of breaking your husband's arm.
Indeed. I was merely trying to defend myself, because—
And yet Tim Allister was grievously wounded!
A victim of this unscrupulous couple who taught Virginia a devastating technique!
Using her to get to her husband: a hard-working man and devoted father, the embodiment of the best of British society.
The Garruds broke far more than a wrist. They broke this man and his sense of self-worth. Let the punishment fit the crime!
Thank you.
Mr. Garrud, as the legal representative of your athletic club, do you wish to plead guilty and benefit from reduced charges?
No, Your Honor!

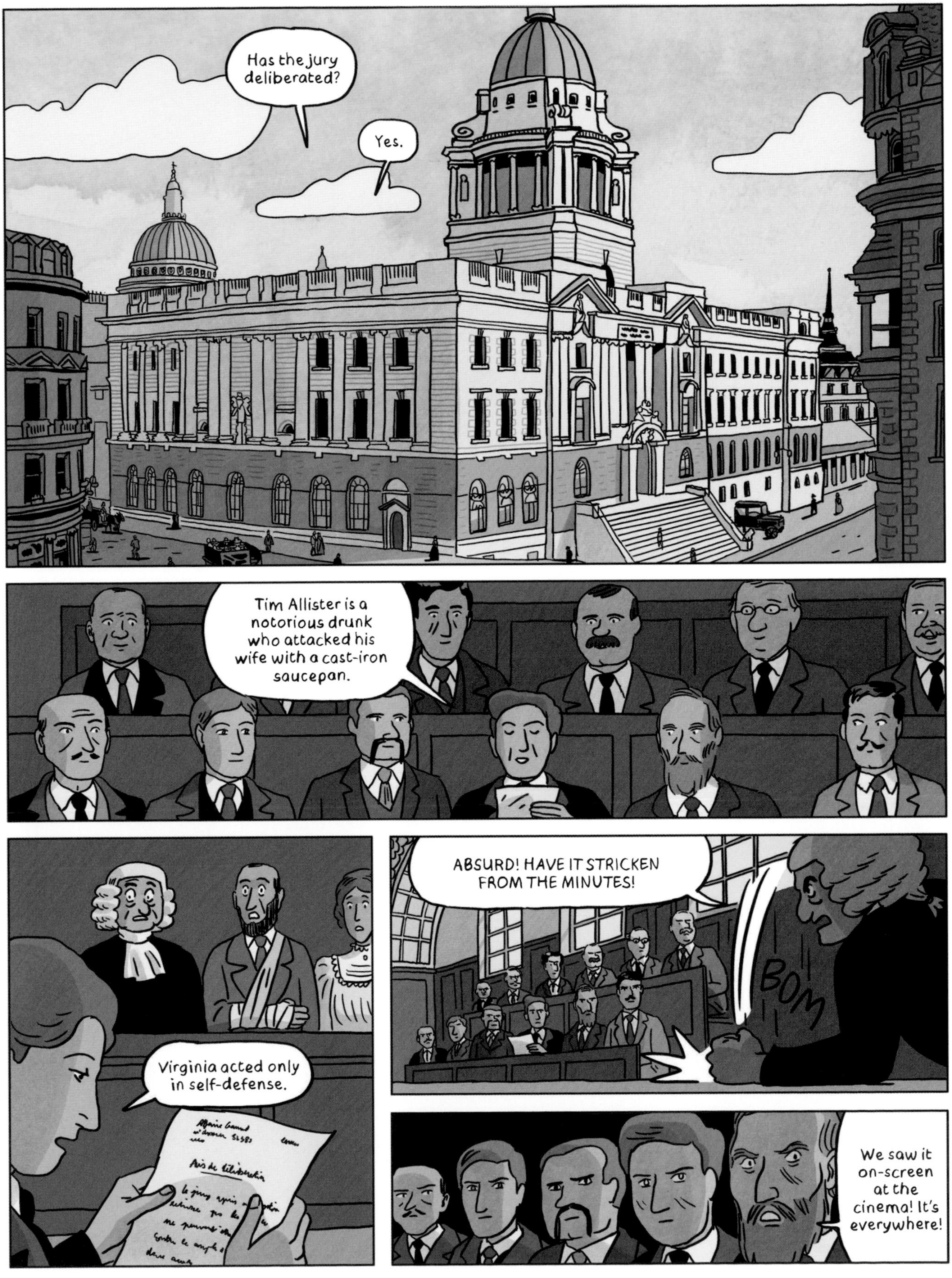
Has the jury deliberated?
Yes.
Tim Allister is a notorious drunk who attacked his wife with a cast-iron saucepan.
Virginia acted only in self-defense.
ABSURD! HAVE IT STRICKEN FROM THE MINUTES!
BOM
We saw it on-screen at the cinema! It's everywhere!

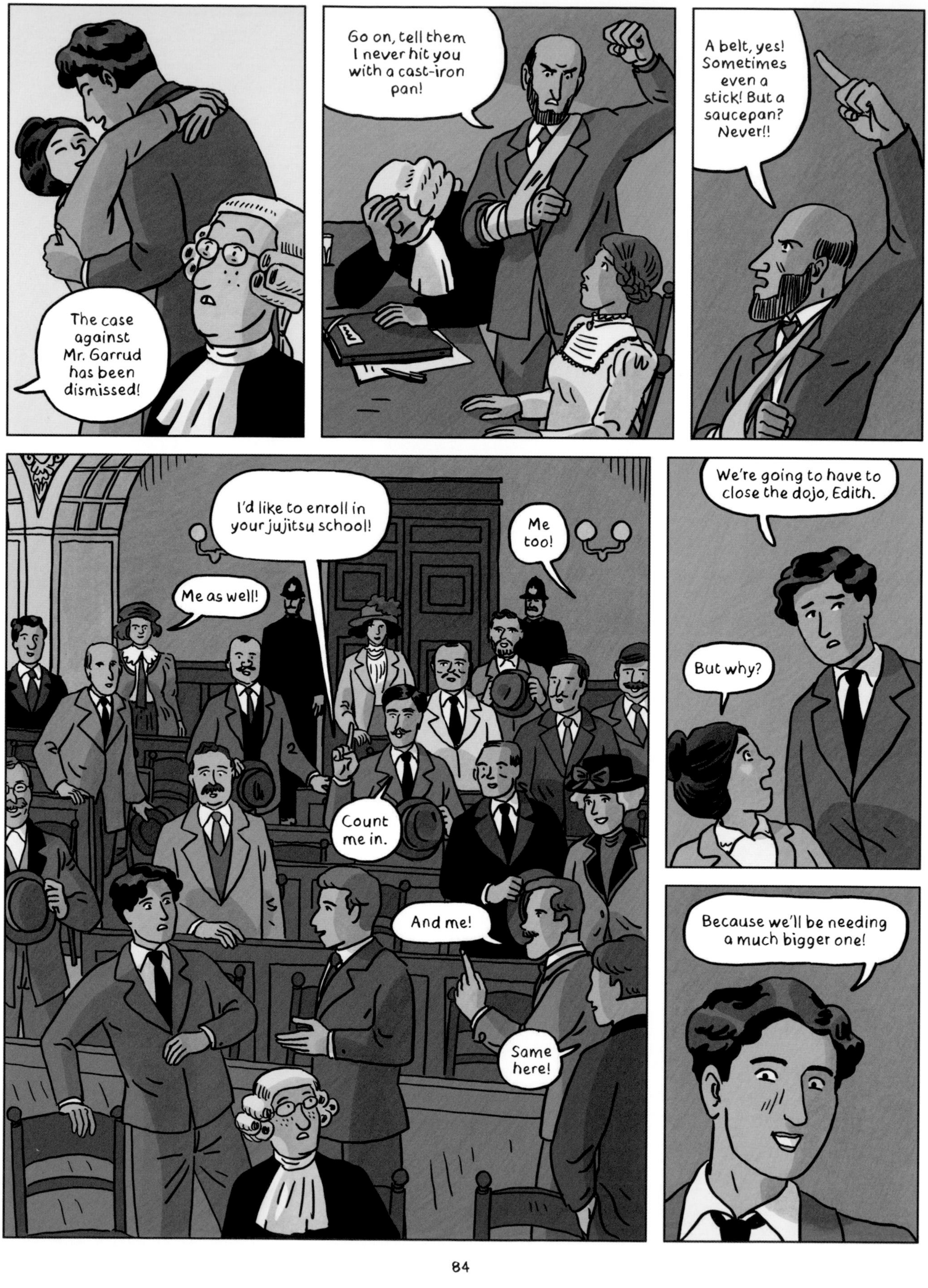
The case against Mr. Garrud has been dismissed!
Go on, tell them I never hit you with a cast-iron pan!
A belt, yes! Sometimes even a stick! But a saucepan? Never!!
I'd like to enroll in your jujitsu school!
Me too!
Me as well!
Count me in.
And me!
Same here!
We're going to have to close the dojo, Edith.
But why?
Because we'll be needing a much bigger one!

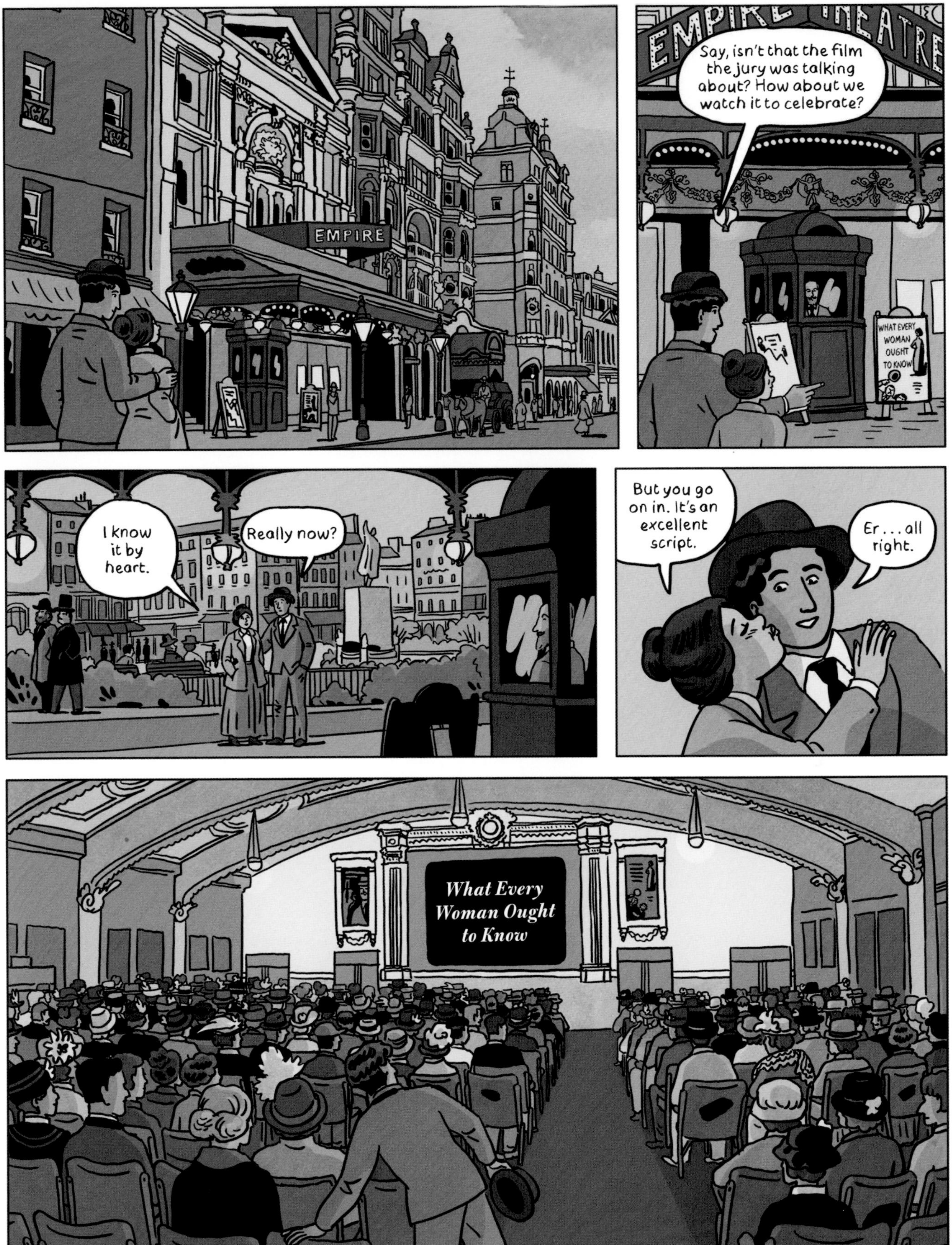
EMPIRE
EMPIRE THEATRE
Say, isn't that the film the jury was talking about? How about we watch it to celebrate?
WHAT EVERY WOMAN OUGHT TO KNOW
I know it by heart.
Really now?
But you go on in. It's an excellent script.
Er . . . all right.
What Every Woman Ought to Know

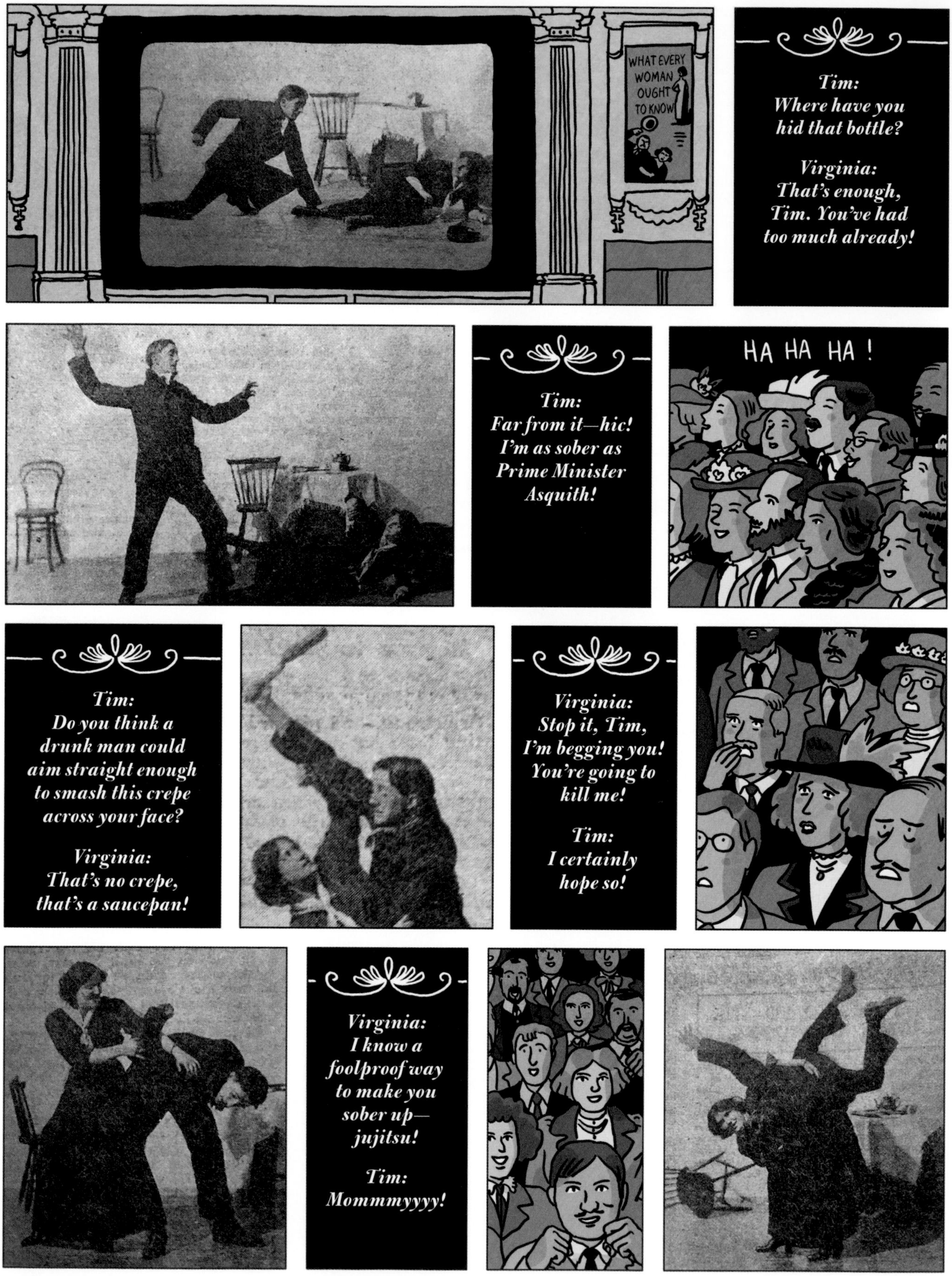
WHAT EVERY WOMAN OUGHT TO KNOW
Tim:
Where have you hid that bottle?
Virginia:
That's enough, Tim. You've had too much already!
Tim:
Far from it—hic! I'm as sober as Prime Minister Asquith!
HA HA HA!
Tim:
Do you think a drunk man could aim straight enough to smash this crepe across your face?
Virginia:
That's no crepe, that's a saucepan!
Virginia:
Stop it, Tim, I'm begging you! You're going to kill me!
Tim:
I certainly hope so!
Virginia:
I know a foolproof way to make you sober up—jujitsu!
Tim:
Mommmyyyy!

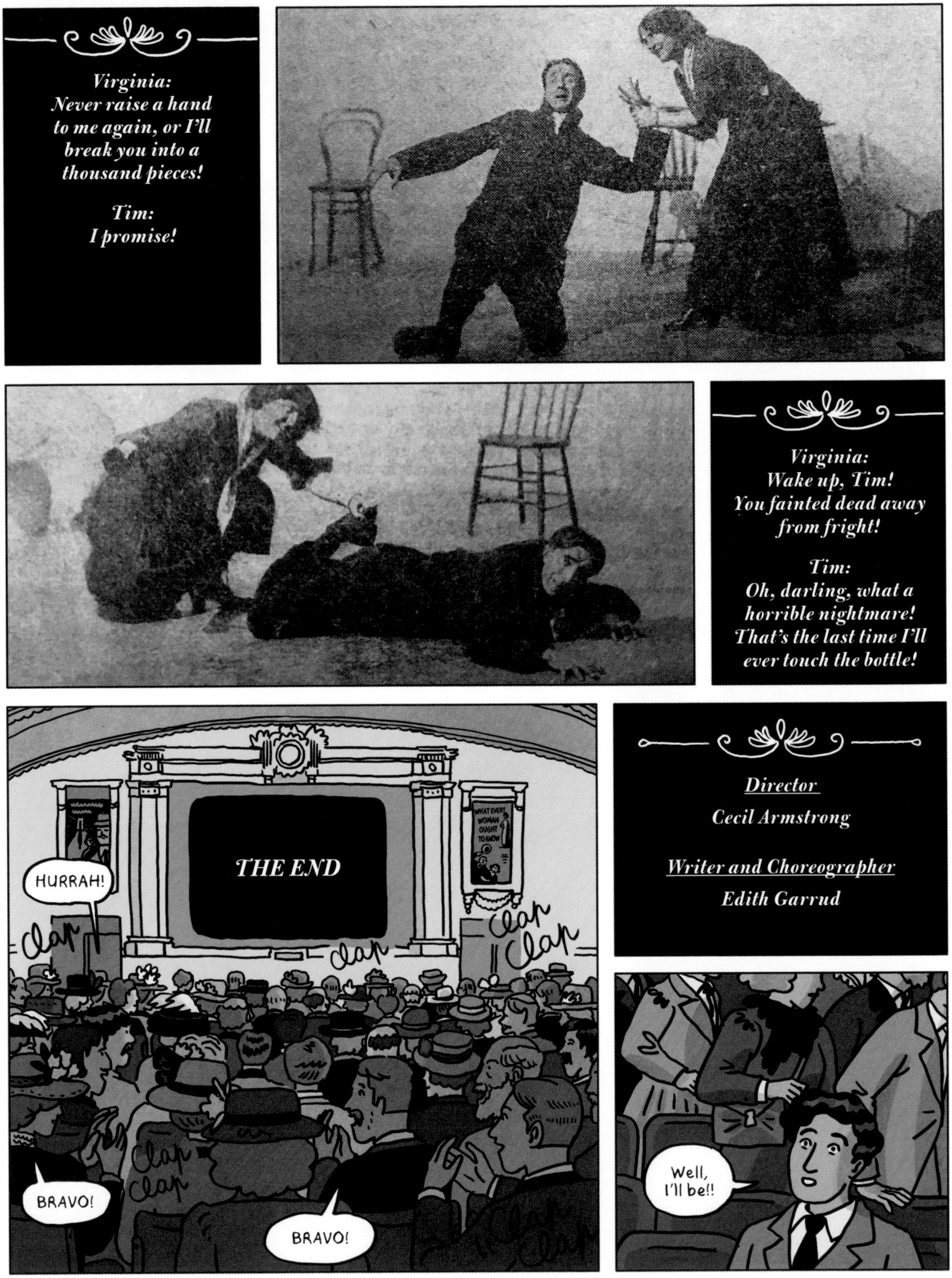

Virginia:
Never raise a hand to me again, or I'll break you into a thousand pieces!
Tim:
I promise!
Virginia:
Wake up, Tim! You fainted dead away from fright!
Tim:
Oh, darling, what a horrible nightmare! That's the last time I'll ever touch the bottle!
THE END
WHAT EVERY WOMAN OUGHT TO KNOW
HURRAH!
clap
clap
clap clap
clap clap
BRAVO!
BRAVO!
Director
Cecil Armstrong
Writer and Choreographer
Edith Garrud
Well, I'll be!!

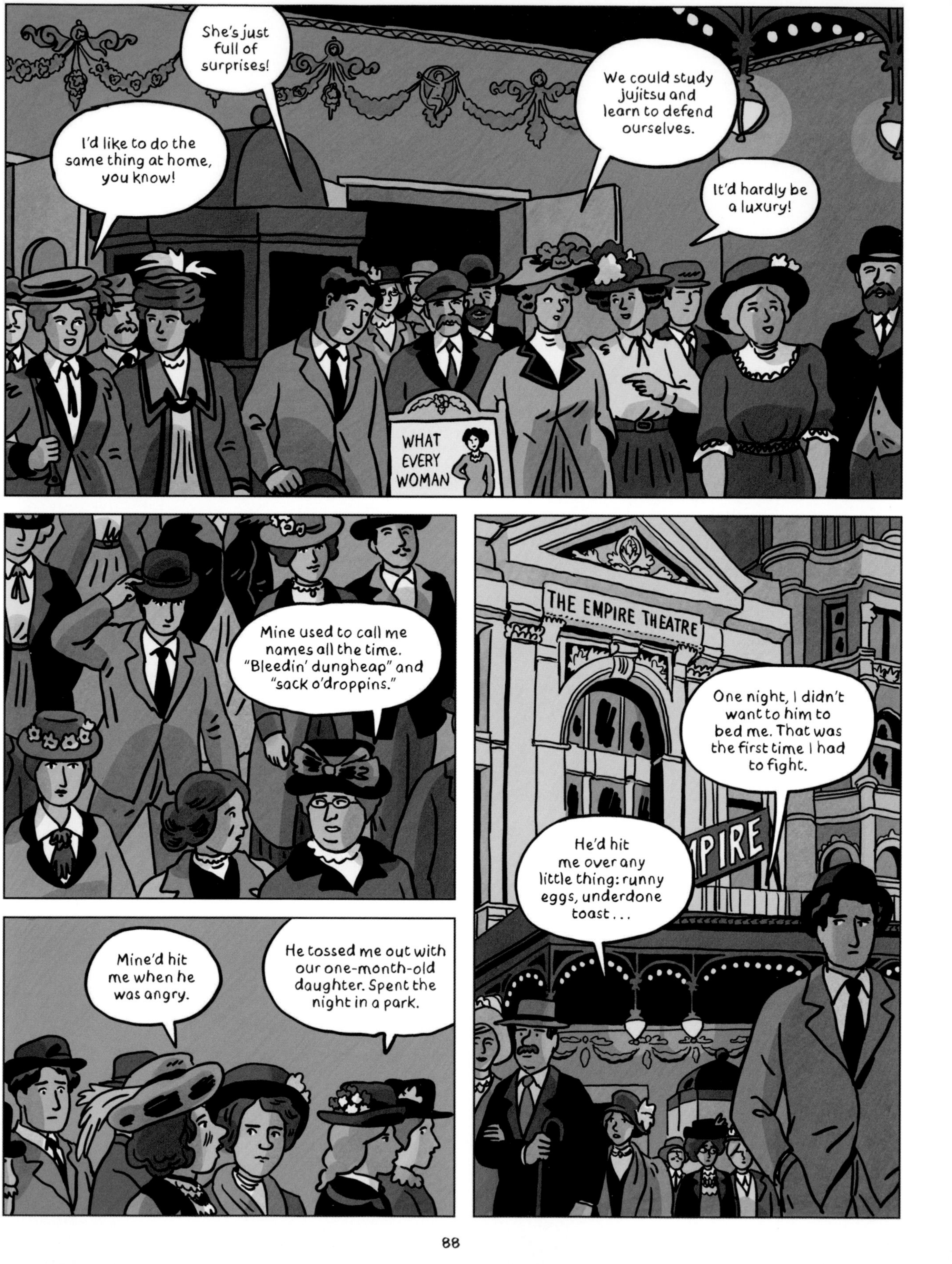
I'd like to do the same thing at home, you know!
She's just full of surprises!
We could study jujitsu and learn to defend ourselves.
It'd hardly be a luxury!
WHAT EVERY WOMAN
Mine used to call me names all the time. "Bleedin' dungheap" and "sack o'droppins."
Mine'd hit me when he was angry.
He tossed me out with our one-month-old daughter. Spent the night in a park.
THE EMPIRE THEATRE
One night, I didn't want to him to bed me. That was the first time I had to fight.
He'd hit me over any little thing: runny eggs, underdone toast...
IPIRE

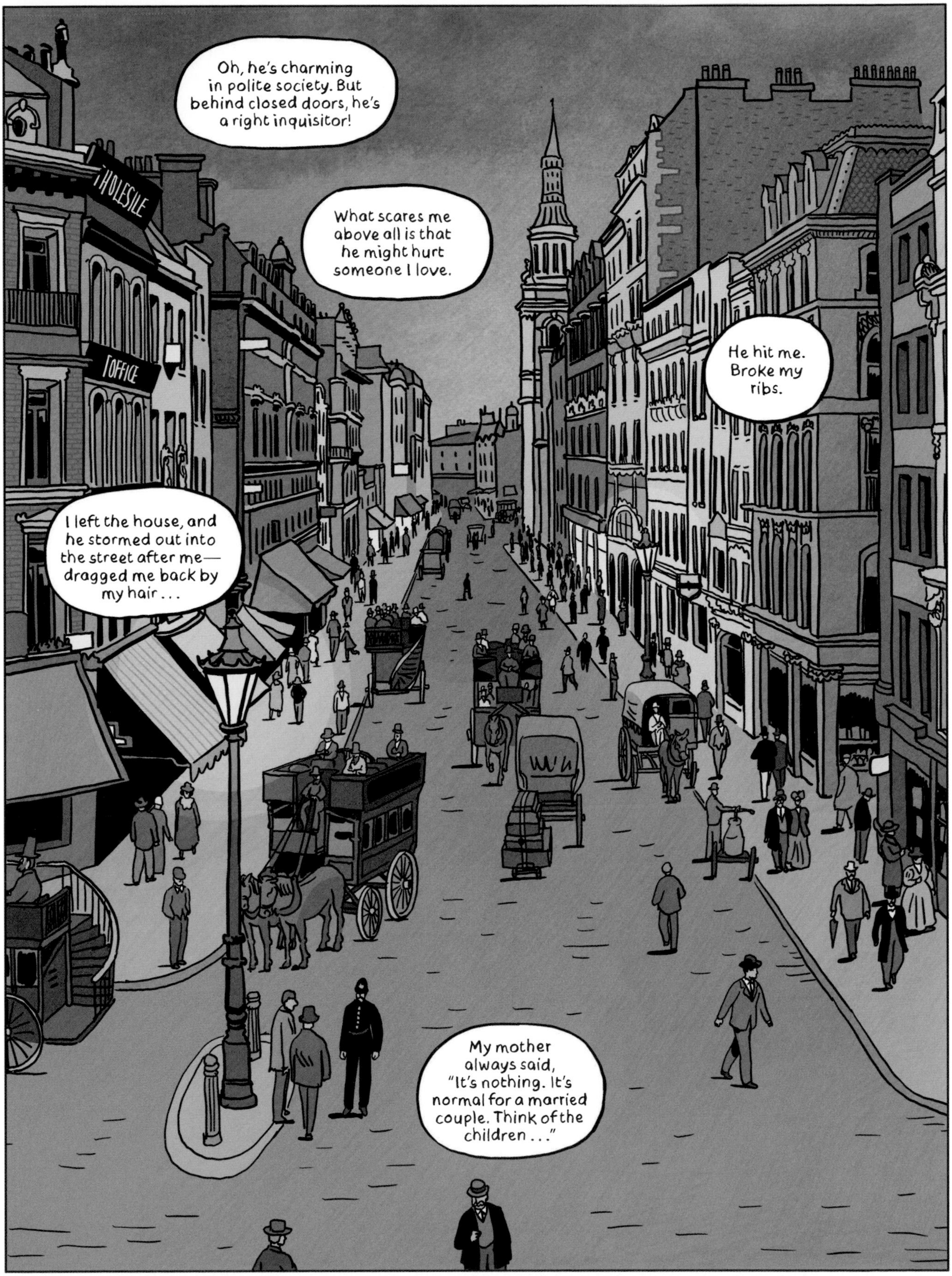
Oh, he's charming in polite society. But behind closed doors, he's a right inquisitor!
What scares me above all is that he might hurt someone I love.
He hit me. Broke my ribs.
I left the house, and he stormed out into the street after me— dragged me back by my hair . . .
My mother always said, "It's nothing. It's normal for a married couple. Think of the children . . ."

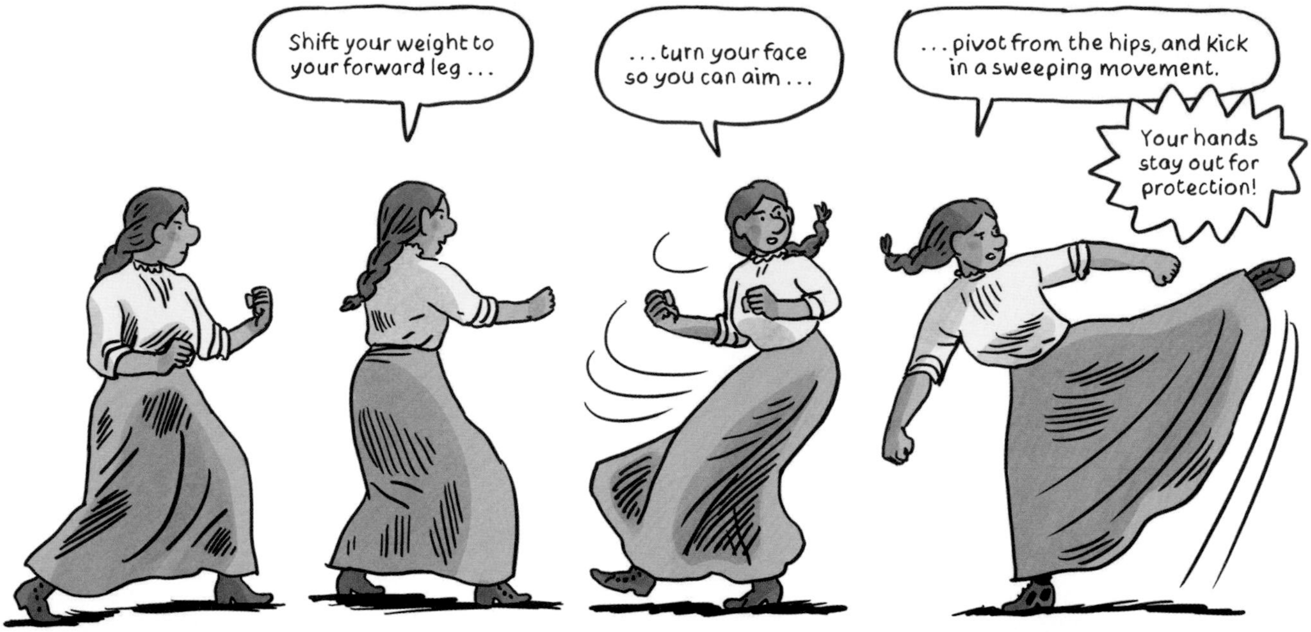
Shift your weight to your forward leg . . .
. . . turn your face so you can aim . . .
. . . pivot from the hips, and kick in a sweeping movement.
Your hands stay out for protection!

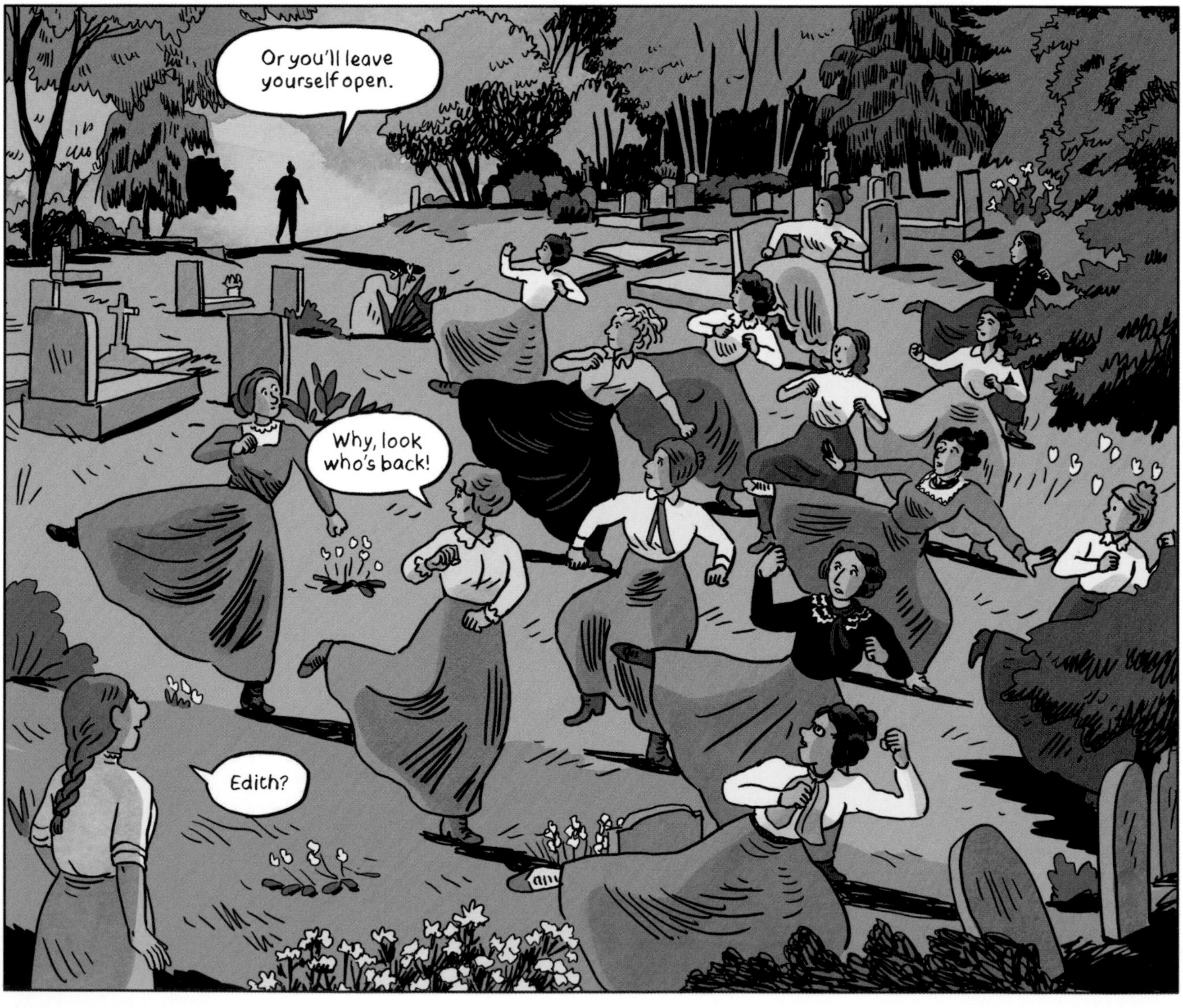
Or you'll leave yourself open.
Why, look who's back!
Edith?

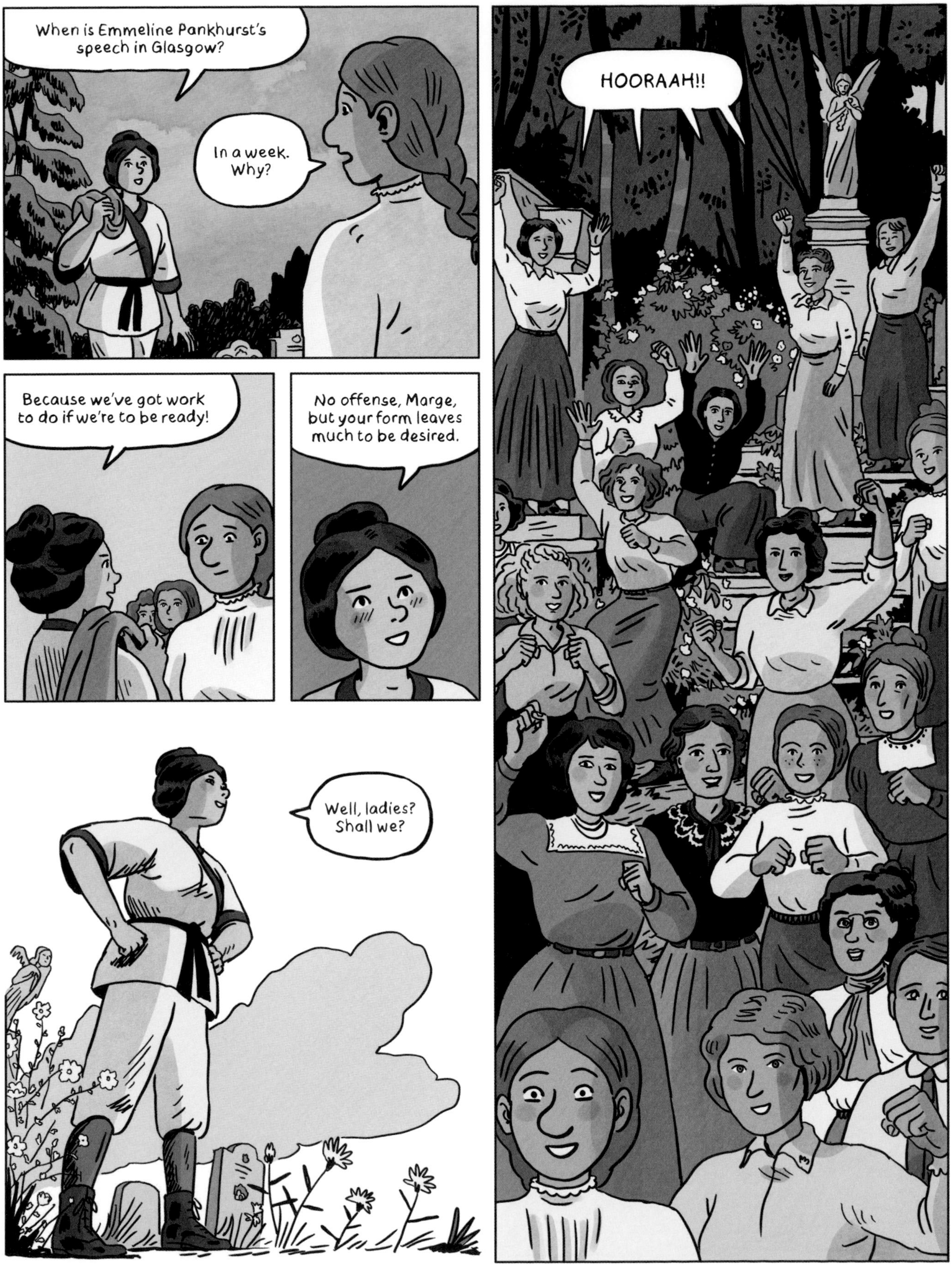
When is Emmeline Pankhurst's speech in Glasgow?
In a week. Why?
Because we've got work to do if we're to be ready!
No offense, Marge, but your form leaves much to be desired.
Well, ladies? Shall we?
HOORAAH!!

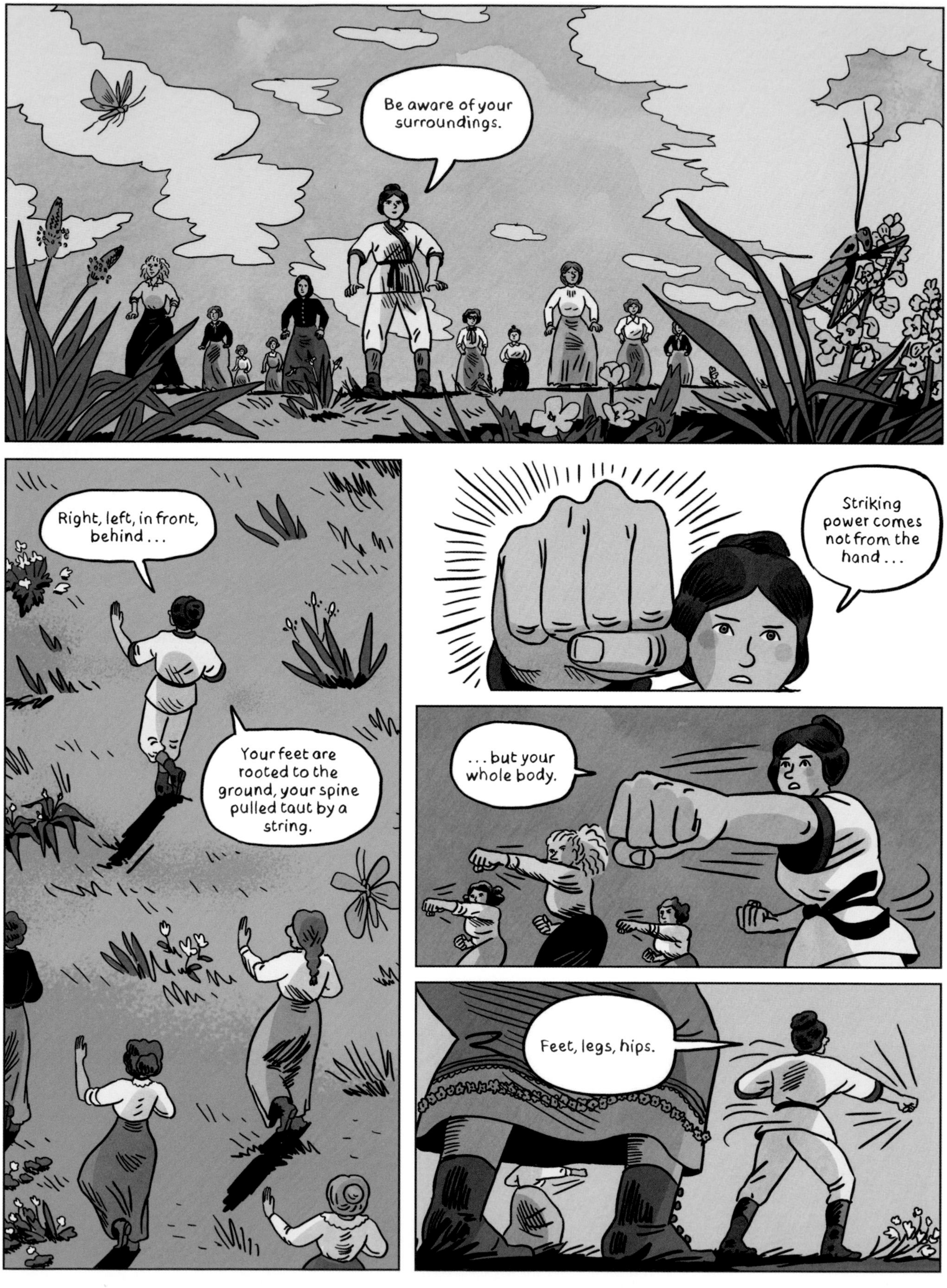
Be aware of your surroundings.
Right, left, in front, behind . . .
Your feet are rooted to the ground, your spine pulled taut by a string.
Striking power comes not from the hand . . .
. . . but your whole body.
Feet, legs, hips.

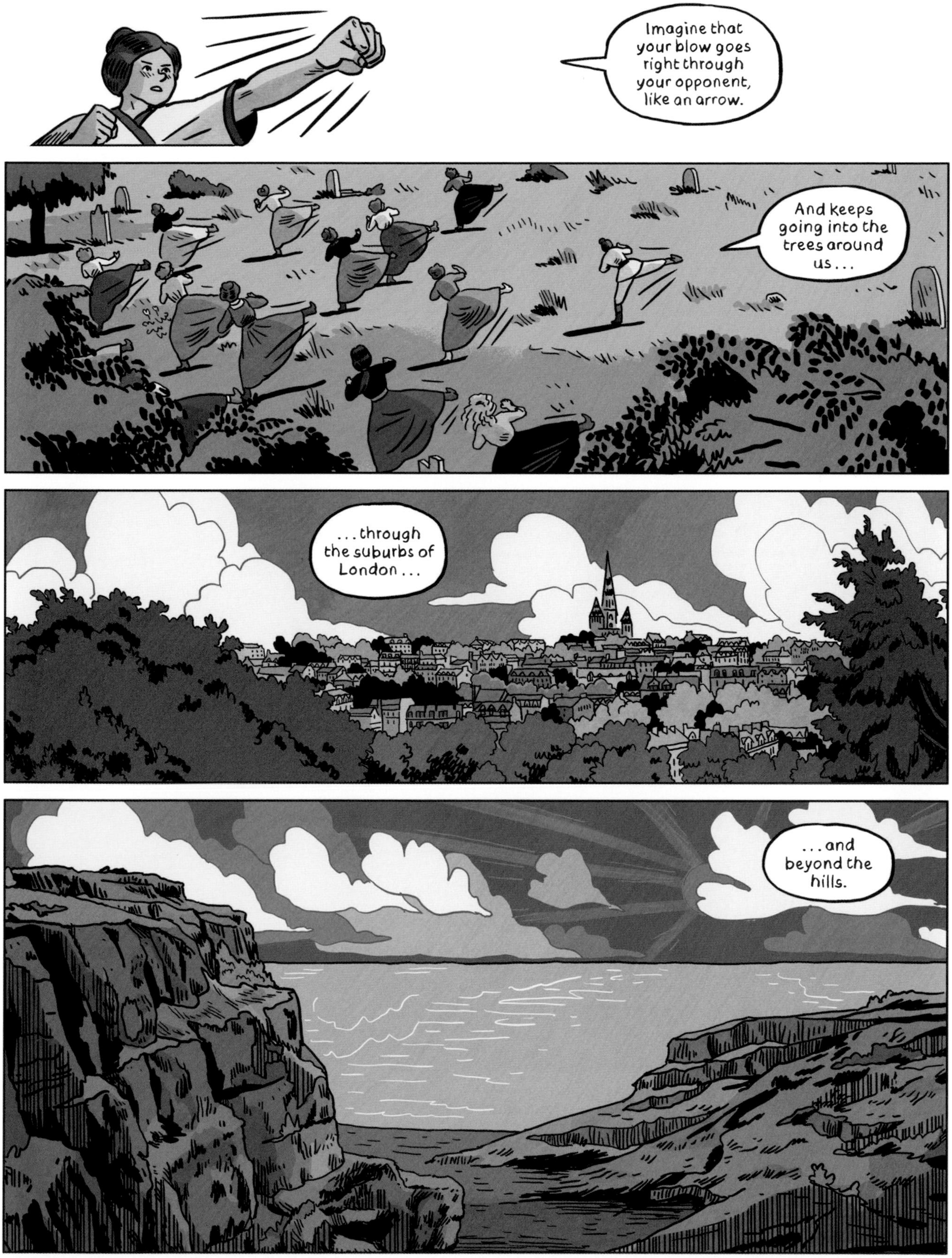
Imagine that your blow goes right through your opponent, like an arrow.
And keeps going into the trees around us...
...through the suburbs of London...
...and beyond the hills.

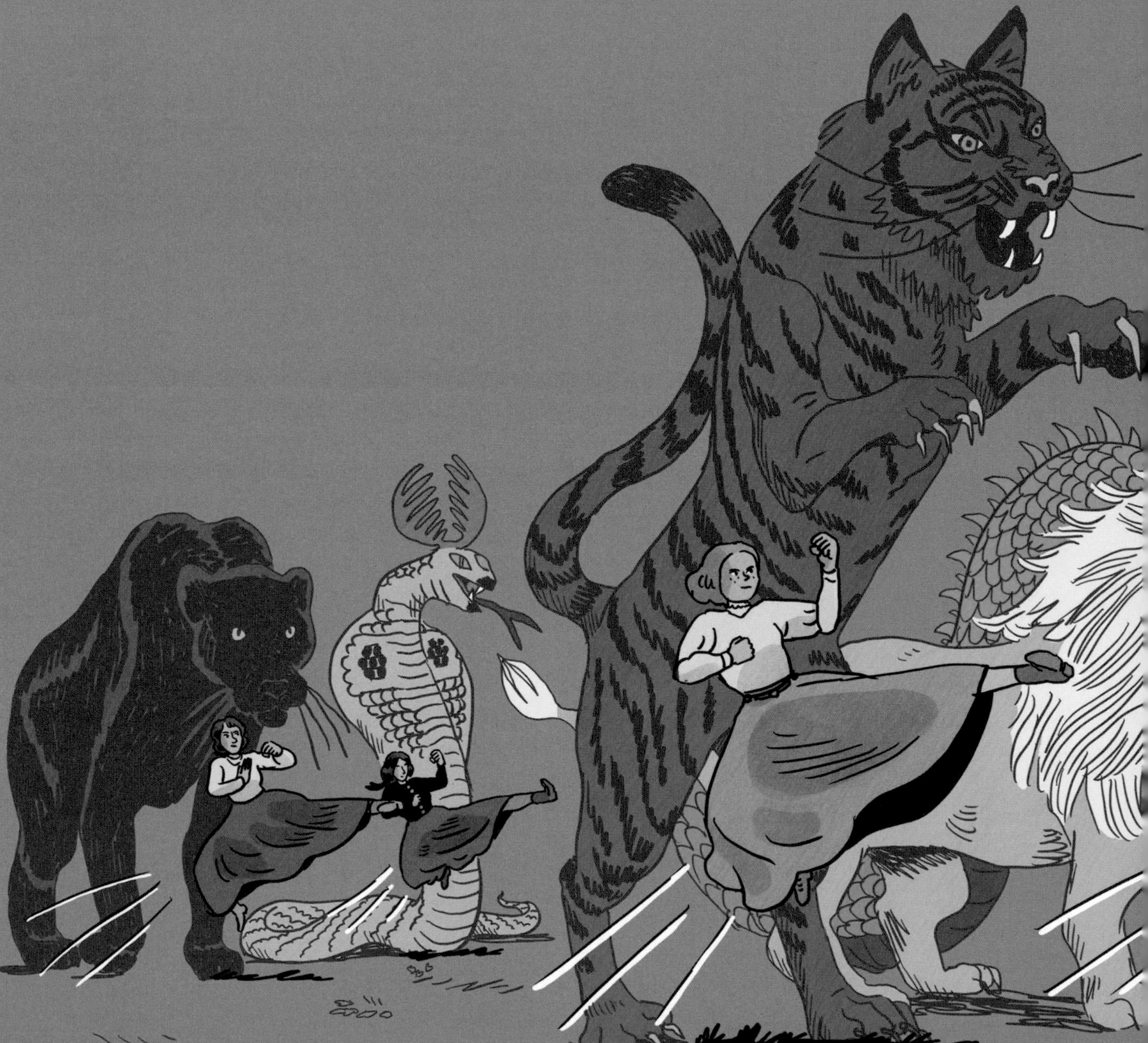
Imagine something in your back pushing you forward, giving you strength.

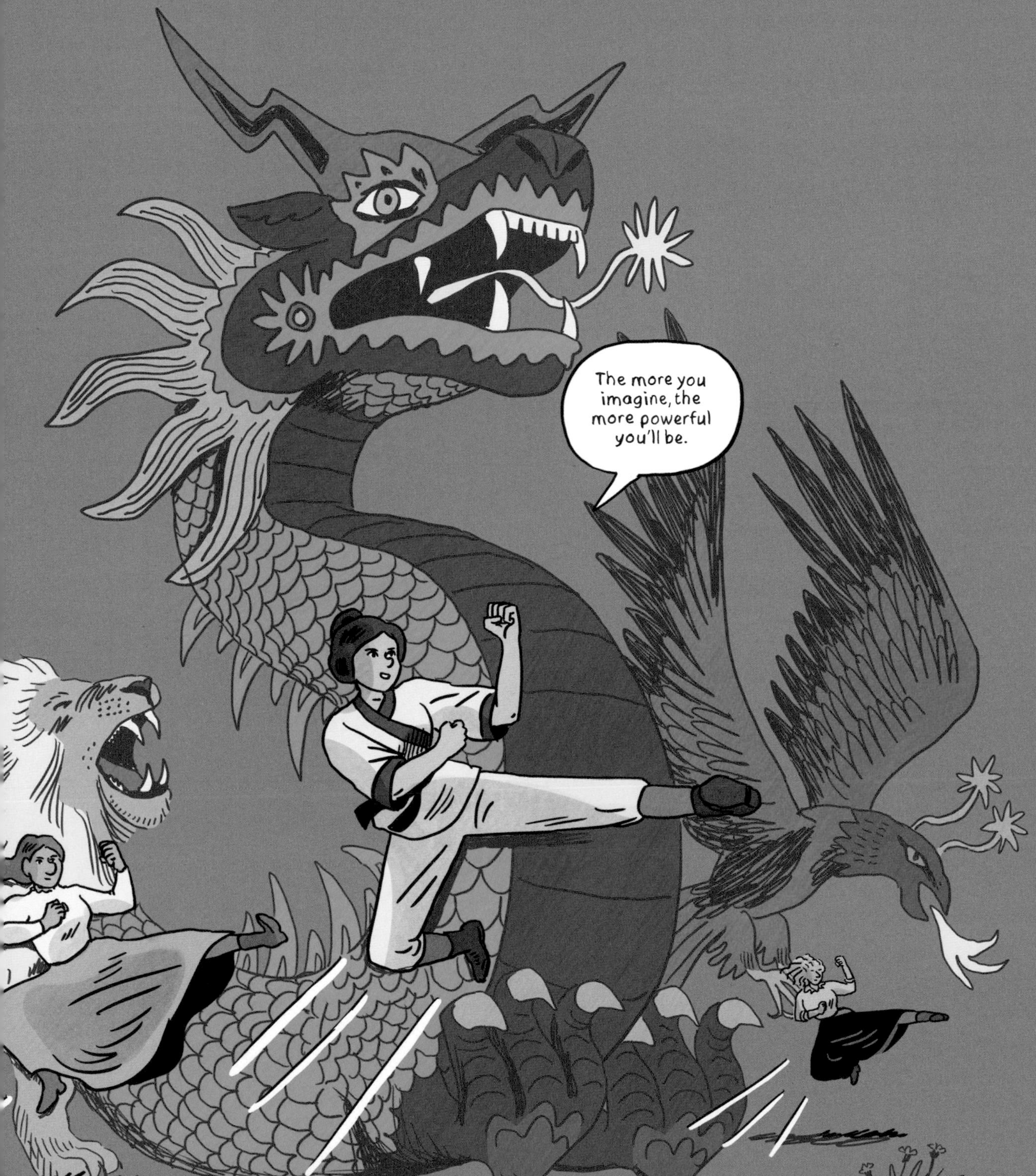
The more you imagine, the more powerful you'll be.

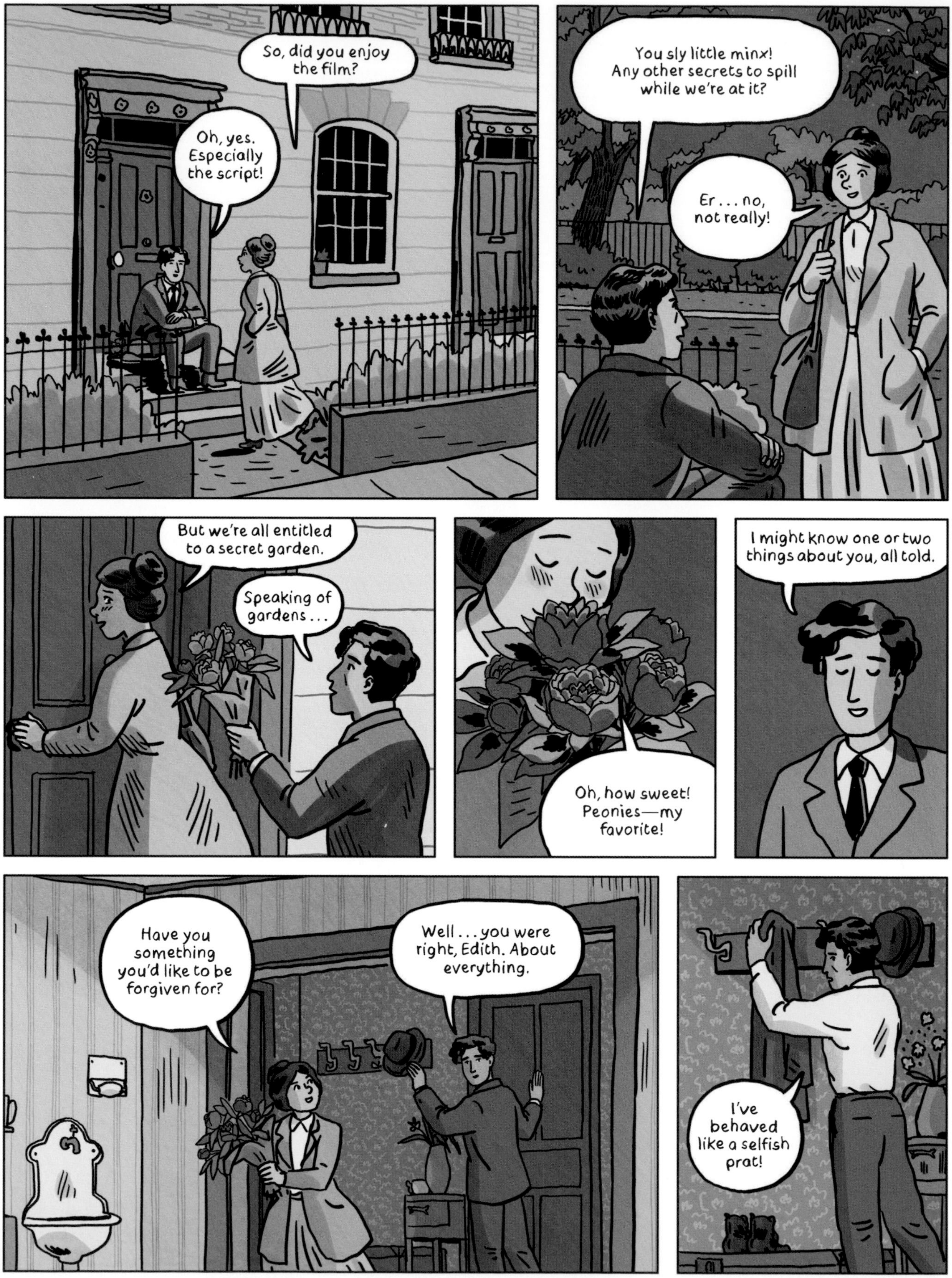
So, did you enjoy the film?
Oh, yes. Especially the script!
You sly little minx! Any other secrets to spill while we're at it?
Er . . . no, not really!
But we're all entitled to a secret garden.
Speaking of gardens . . .
Oh, how sweet! Peonies—my favorite!
I might know one or two things about you, all told.
Have you something you'd like to be forgiven for?
Well . . . you were right, Edith. About everything.
I've behaved like a selfish prat!

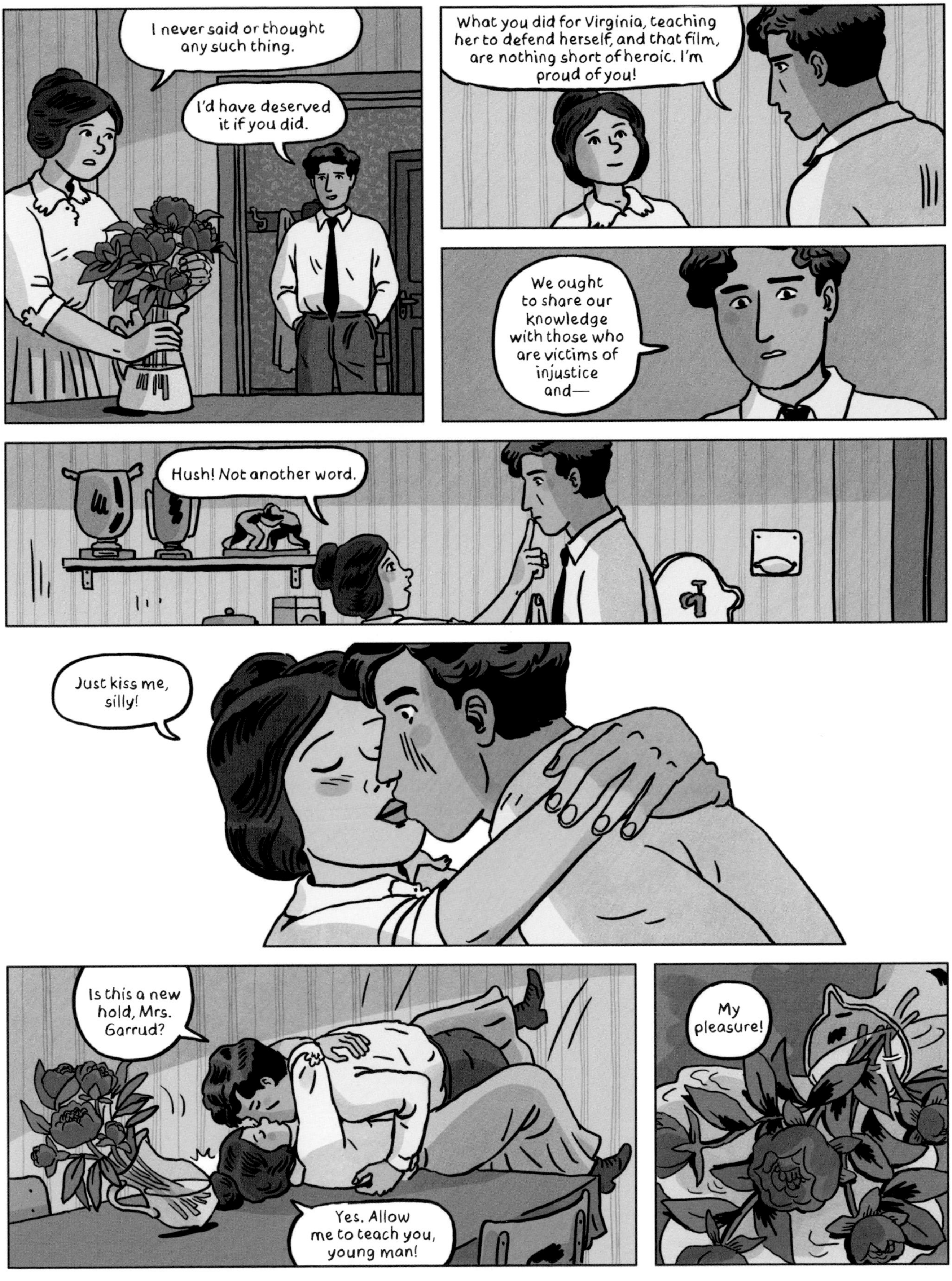
I never said or thought any such thing.
I'd have deserved it if you did.
What you did for Virginia, teaching her to defend herself, and that film, are nothing short of heroic. I'm proud of you!
We ought to share our knowledge with those who are victims of injustice and—
Hush! Not another word.
Just kiss me, silly!
Is this a new hold, Mrs. Garrud?
Yes. Allow me to teach you, young man!
My pleasure!

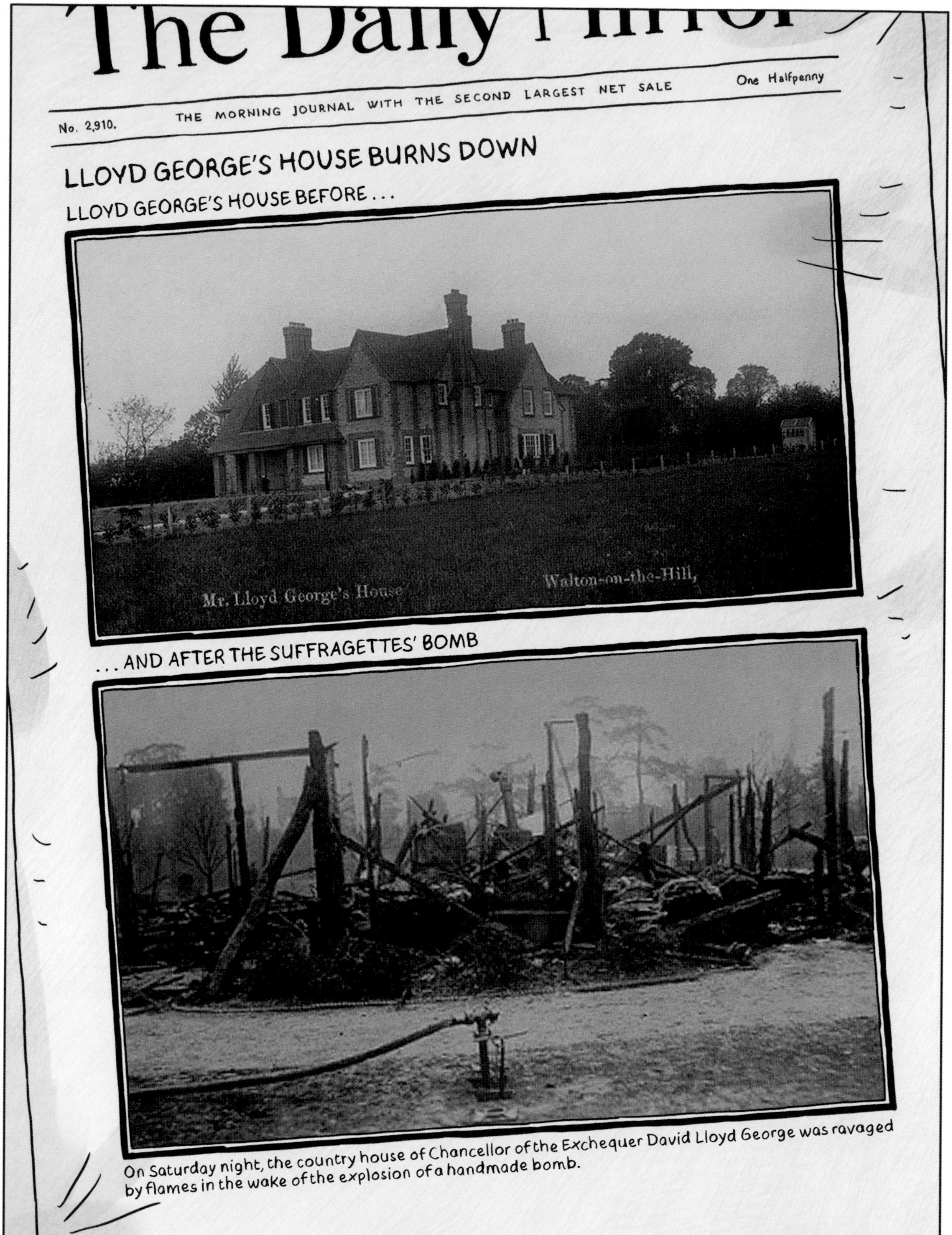
The Daily Mirror
No. 2,910.
THE MORNING JOURNAL WITH THE SECOND LARGEST NET SALE
One Halfpenny
LLOYD GEORGE'S HOUSE BURNS DOWN
LLOYD GEORGE'S HOUSE BEFORE . . .
Mr. Lloyd George's House
Walton-on-the-Hill,
. . . AND AFTER THE SUFFRAGETTES' BOMB
On Saturday night, the country house of Chancellor of the Exchequer David Lloyd George was ravaged by flames in the wake of the explosion of a handmade bomb.

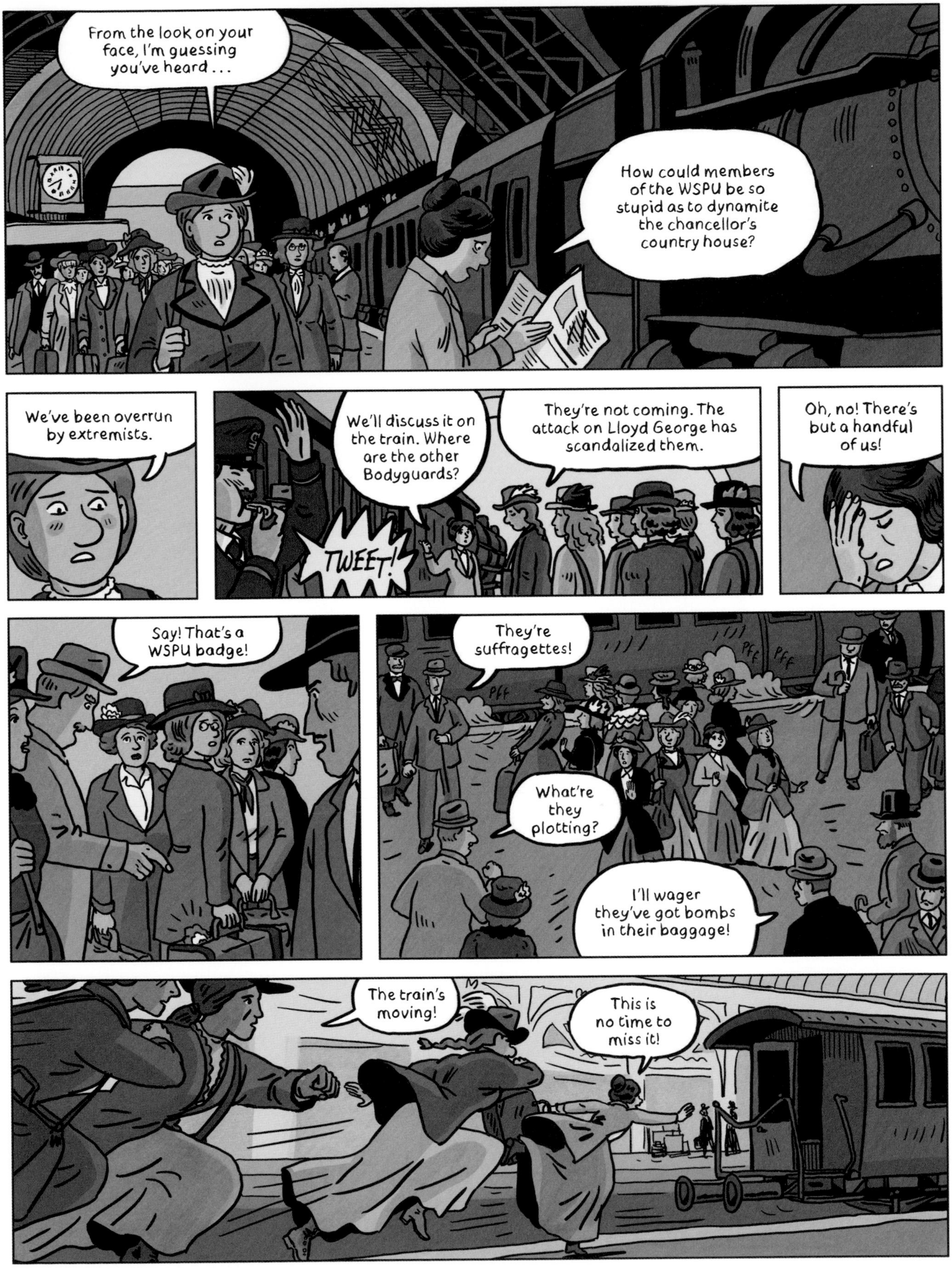
From the look on your face, I'm guessing you've heard . . .
How could members of the WSPU be so stupid as to dynamite the chancellor's country house?
We've been overrun by extremists.
We'll discuss it on the train. Where are the other Bodyguards?
TWEET!
They're not coming. The attack on Lloyd George has scandalized them.
Oh, no! There's but a handful of us!
Say! That's a WSPU badge!
They're suffragettes!
PFF
What're they plotting?
I'll wager they've got bombs in their baggage!
The train's moving!
This is no time to miss it!

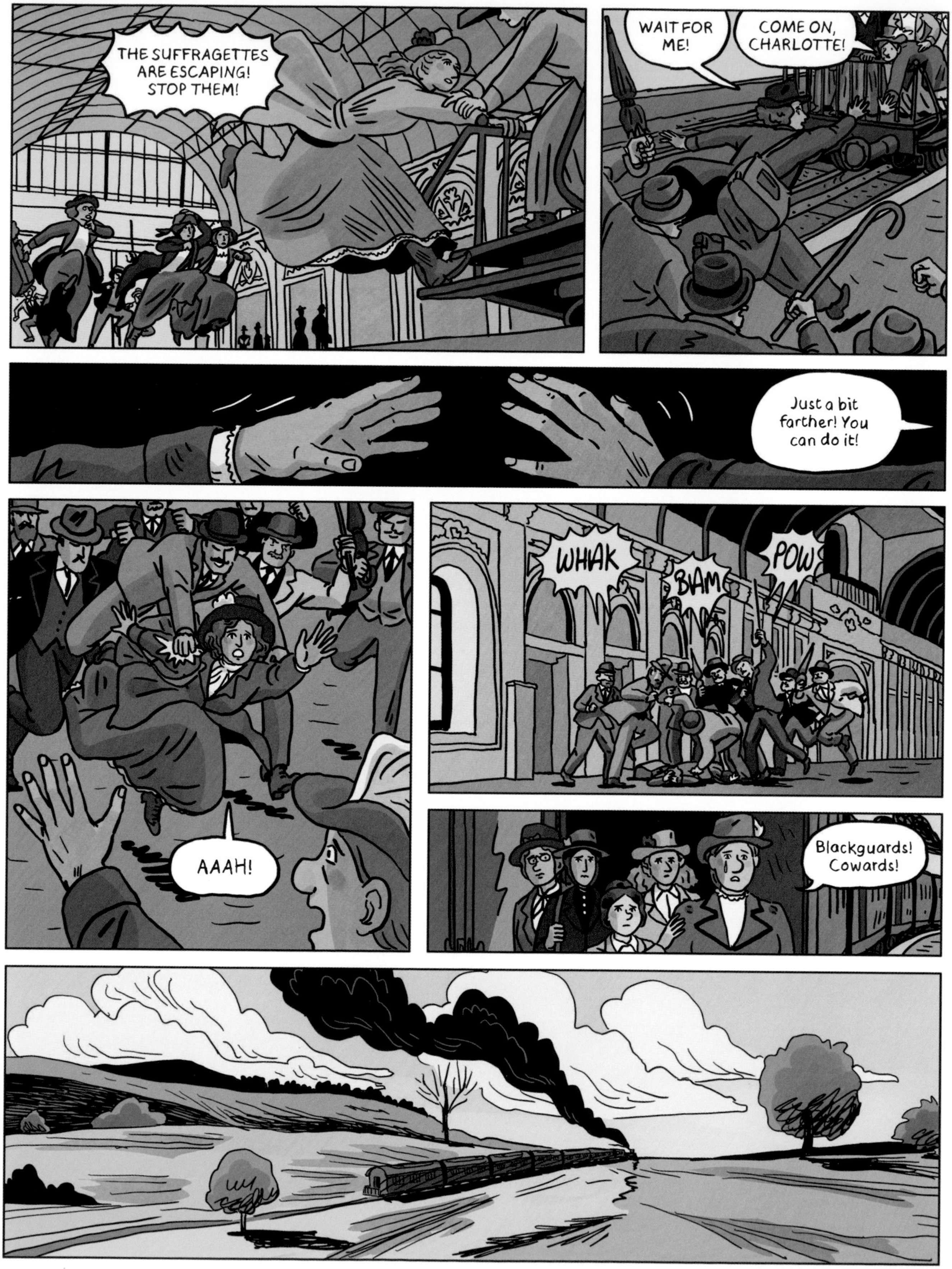
THE SUFFRAGETTES ARE ESCAPING! STOP THEM!
WAIT FOR ME!
COME ON, CHARLOTTE!
Just a bit farther! You can do it!
AAAH!
WHAK
BAM
POW
Blackguards! Cowards!

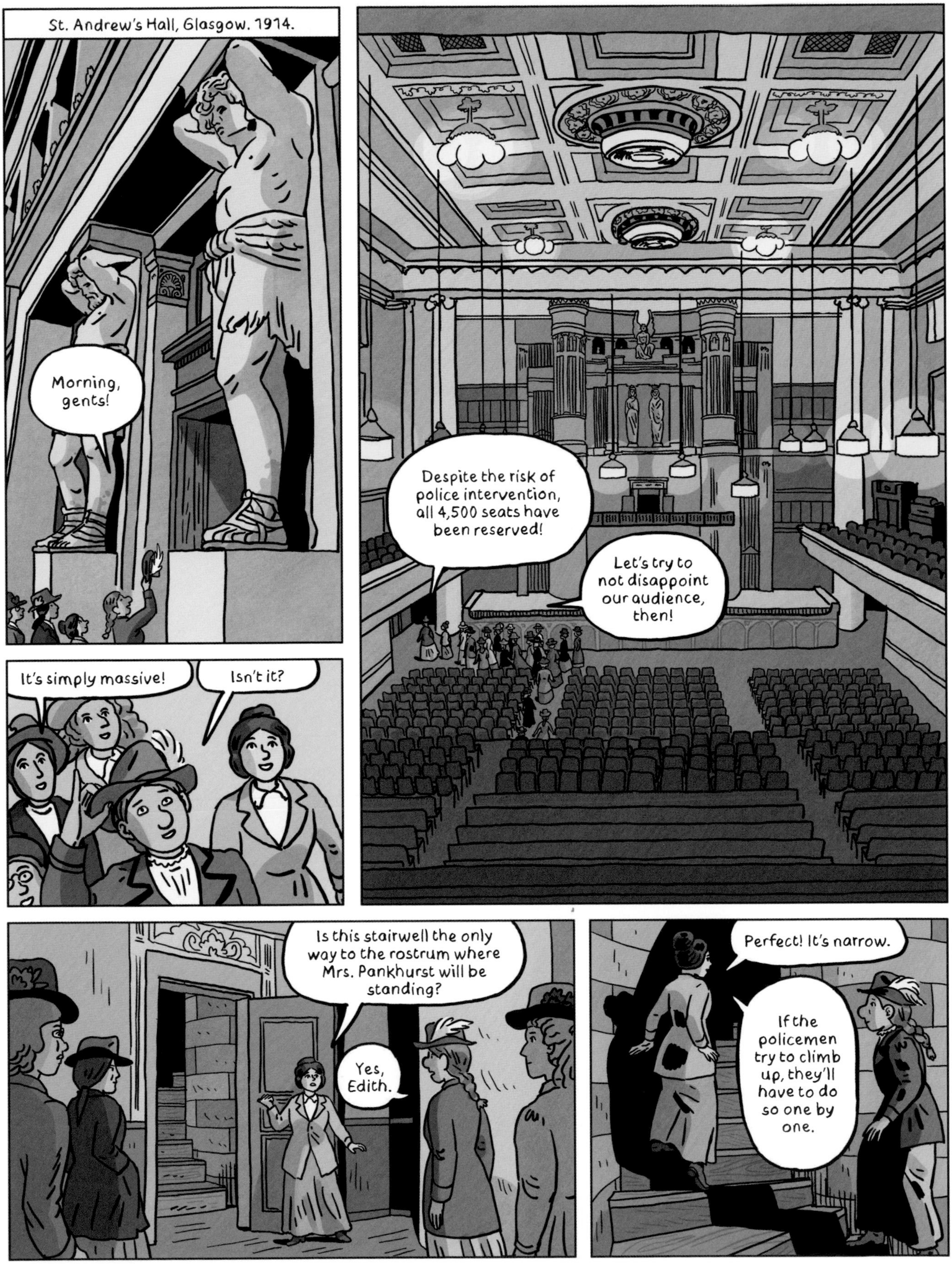
St. Andrew's Hall, Glasgow. 1914.
Morning, gents!
It's simply massive!
Isn't it?
Despite the risk of police intervention, all 4,500 seats have been reserved!
Let's try to not disappoint our audience, then!
Is this stairwell the only way to the rostrum where Mrs. Pankhurst will be standing?
Yes, Edith.
Perfect! It's narrow.
If the policemen try to climb up, they'll have to do so one by one.

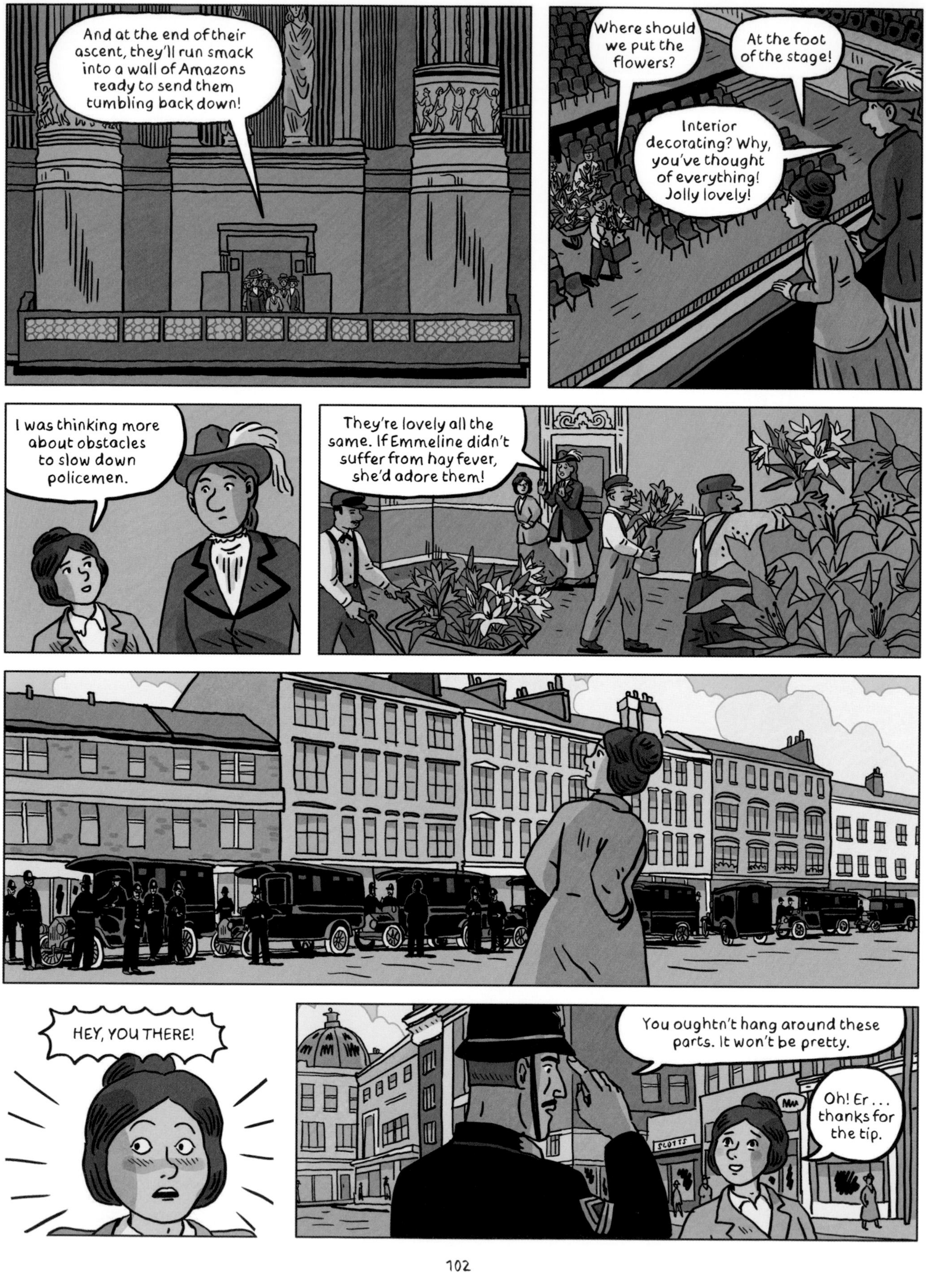

And at the end of their ascent, they'll run smack into a wall of Amazons ready to send them tumbling back down!
Where should we put the flowers?
At the foot of the stage!
Interior decorating? Why, you've thought of everything! Jolly lovely!
I was thinking more about obstacles to slow down policemen.
They're lovely all the same. If Emmeline didn't suffer from hay fever, she'd adore them!
HEY, YOU THERE!
You oughtn't hang around these parts. It won't be pretty.
Oh! Er . . . thanks for the tip.

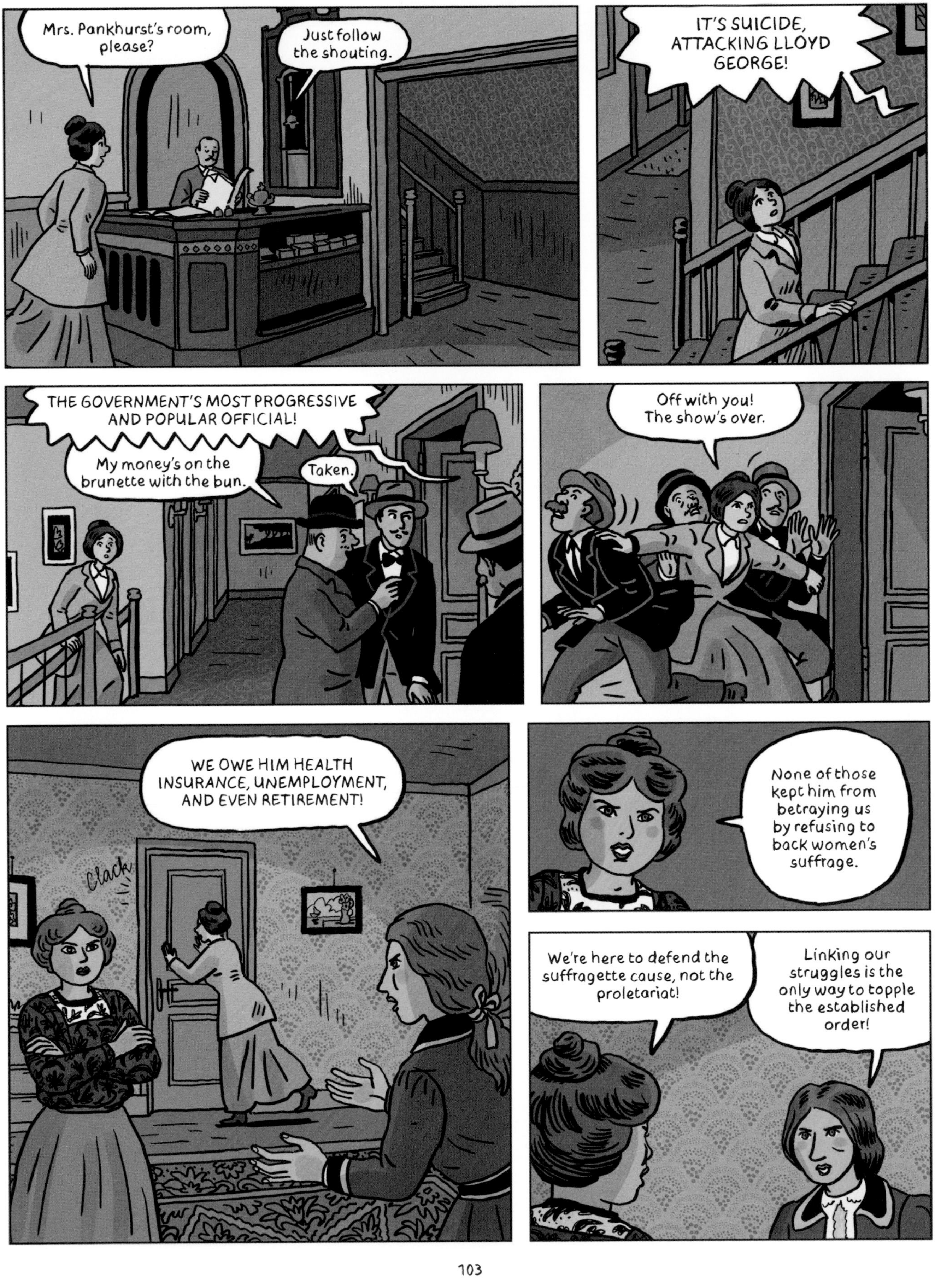
Mrs. Pankhurst's room, please?
Just follow the shouting.
IT'S SUICIDE, ATTACKING LLOYD GEORGE!
THE GOVERNMENT'S MOST PROGRESSIVE AND POPULAR OFFICIAL!
My money's on the brunette with the bun.
Taken.
Off with you! The show's over.
WE OWE HIM HEALTH INSURANCE, UNEMPLOYMENT, AND EVEN RETIREMENT!
Clack
None of those kept him from betraying us by refusing to back women's suffrage.
We're here to defend the suffragette cause, not the proletariat!
Linking our struggles is the only way to topple the established order!

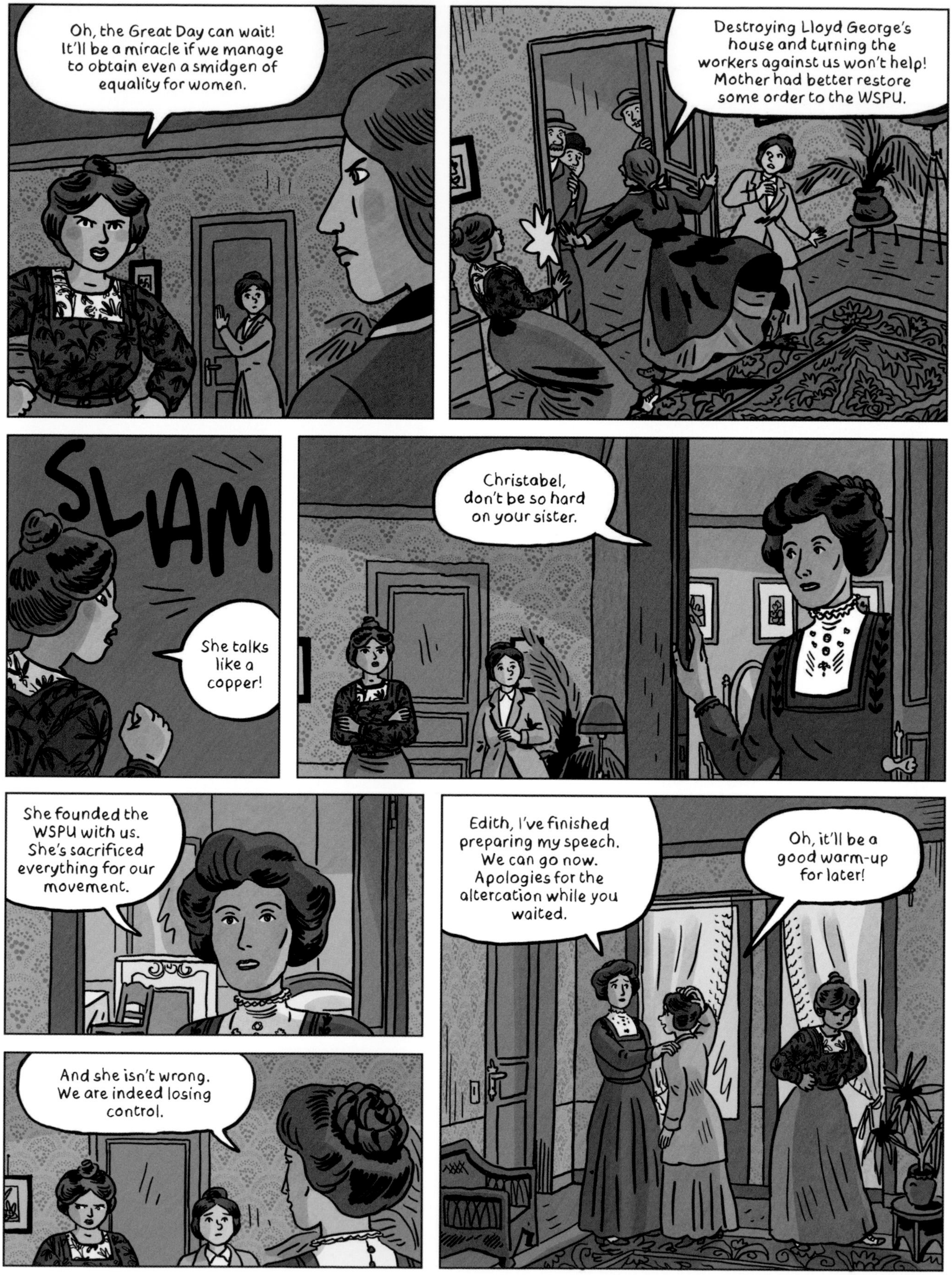
Oh, the Great Day can wait! It'll be a miracle if we manage to obtain even a smidgen of equality for women.
Destroying Lloyd George's house and turning the workers against us won't help! Mother had better restore some order to the WSPU.
SLAM
She talks like a copper!
Christabel, don't be so hard on your sister.
She founded the WSPU with us. She's sacrificed everything for our movement.
And she isn't wrong. We are indeed losing control.
Edith, I've finished preparing my speech. We can go now. Apologies for the altercation while you waited.
Oh, it'll be a good warm-up for later!

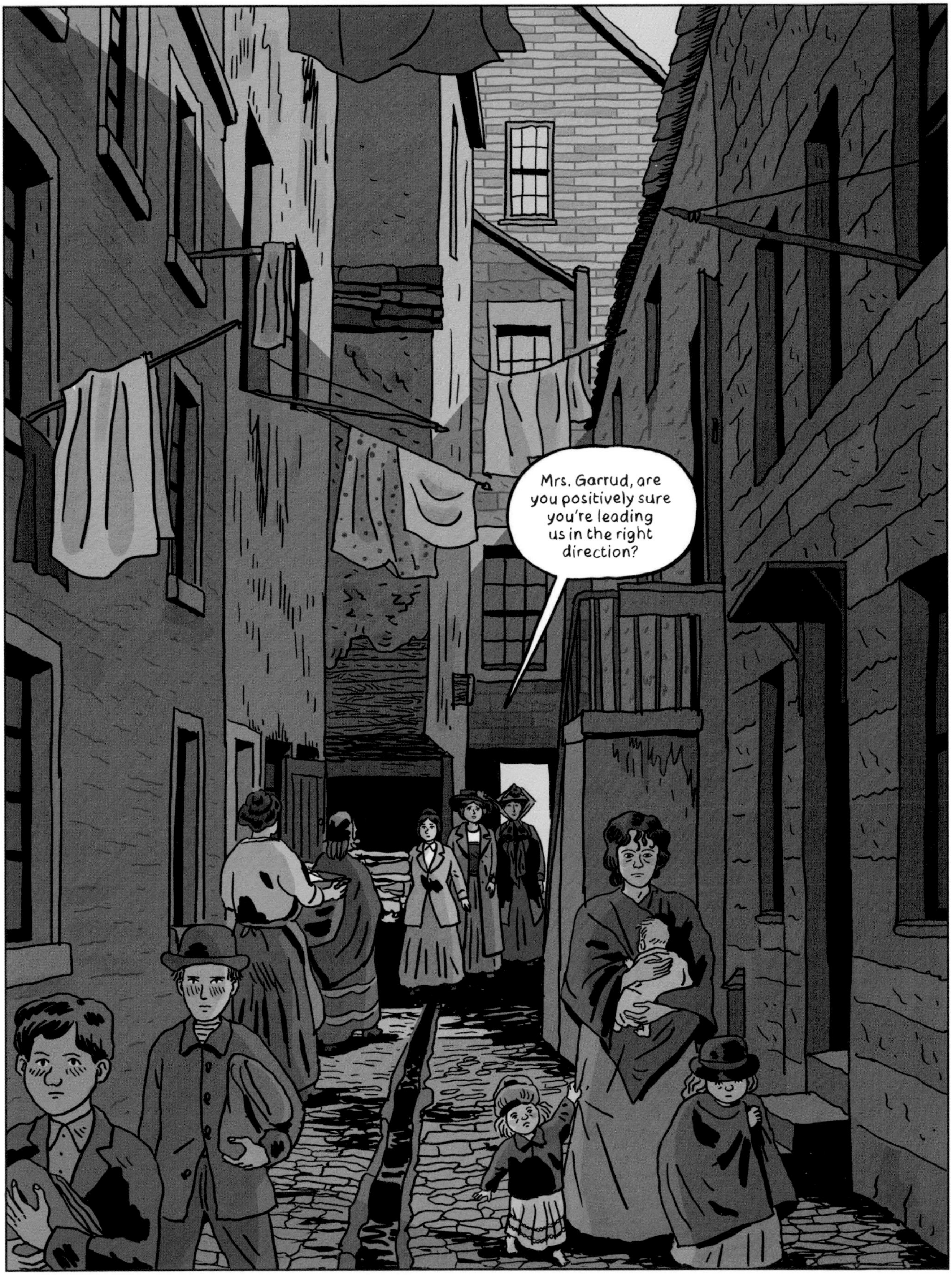
Mrs. Garrud, are you positively sure you're leading us in the right direction?

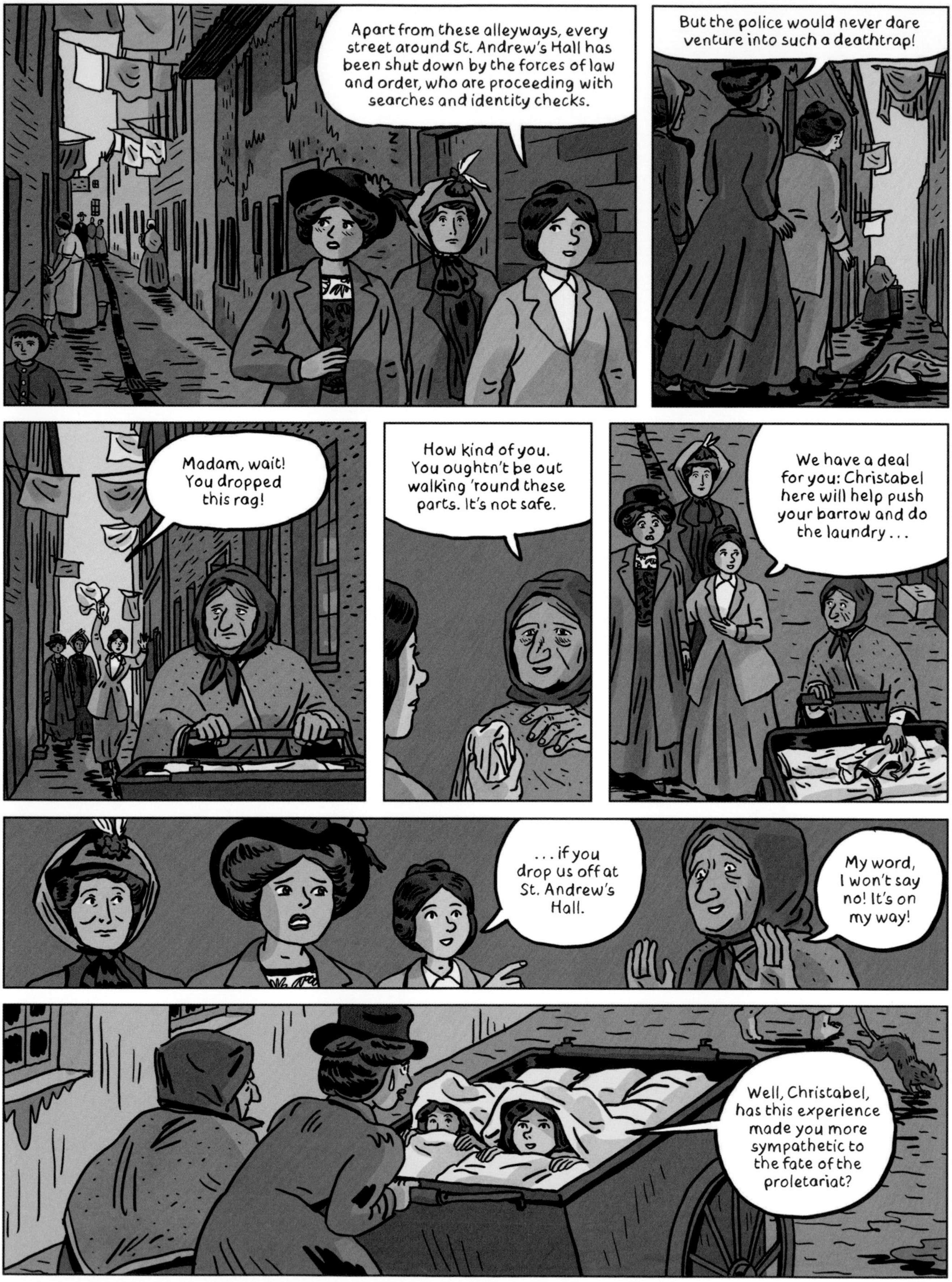
Apart from these alleyways, every street around St. Andrew's Hall has been shut down by the forces of law and order, who are proceeding with searches and identity checks.
But the police would never dare venture into such a deathtrap!
Madam, wait! You dropped this rag!
How kind of you. You oughtn't be out walking 'round these parts. It's not safe.
We have a deal for you: Christabel here will help push your barrow and do the laundry . . .
. . . if you drop us off at St. Andrew's Hall.
My word, I won't say no! It's on my way!
Well, Christabel, has this experience made you more sympathetic to the fate of the proletariat?

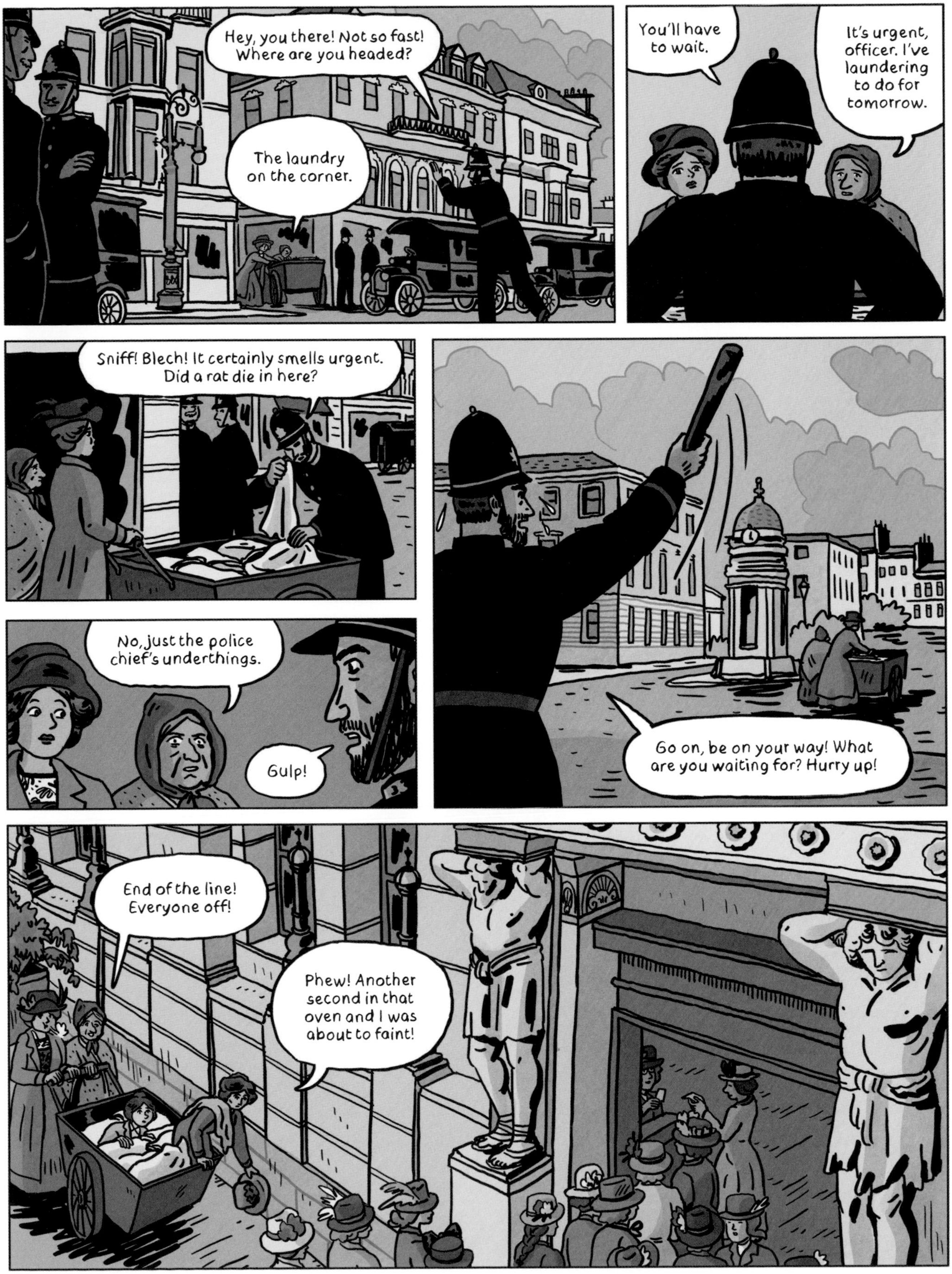
Hey, you there! Not so fast! Where are you headed?
The laundry on the corner.
You'll have to wait.
It's urgent, officer. I've laundering to do for tomorrow.
Sniff! Blech! It certainly smells urgent. Did a rat die in here?
No, just the police chief's underthings.
Gulp!
Go on, be on your way! What are you waiting for? Hurry up!
End of the line! Everyone off!
Phew! Another second in that oven and I was about to faint!

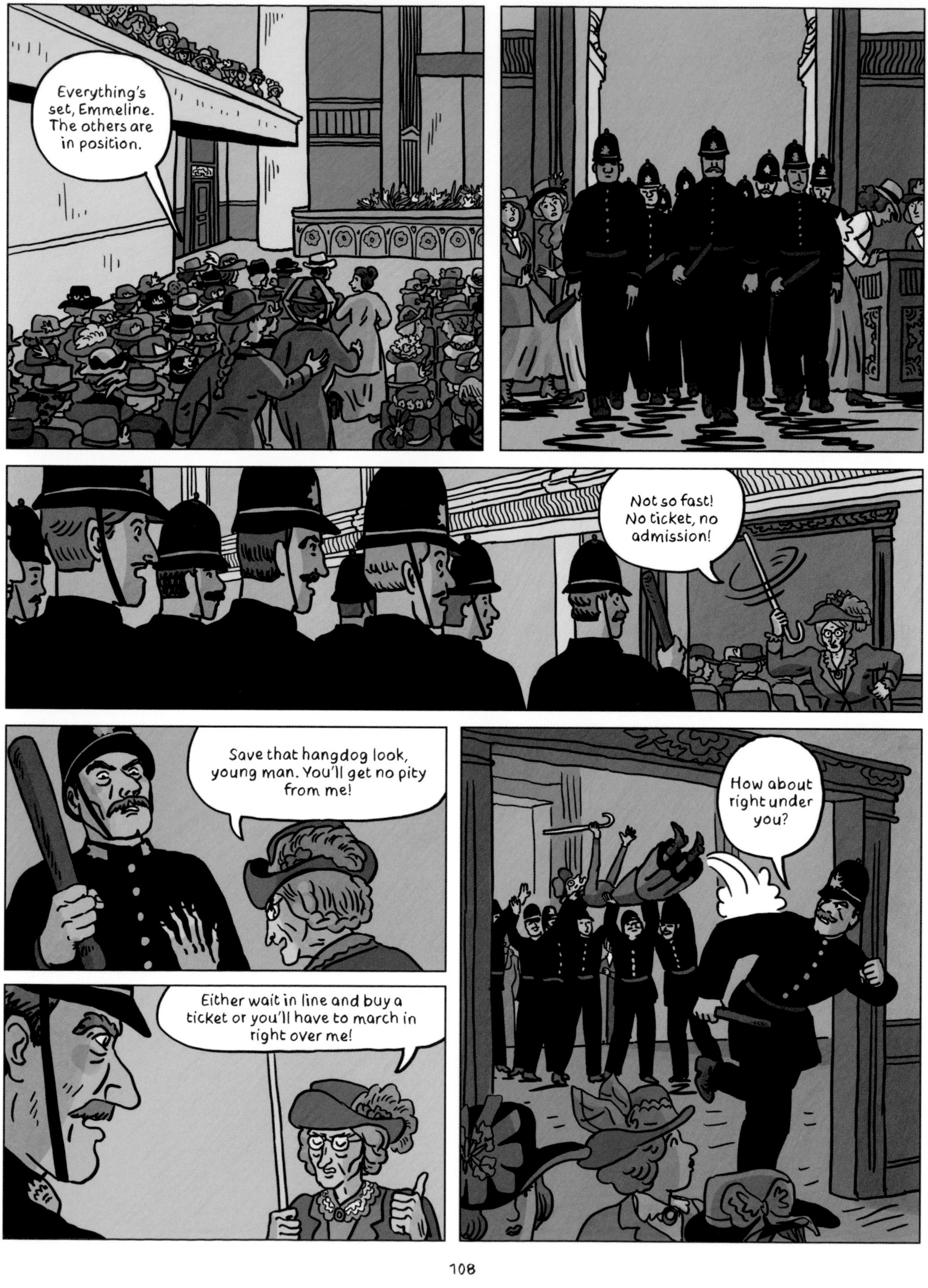
Everything's set, Emmeline. The others are in position.
Not so fast! No ticket, no admission!
Save that hangdog look, young man. You'll get no pity from me!
Either wait in line and buy a ticket or you'll have to march in right over me!
How about right under you?

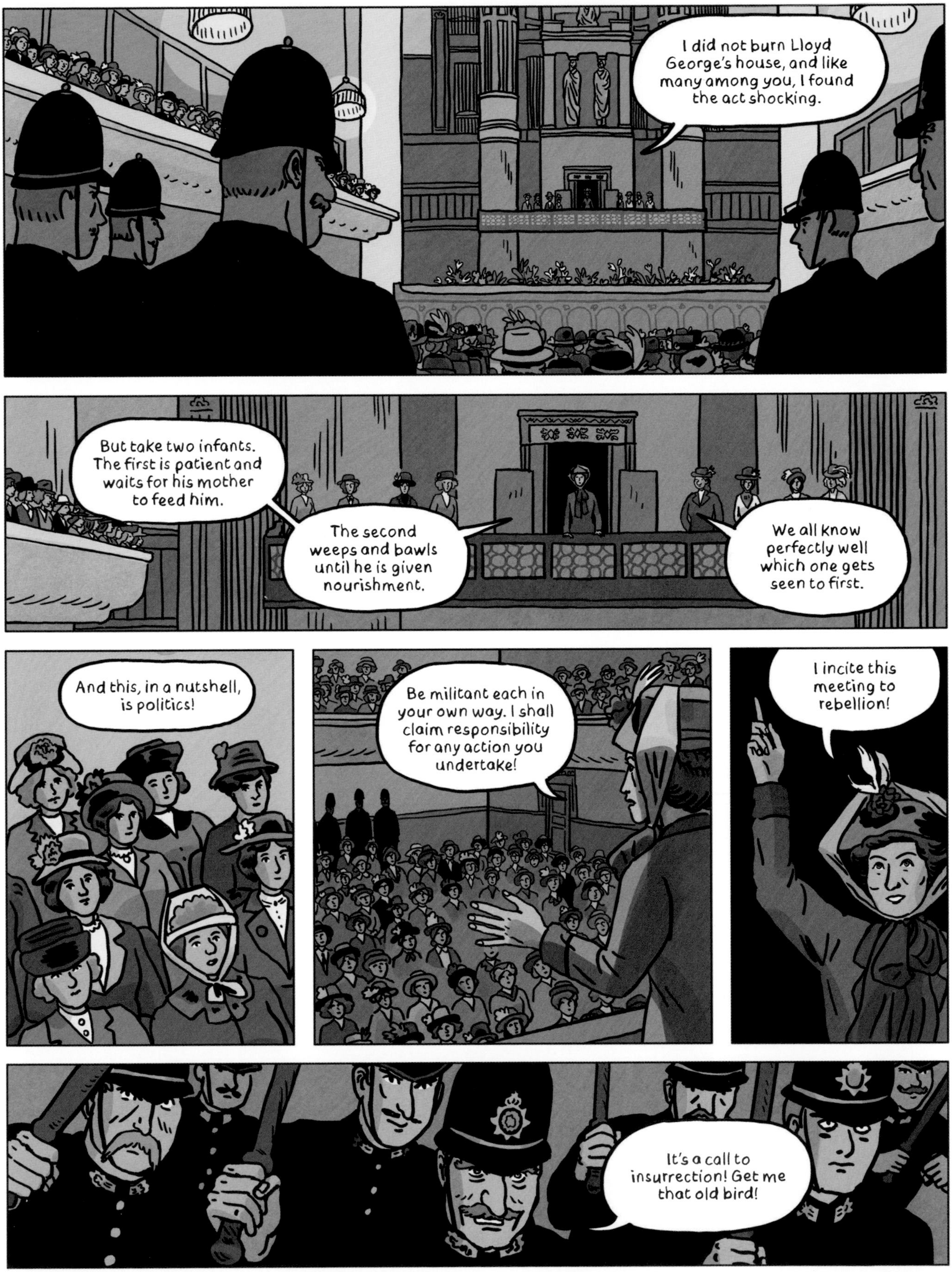
I did not burn Lloyd George's house, and like many among you, I found the act shocking.
But take two infants. The first is patient and waits for his mother to feed him.
The second weeps and bawls until he is given nourishment.
We all know perfectly well which one gets seen to first.
And this, in a nutshell, is politics!
Be militant each in your own way. I shall claim responsibility for any action you undertake!
I incite this meeting to rebellion!
It's a call to insurrection! Get me that old bird!

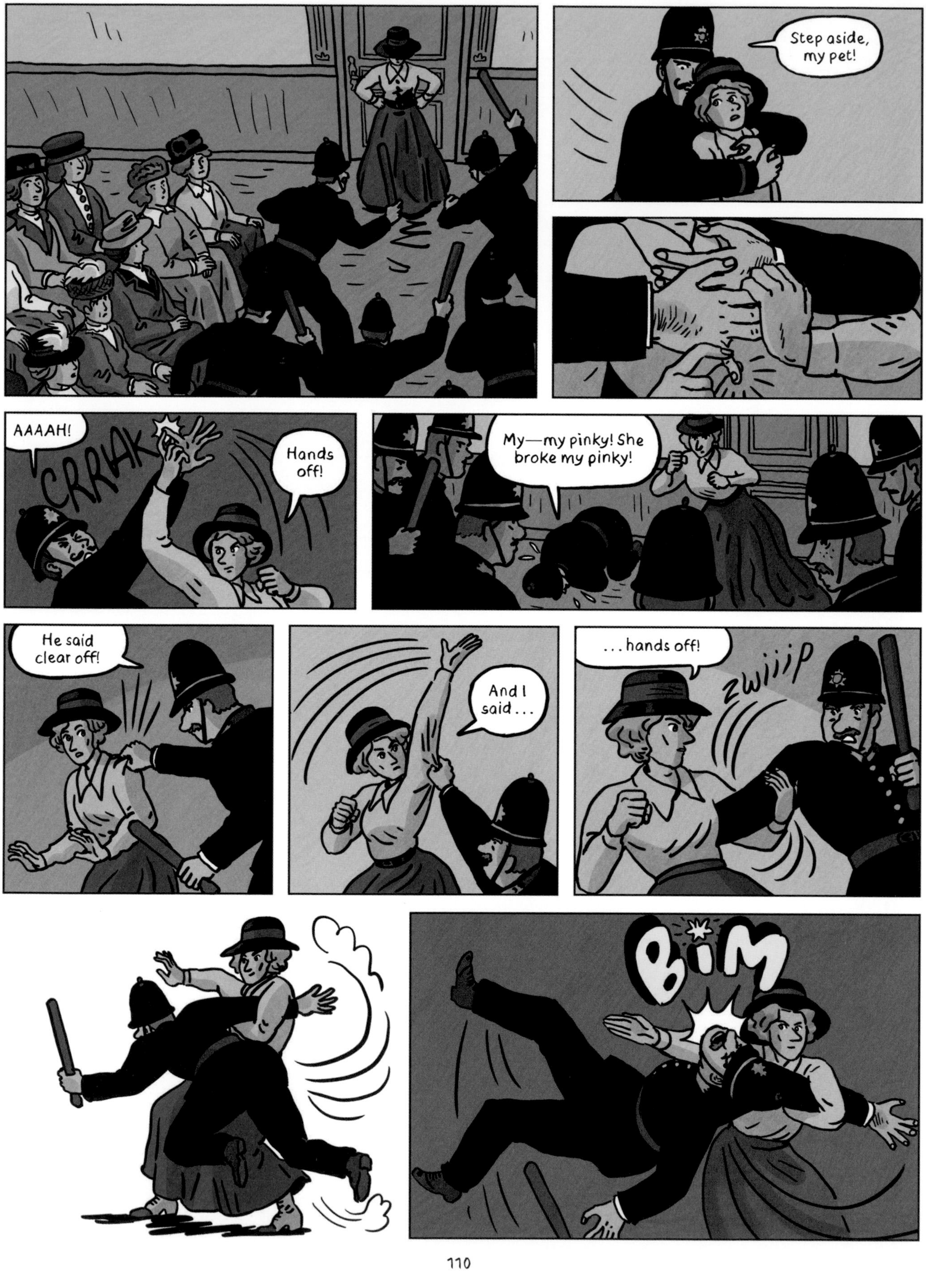

Step aside, my pet!
AAAAH!
CRRK
Hands off!
My—my pinky! She broke my pinky!
He said clear off!
And I said . . .
. . . hands off!
ZWiiiP
BiM

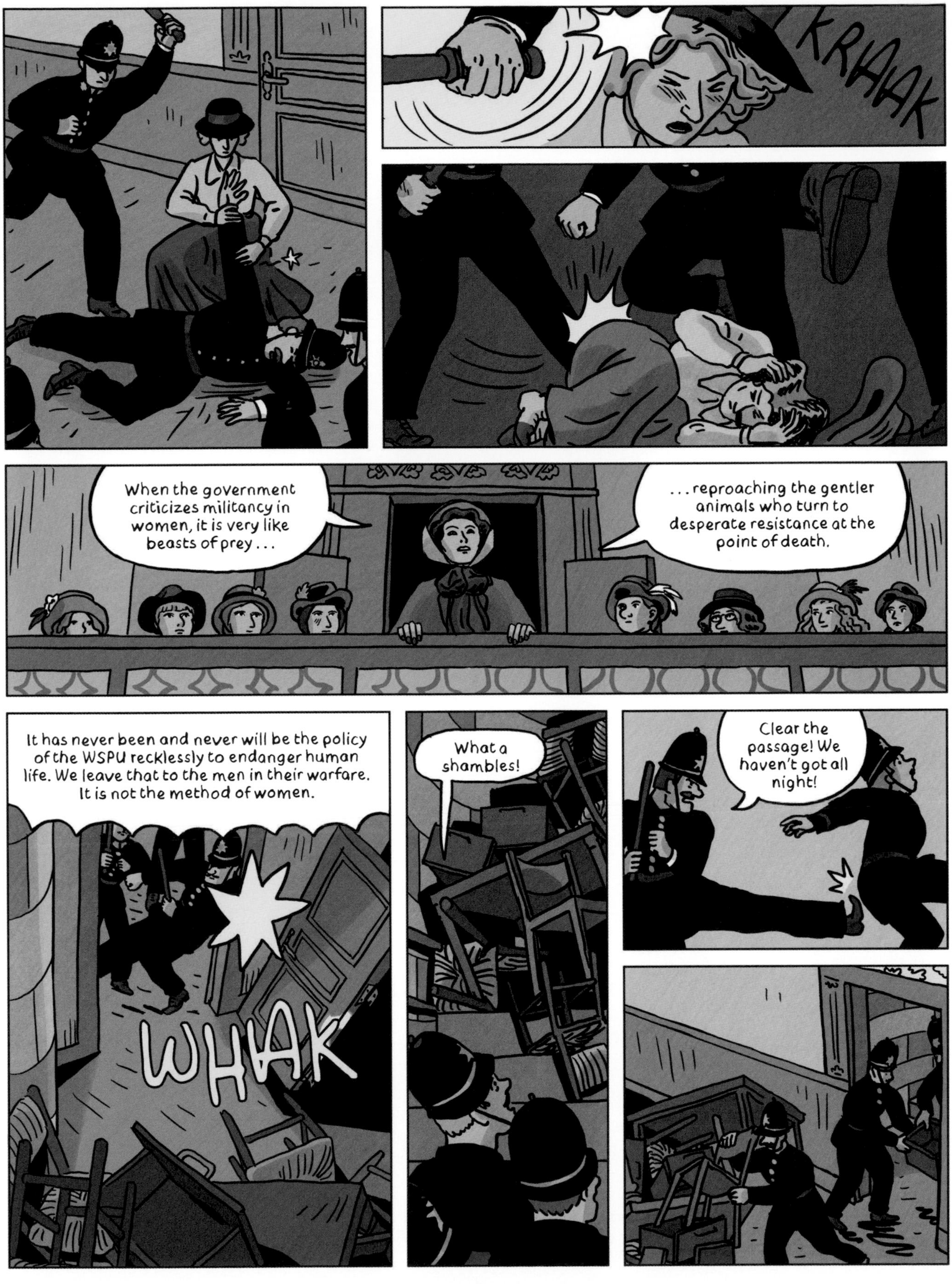
KRAAAK
When the government criticizes militancy in women, it is very like beasts of prey . . .
. . . reproaching the gentler animals who turn to desperate resistance at the point of death.
It has never been and never will be the policy of the WSPU recklessly to endanger human life. We leave that to the men in their warfare. It is not the method of women.
WHAAK
What a shambles!
Clear the passage! We haven't got all night!

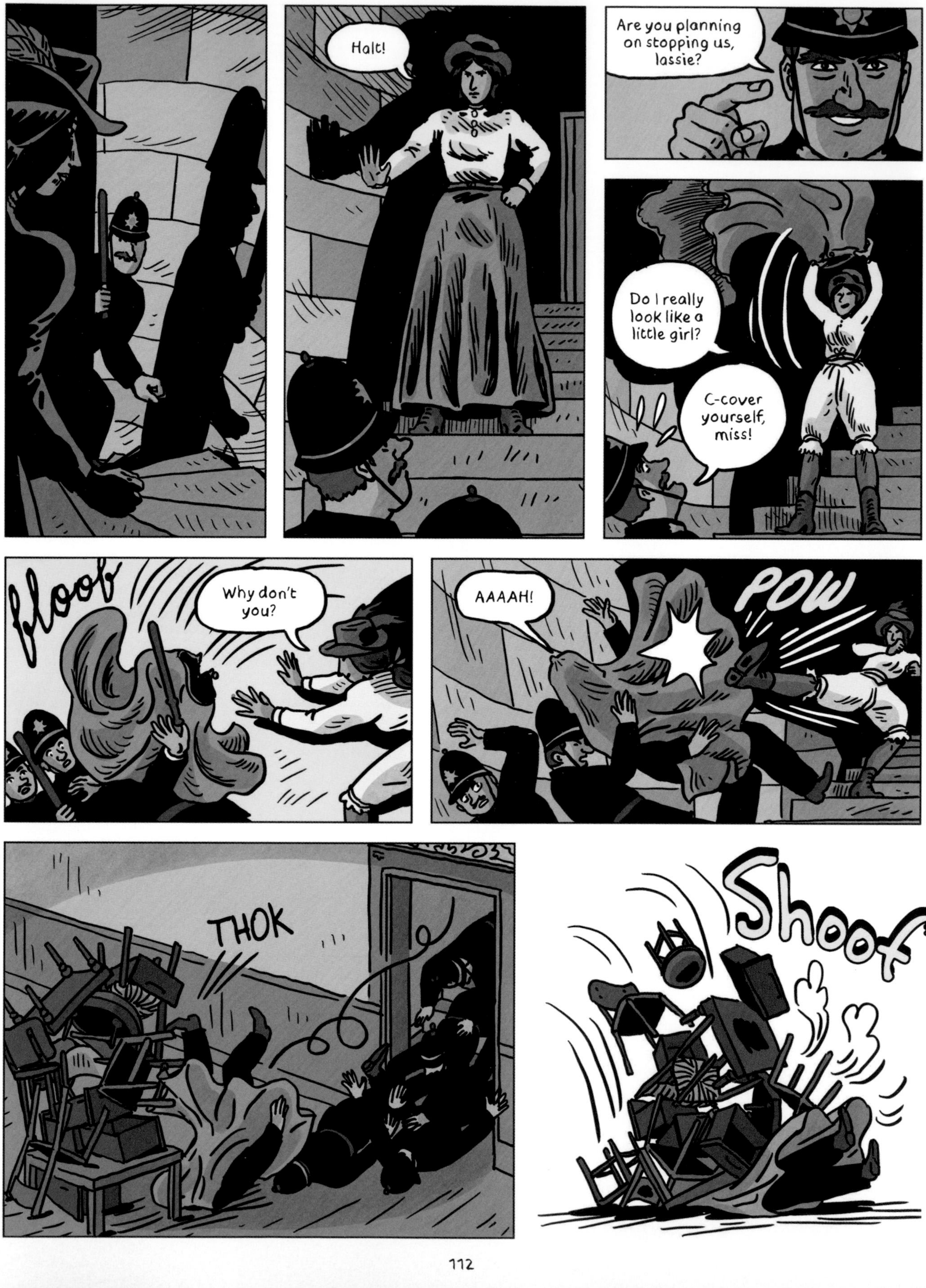
Halt!
Are you planning on stopping us, lassie?
Do I really look like a little girl?
C-cover yourself, miss!
floof
Why don't you?
AAAAH!
POW
THOK
Shoof

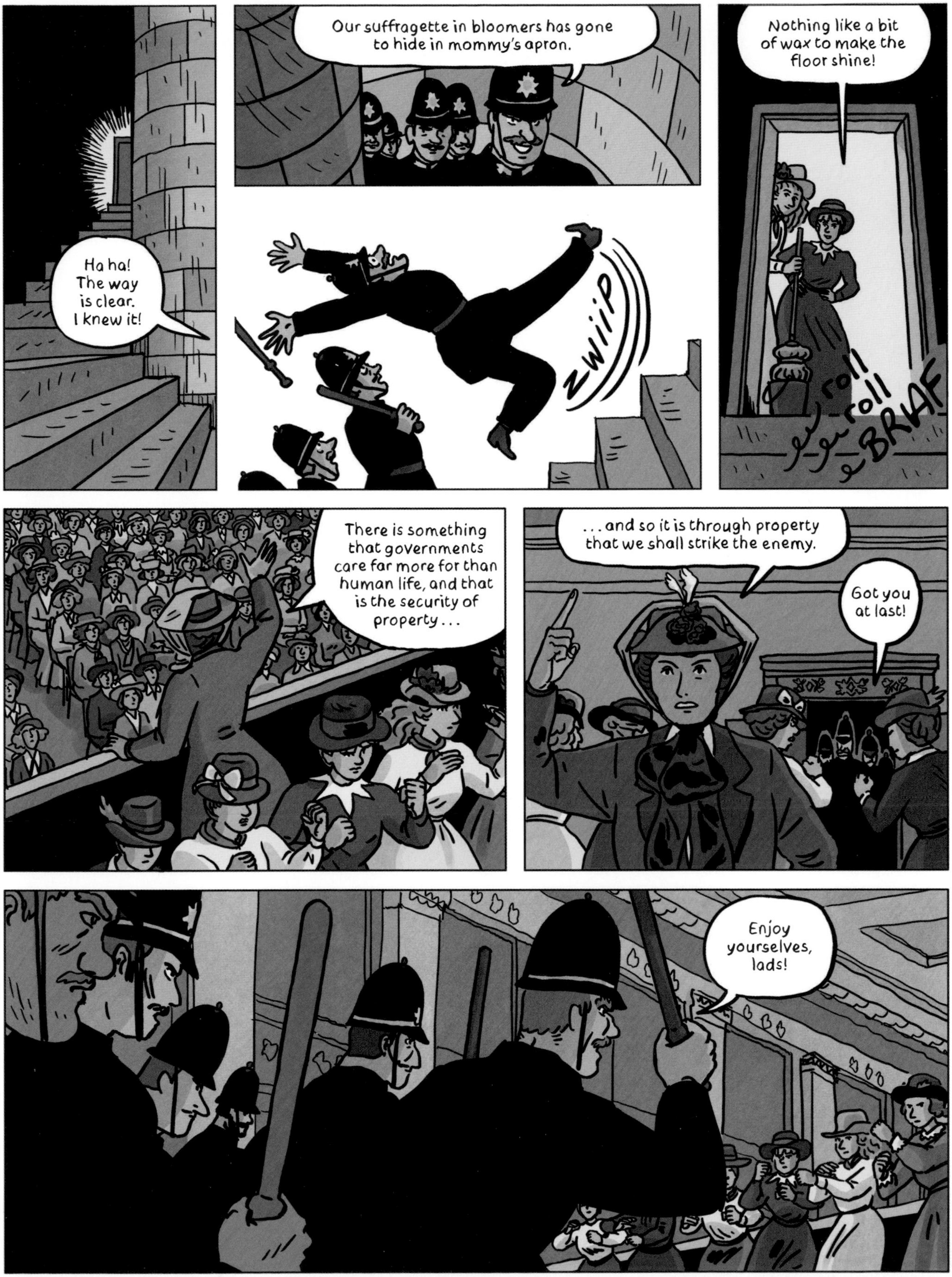
Ha ha! The way is clear. I knew it!
Our suffragette in bloomers has gone to hide in mommy's apron.
ZWIIIP
Nothing like a bit of wax to make the floor shine!
roll roll BRAF
There is something that governments care far more for than human life, and that is the security of property . . .
. . . and so it is through property that we shall strike the enemy.
Got you at last!
Enjoy yourselves, lads!

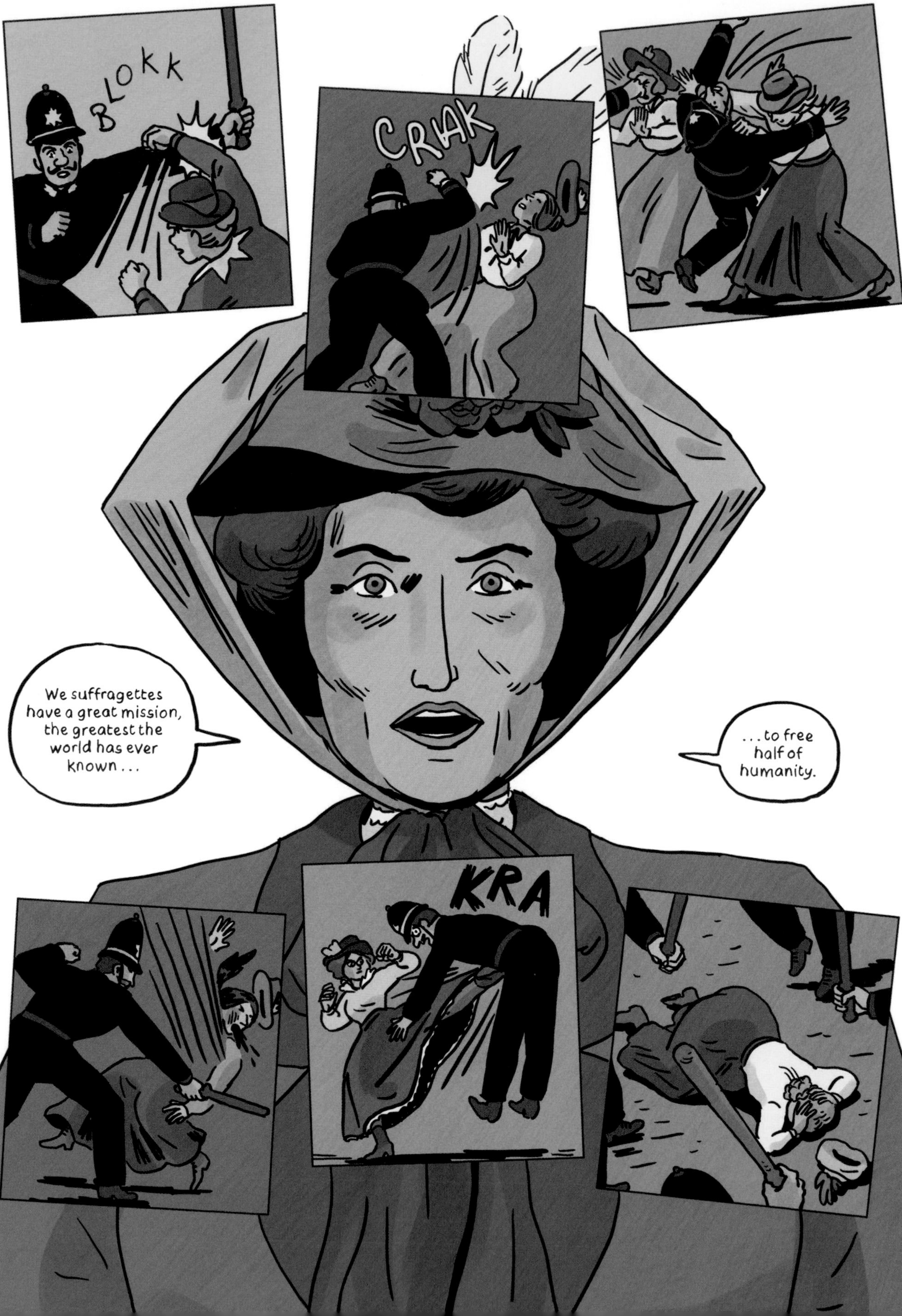
BLOKK
CRAK
We suffragettes have a great mission, the greatest the world has ever known . . .
. . . to free half of humanity.
KRA

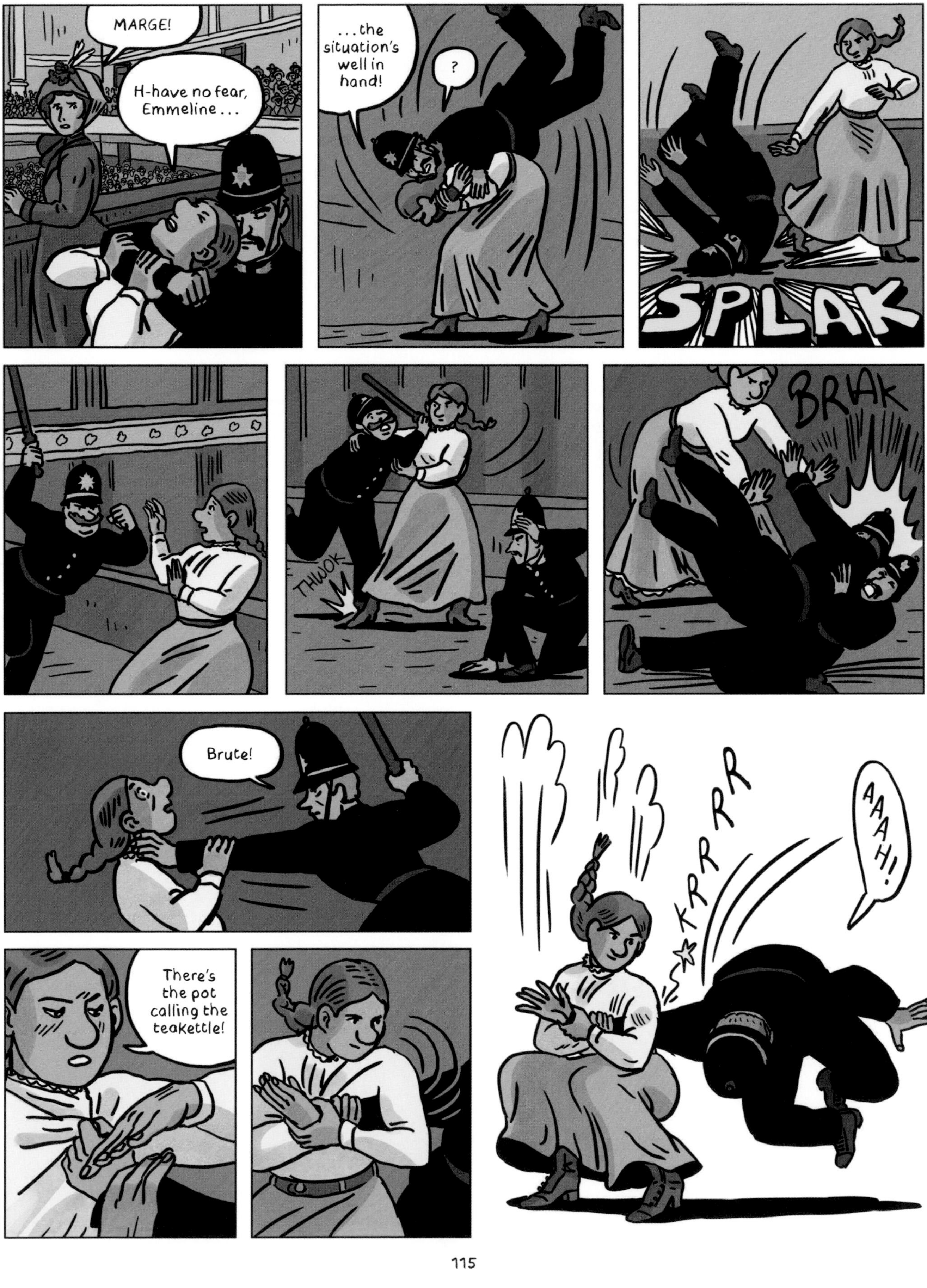
MARGE!
H-have no fear, Emmeline . . .
. . . the situation's well in hand!
?
SPLAK
BRAK
THWOK
Brute!
There's the pot calling the teakettle!
KRRRRR
AAAAH!

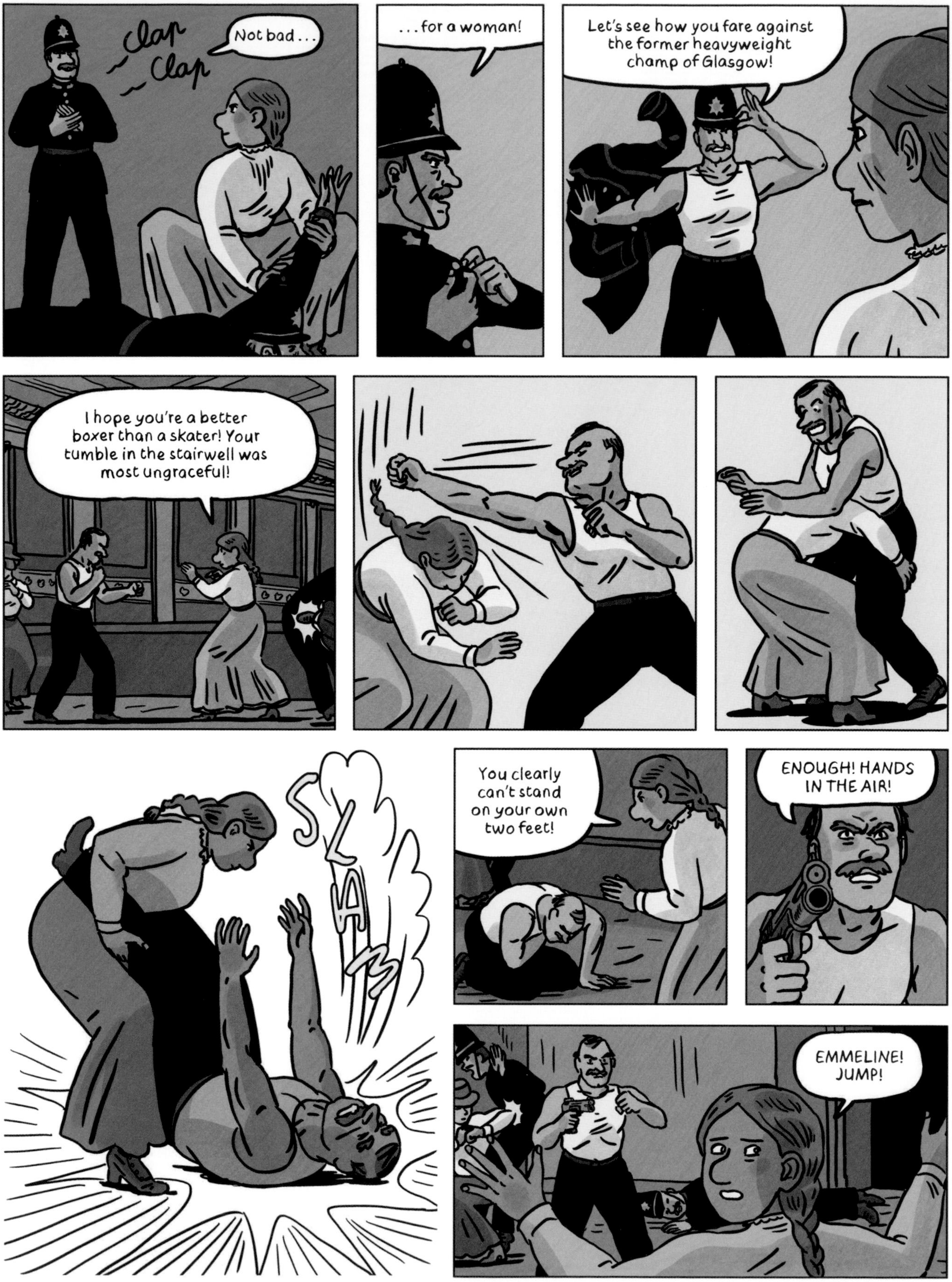

~Clap
~Clap
Not bad...
...for a woman!
Let's see how you fare against the former heavyweight champ of Glasgow!
I hope you're a better boxer than a skater! Your tumble in the stairwell was most ungraceful!
SLAM
You clearly can't stand on your own two feet!
ENOUGH! HANDS IN THE AIR!
EMMELINE! JUMP!

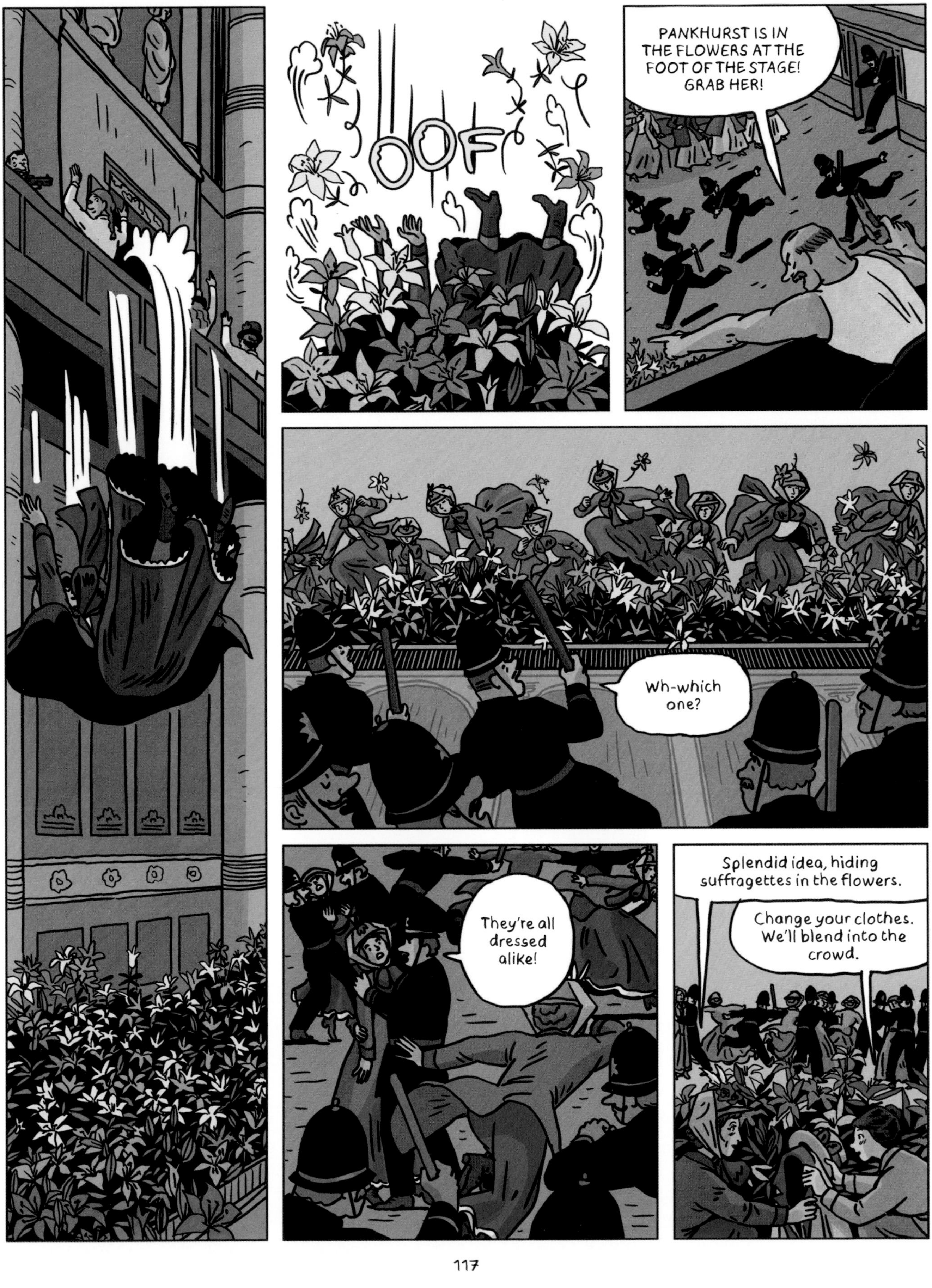
OOF
PANKHURST IS IN THE FLOWERS AT THE FOOT OF THE STAGE! GRAB HER!
Wh-which one?
They're all dressed alike!
Splendid idea, hiding suffragettes in the flowers.
Change your clothes. We'll blend into the crowd.

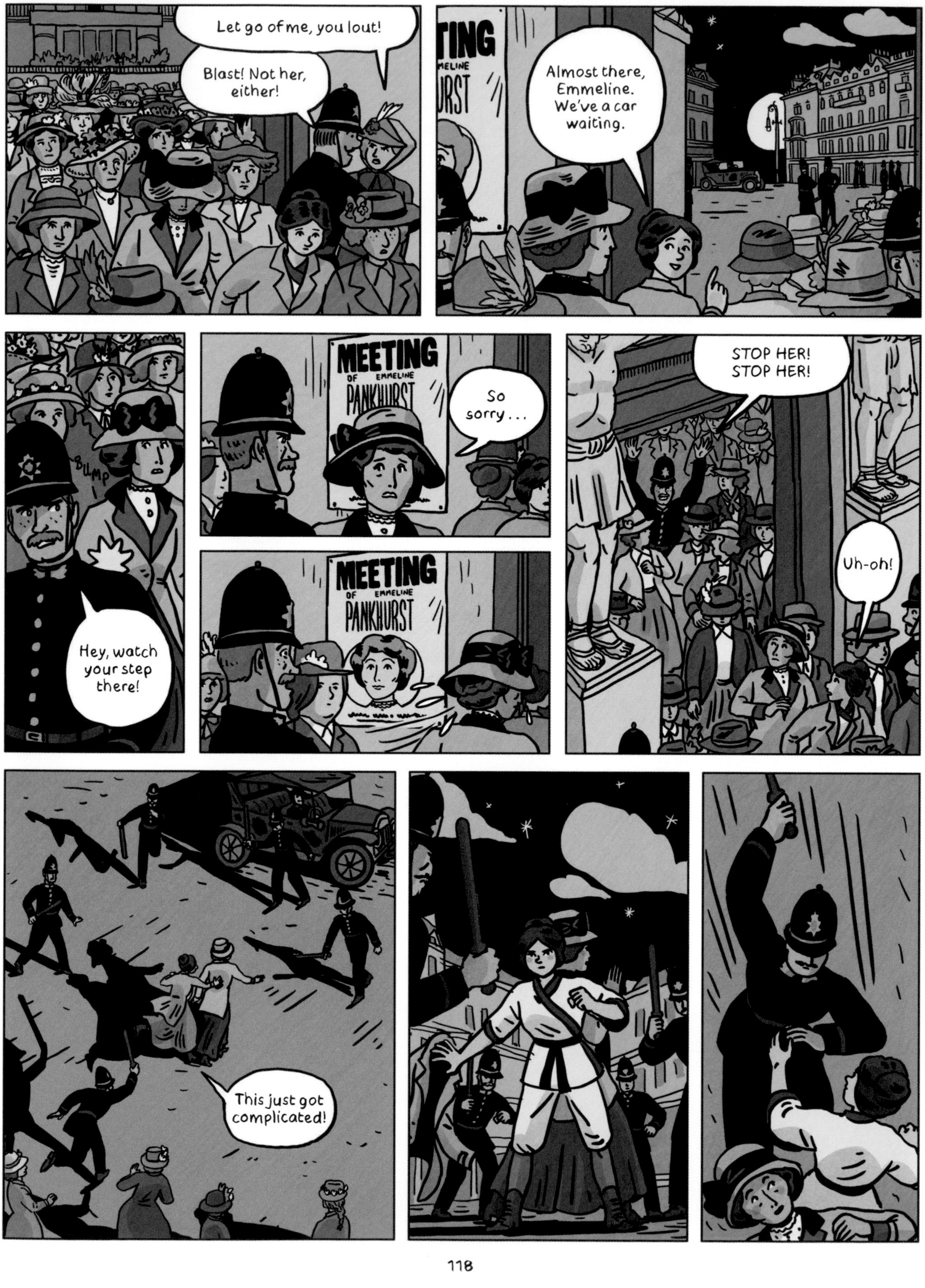
Let go of me, you lout!
Blast! Not her, either!
TING
MELINE
URST
Almost there, Emmeline. We've a car waiting.
BUMP
Hey, watch your step there!
MEETING OF EMMELINE PANKHURST
So sorry . . .
MEETING OF EMMELINE PANKHURST
STOP HER! STOP HER!
Uh-oh!
This just got complicated!

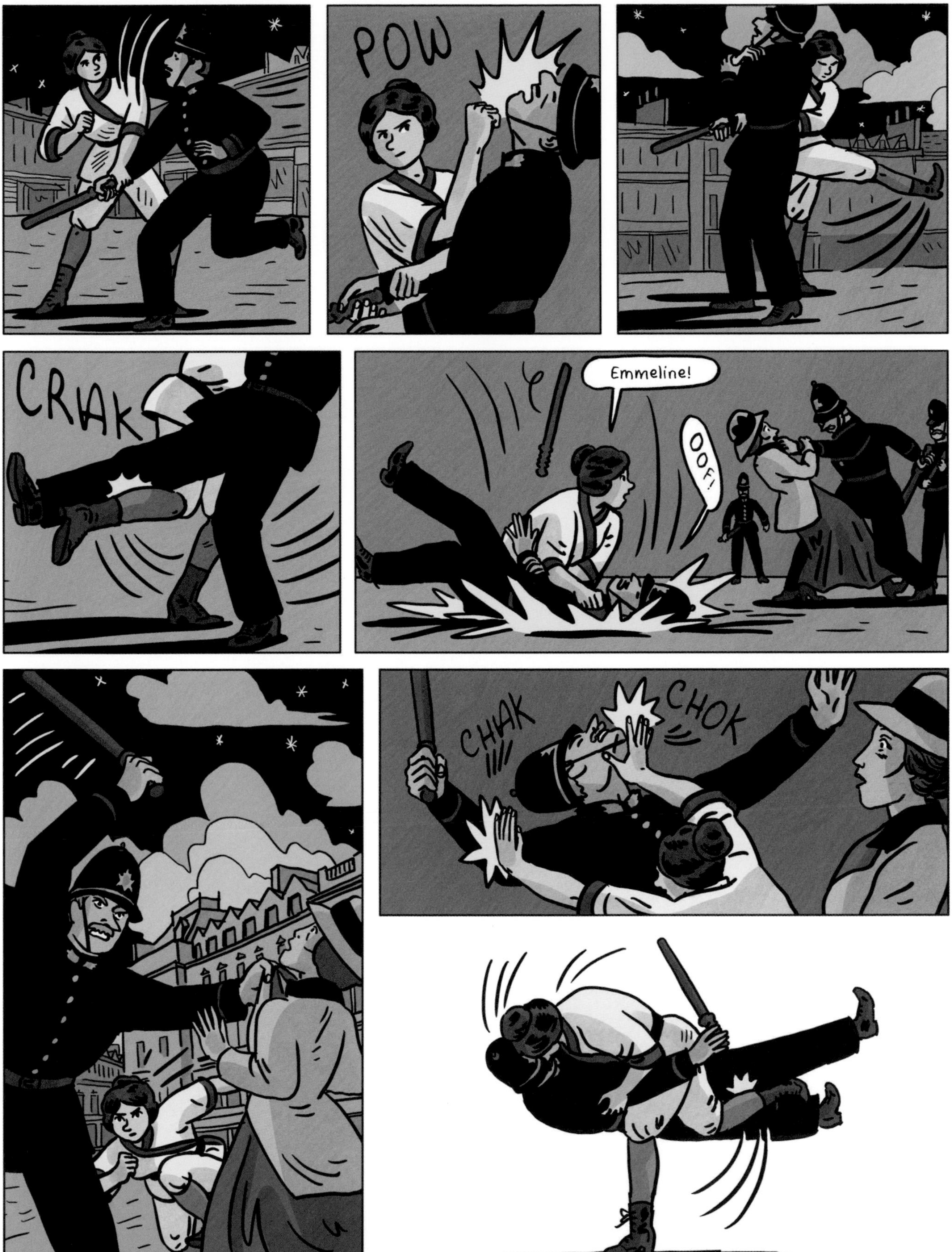
POW
CRAK
Emmeline!
OOF!
CHAK
CHOK

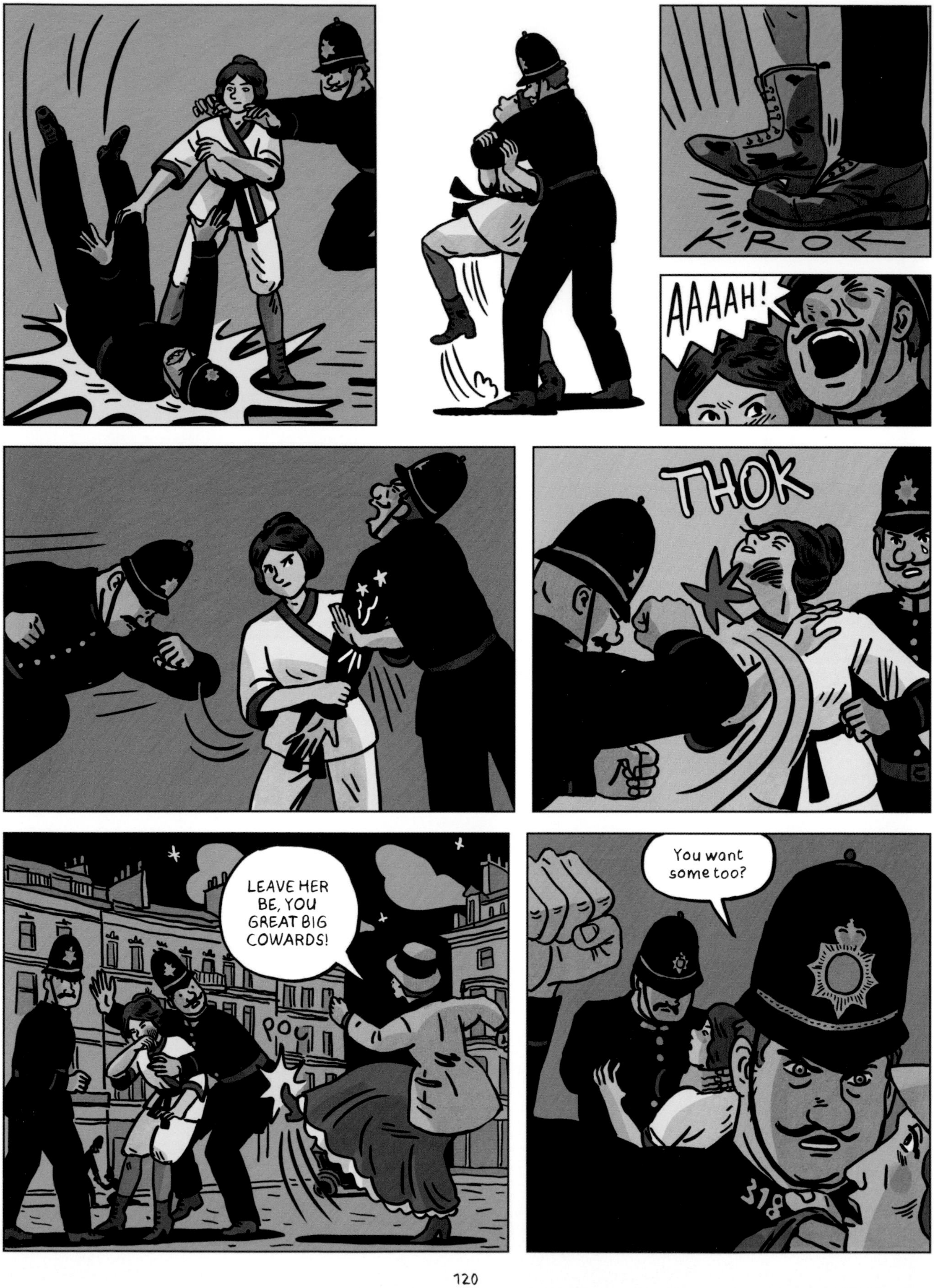
KROK
AAAAH!
THOK
LEAVE HER BE, YOU GREAT BIG COWARDS!
You want some too?

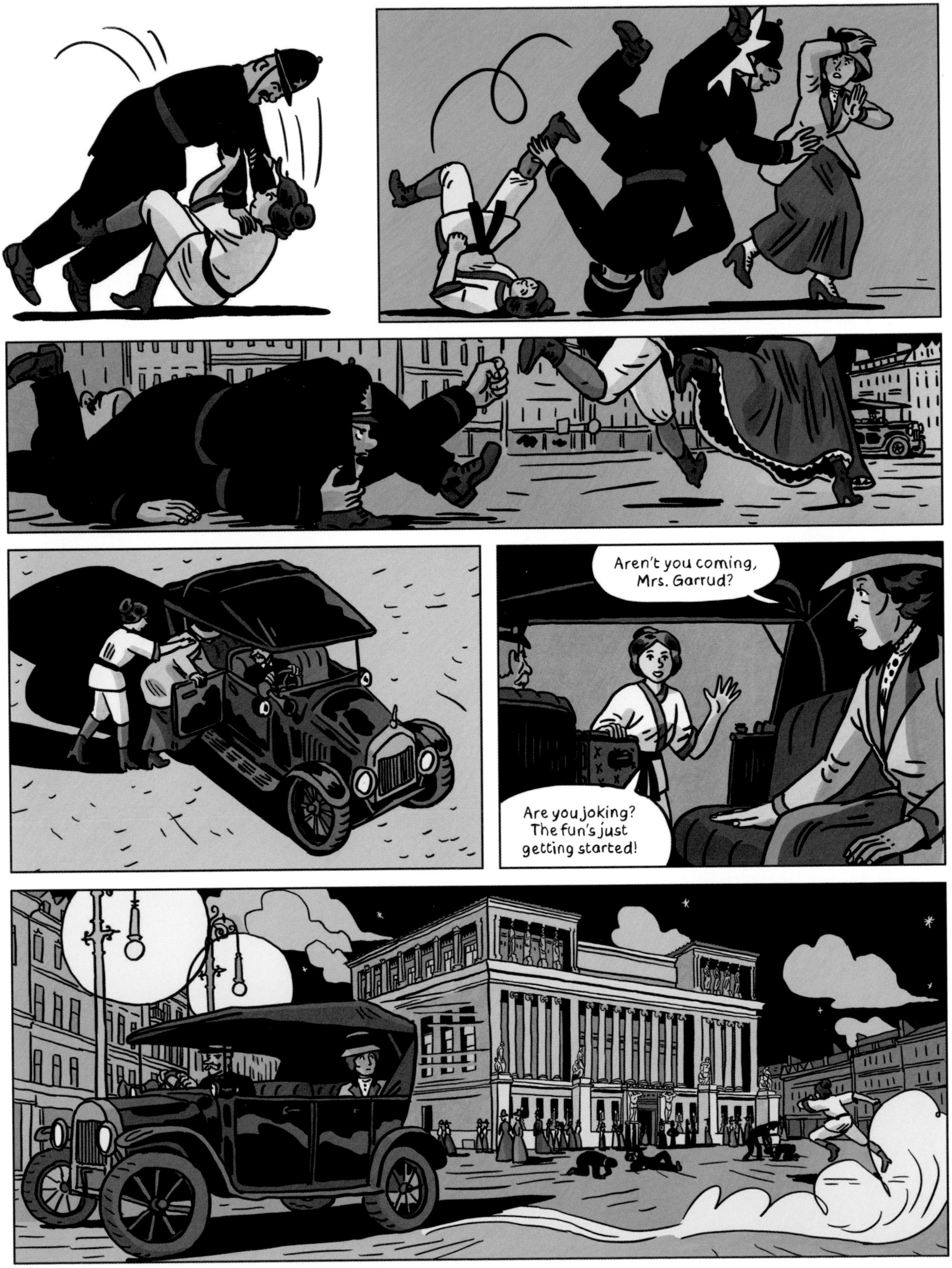
Aren't you coming,
Mrs. Garrud?
Are you joking?
The fun's just
getting started!

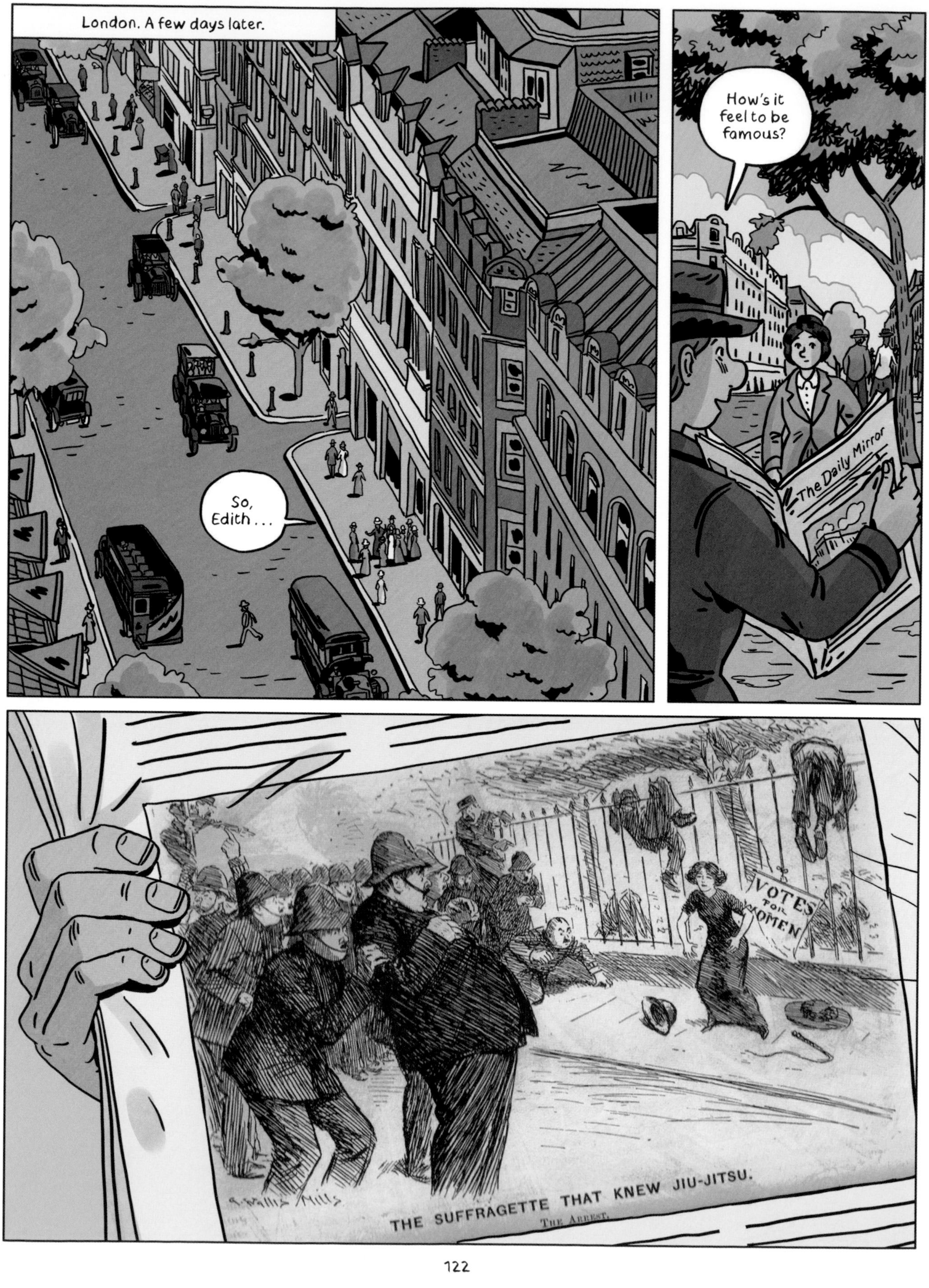
London. A few days later.
So, Edith...
How's it feel to be famous?
The Daily Mirror
VOTES FOR WOMEN
THE SUFFRAGETTE THAT KNEW JIU-JITSU.
THE ARREST.

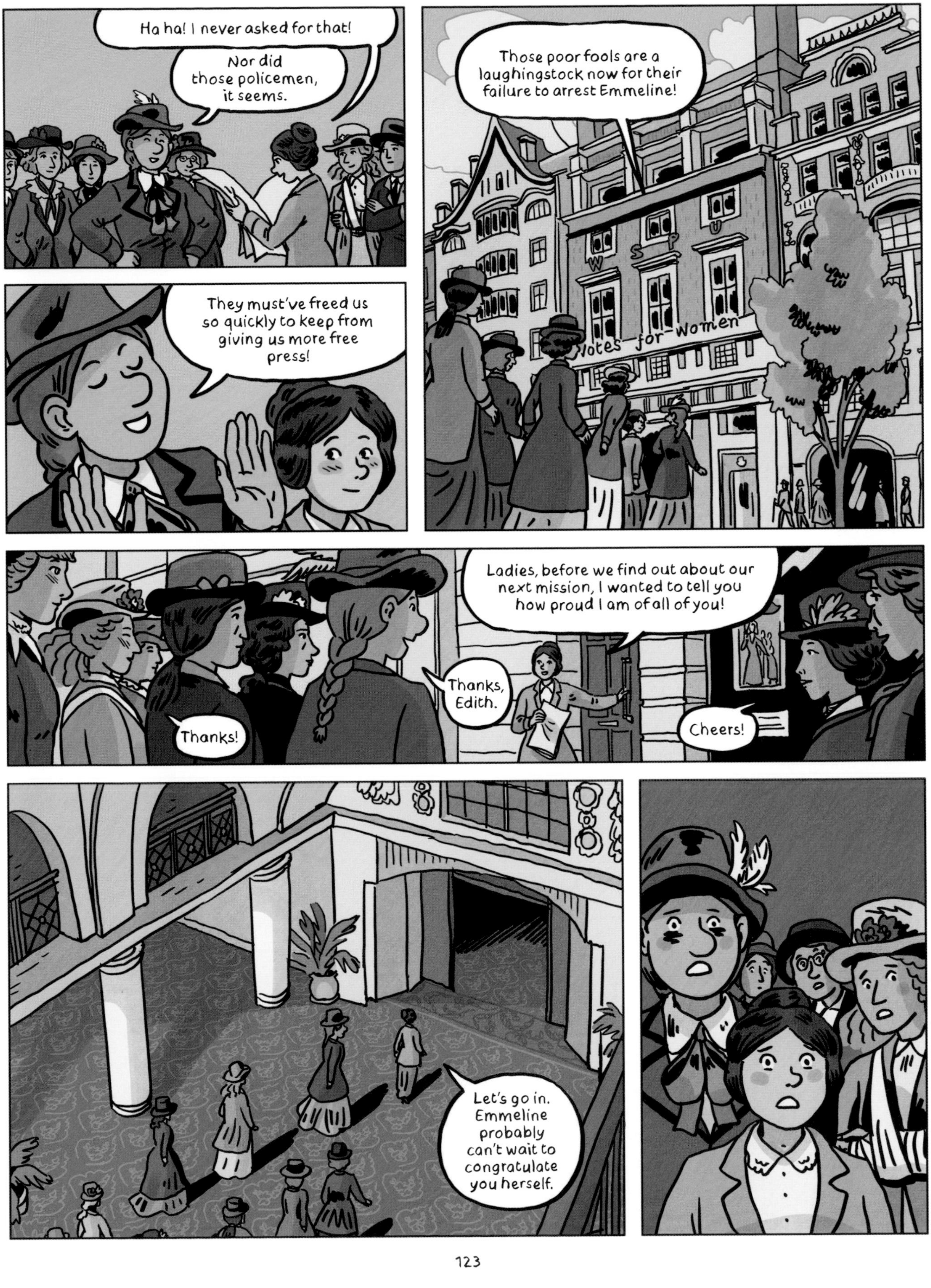
Ha ha! I never asked for that!
Nor did those policemen, it seems.
Those poor fools are a laughingstock now for their failure to arrest Emmeline!
They must've freed us so quickly to keep from giving us more free press!
W S P U
Votes for Women
Ladies, before we find out about our next mission, I wanted to tell you how proud I am of all of you!
Thanks!
Thanks, Edith.
Cheers!
Let's go in. Emmeline probably can't wait to congratulate you herself.

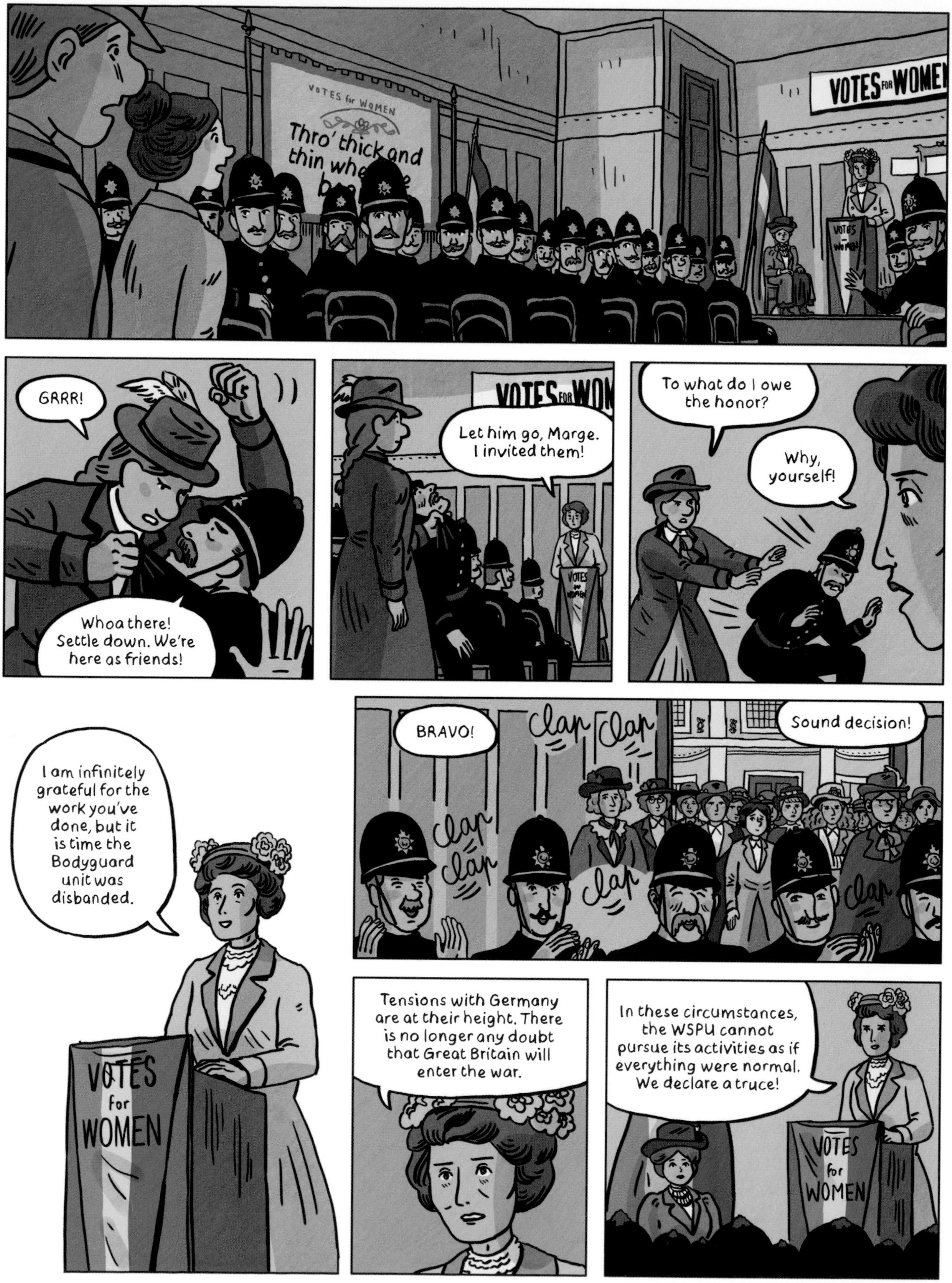
VOTES for WOMEN
Thro' thick and thin whe
VOTES for WOMEN
GRRR!
Whoa there! Settle down. We're here as friends!
VOTES for WOM
Let him go, Marge. I invited them!
To what do I owe the honor?
Why, yourself!
I am infinitely grateful for the work you've done, but it is time the Bodyguard unit was disbanded.
VOTES for WOMEN
BRAVO!
clap clap
Sound decision!
clap clap
clap
clap
Tensions with Germany are at their height. There is no longer any doubt that Great Britain will enter the war.
In these circumstances, the WSPU cannot pursue its activities as if everything were normal. We declare a truce!
VOTES for WOMEN

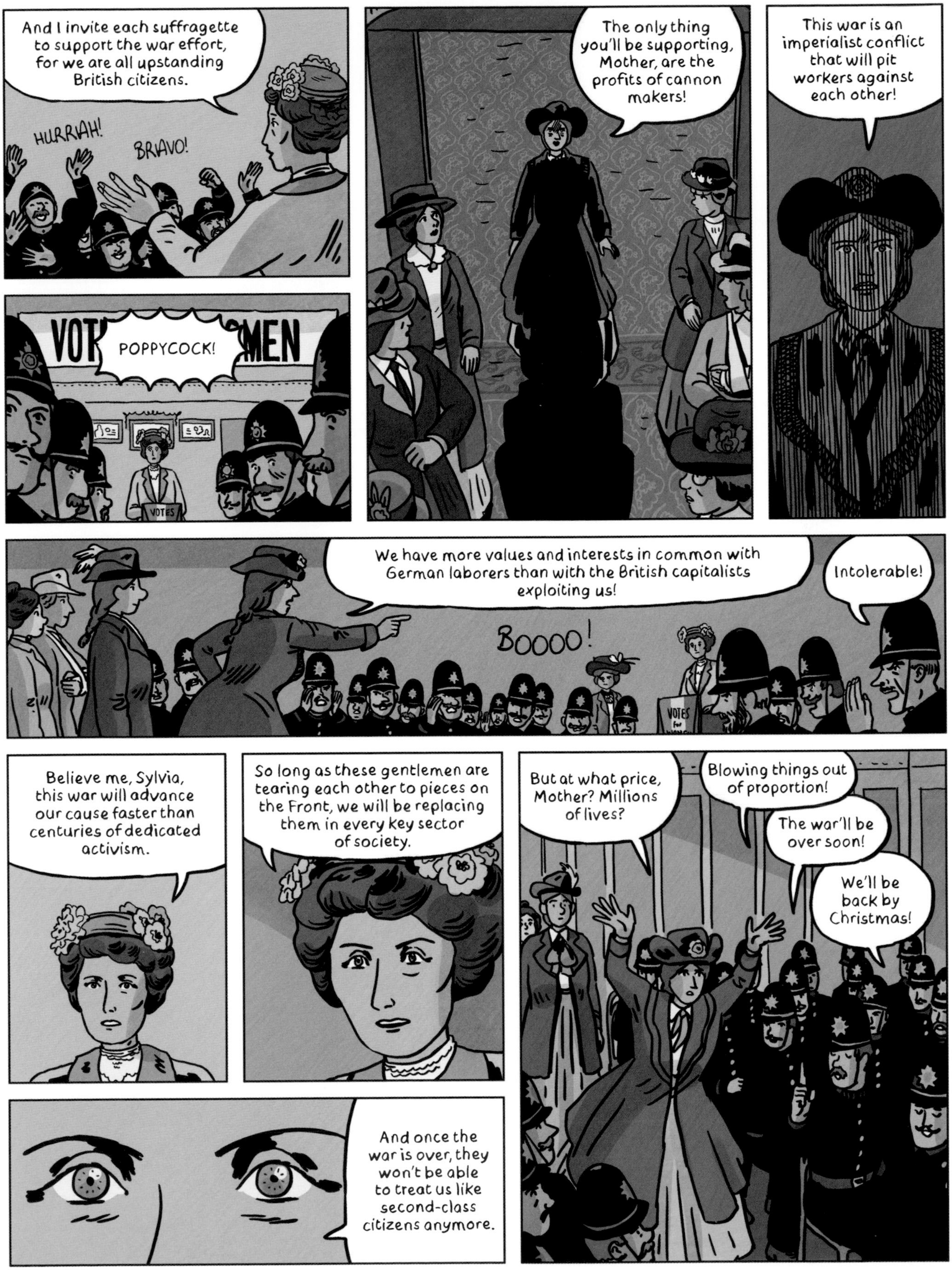
And I invite each suffragette to support the war effort, for we are all upstanding British citizens.
HURRAH!
BRAVO!
VOT
MEN
POPPYCOCK!
VOTES
The only thing you'll be supporting, Mother, are the profits of cannon makers!
This war is an imperialist conflict that will pit workers against each other!
We have more values and interests in common with German laborers than with the British capitalists exploiting us!
Intolerable!
BOOOO!
VOTES
Believe me, Sylvia, this war will advance our cause faster than centuries of dedicated activism.
So long as these gentlemen are tearing each other to pieces on the Front, we will be replacing them in every key sector of society.
But at what price, Mother? Millions of lives?
Blowing things out of proportion!
The war'll be over soon!
We'll be back by Christmas!
And once the war is over, they won't be able to treat us like second-class citizens anymore.

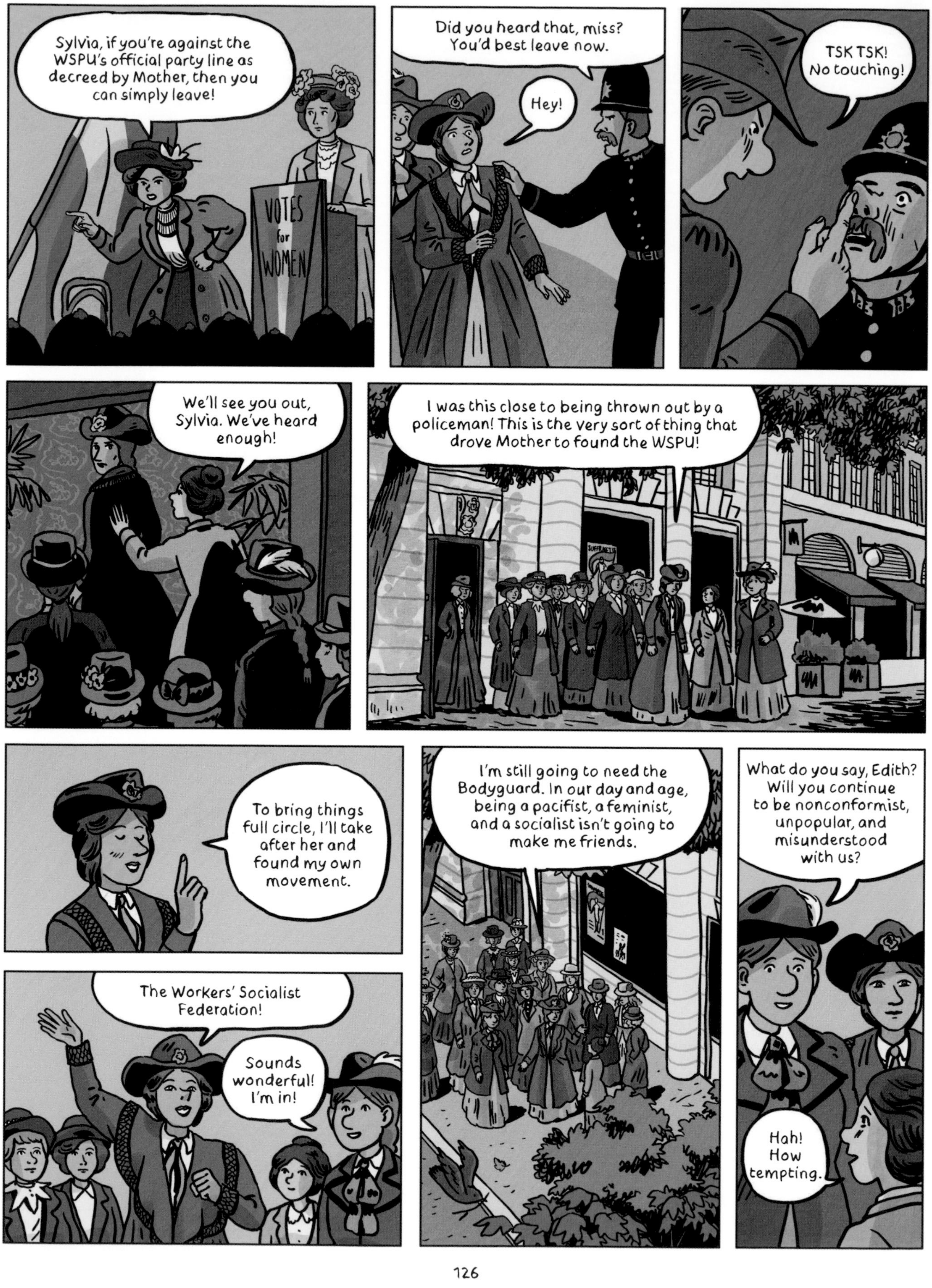

Sylvia, if you're against the WSPU's official party line as decreed by Mother, then you can simply leave!
VOTES for WOMEN
Did you heard that, miss? You'd best leave now.
Hey!
TSK TSK! No touching!
We'll see you out, Sylvia. We've heard enough!
I was this close to being thrown out by a policeman! This is the very sort of thing that drove Mother to found the WSPU!
To bring things full circle, I'll take after her and found my own movement.
The Workers' Socialist Federation!
Sounds wonderful! I'm in!
I'm still going to need the Bodyguard. In our day and age, being a pacifist, a feminist, and a socialist isn't going to make me friends.
What do you say, Edith? Will you continue to be nonconformist, unpopular, and misunderstood with us?
Hah! How tempting.

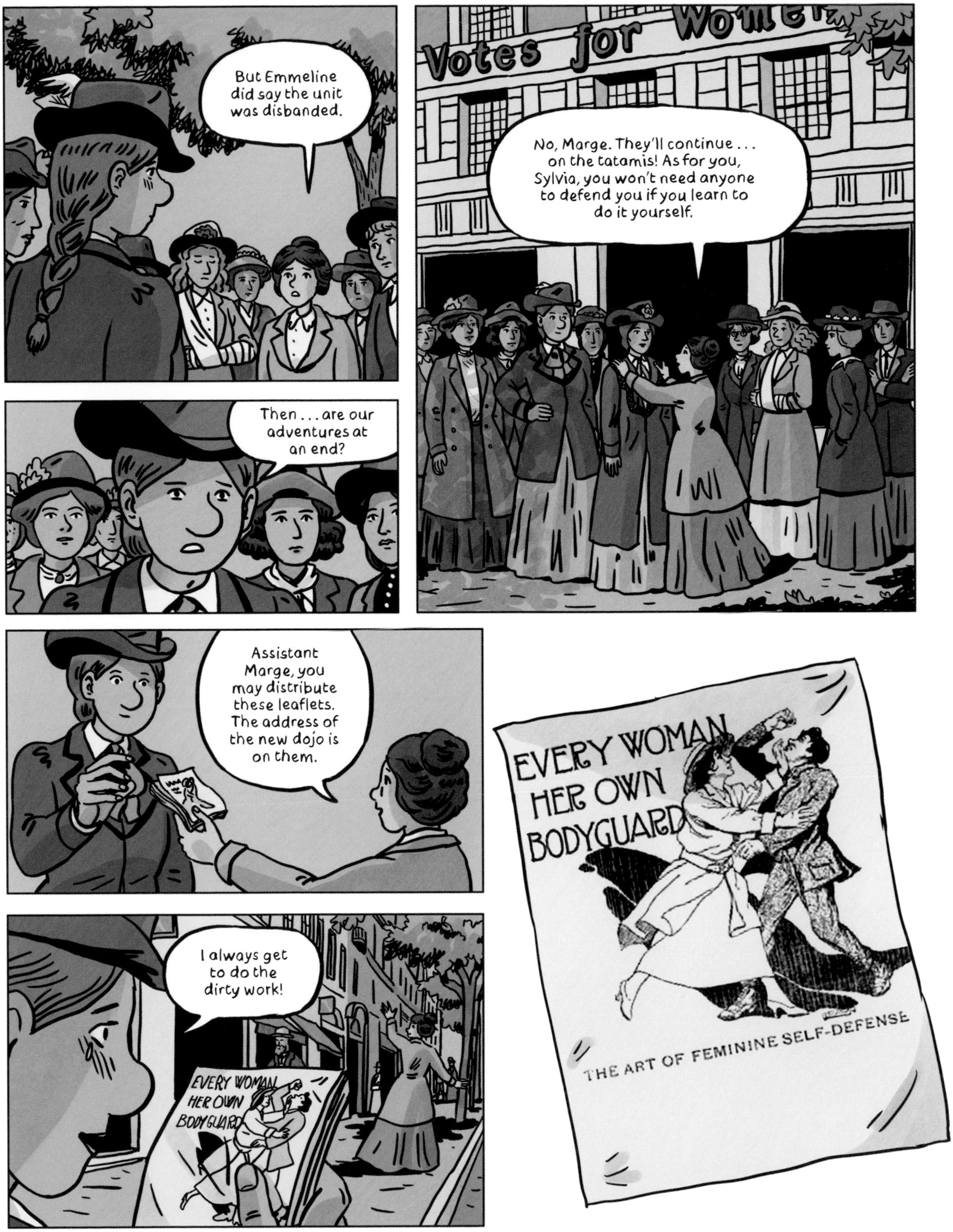

Votes for Wom
But Emmeline did say the unit was disbanded.
Then . . . are our adventures at an end?
No, Marge. They'll continue . . . on the tatamis! As for you, Sylvia, you won't need anyone to defend you if you learn to do it yourself.
Assistant Marge, you may distribute these leaflets. The address of the new dojo is on them.
I always get to do the dirty work!
EVERY WOMAN HER OWN BODYGUARD
EVERY WOMAN HER OWN BODYGUARD
THE ART OF FEMININE SELF-DEFENSE

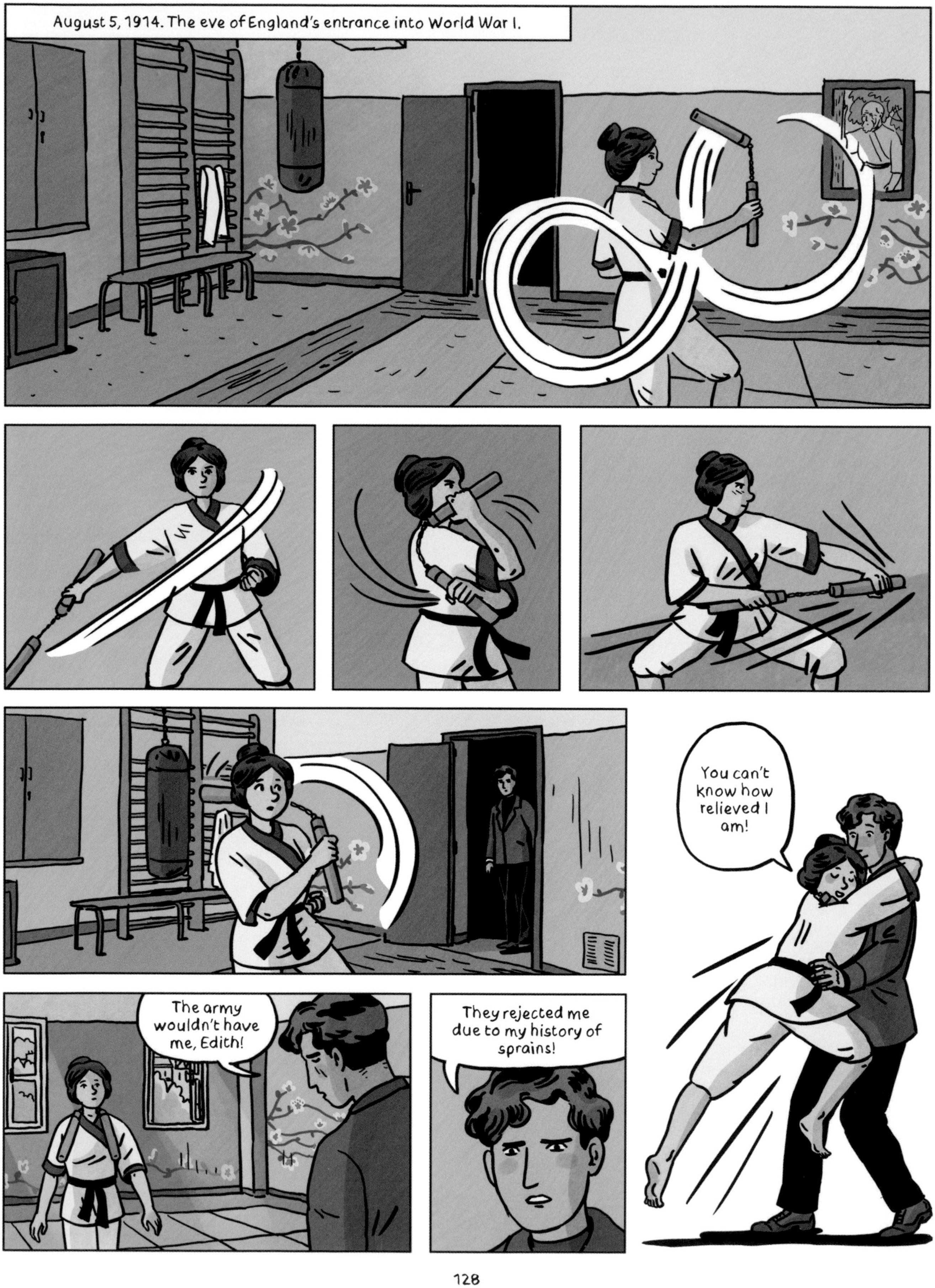
August 5, 1914. The eve of England's entrance into World War I.
You can't know how relieved I am!
The army wouldn't have me, Edith!
They rejected me due to my history of sprains!

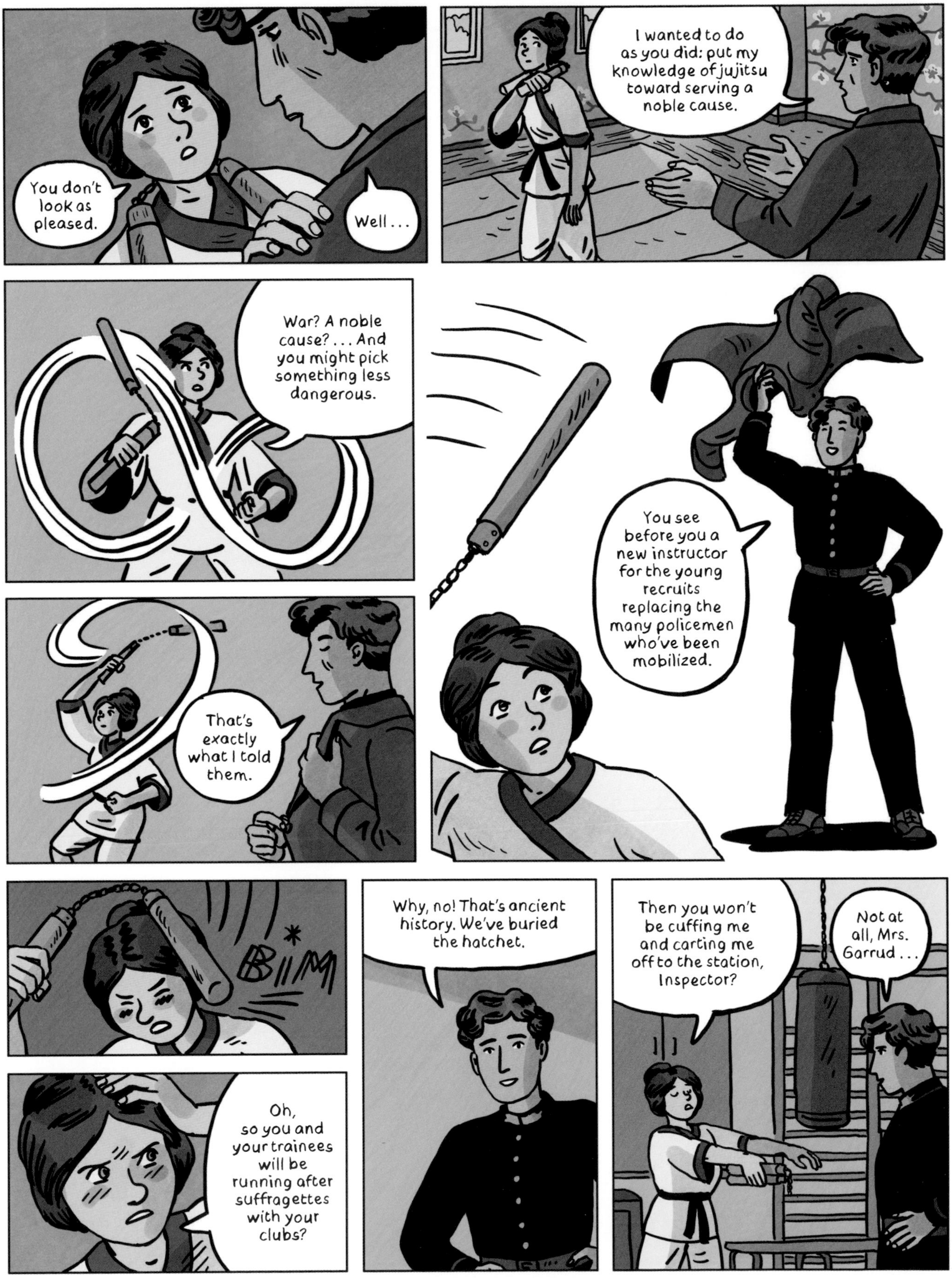
You don't look as pleased.
Well . . .
I wanted to do as you did: put my knowledge of jujitsu toward serving a noble cause.
War? A noble cause? . . . And you might pick something less dangerous.
That's exactly what I told them.
You see before you a new instructor for the young recruits replacing the many policemen who've been mobilized.
BIIM
Oh, so you and your trainees will be running after suffragettes with your clubs?
Why, no! That's ancient history. We've buried the hatchet.
Then you won't be cuffing me and carting me off to the station, Inspector?
Not at all, Mrs. Garrud . . .

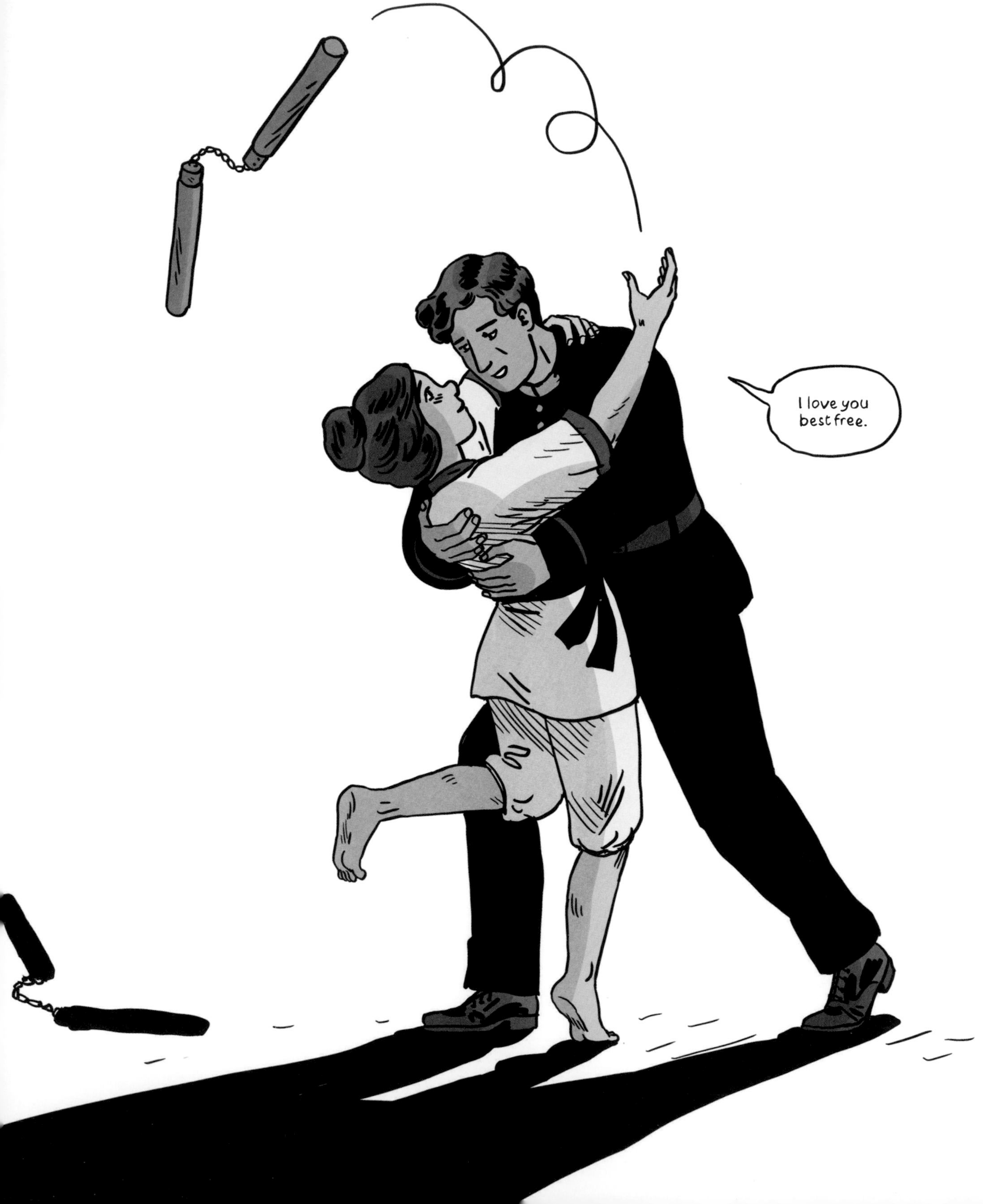
I love you
best free.

After the Bodyguard

Emmeline Pankhurst, photographed in 1913, several years into a civil-disobedience campaign for British women's right to vote.

Emmeline Pankhurst was right: the First World War was a key moment for the liberties of women. Called to support the war effort, British women took the places of men who left for the front lines. They entered the British workforce in unprecedented numbers, demonstrating the ability to perform tasks that were previously forbidden to them. To aid this process, British society made changes to assist women in their daily lives, including the creation of countless daycares.

In 1918, at the end of the monstrous war, British women age thirty and older received the right to vote. (Men of the time were able to vote at age twenty-one.) Further gains in the form of a change in this age difference did not occur until 1928, a month after the death of Emmeline Pankhurst. She did not live to see her dream of universal suffrage come true but had tremendous influence in making it happen.

Sylvia Pankhurst abandoned progressive salons for lower-income neighborhoods of East London after she broke away from her mother. There she advocated for initiatives such as pediatric clinics and restaurants that sold meals at cost. In contrast to her mother and sister Christabel, she in 1915 supported the International Women's Peace Congress. In the years afterward, she belonged to a series of organizations dedicated to advancing communist ideals. However, she also found herself disagreeing with the policies of some of these organizations and with some of the opinions of Russian communist revolutionary Vladimir Lenin.

Sylvia Pankhurst in London at the start of 1932, protesting international policies of the British government.

After a series of criticisms of the Communist International, Sylvia Pankhurst instead devoted herself to combating the rise of fascism. Beginning in the 1930s, she began to advocate for Ethiopia, which was under invasion from Italy's fascist regime under Benito Mussolini. By 1956, she had moved to the capital of Ethiopia, Addis Ababa, where she died in 1960.

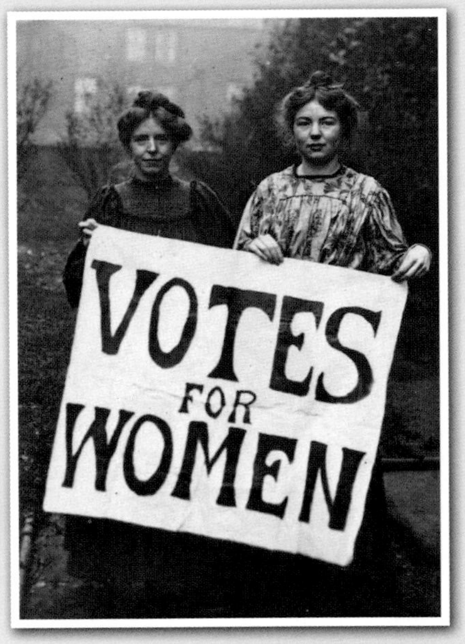
VOTES
FOR
WOMEN

Suffragists Annie Kenney (*left*) and Christabel Pankhurst (*right*), displaying a protest sign in 1908.

Edith and William Garrud continued to teach jujitsu until 1925. Edith made her final appearance in the press forty years later, when in 1965 a magazine interviewed her on her 94th birthday. Although the journalist who interviewed her was somewhat condescending, Edith nevertheless responded politely to his questions. As the interviewer prepared to leave, Edith prepared to shake his hand, then grabbed his wrist and administered an armbar. The jujitsu teacher had lost none of her reflexes.

Edith died in 1971 at age 99. In addition to having democratized jujitsu and shared the art with many practitioners, she left behind an essential text: *The World We Live In: Self-Defence* (1910). Considered an early manifesto of modern self-defense, it continues to inspire many women.

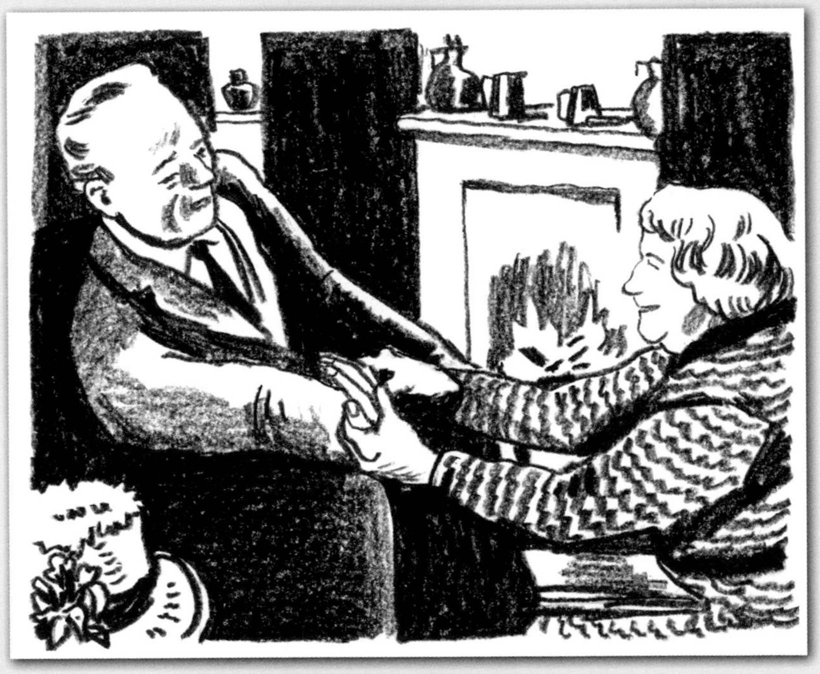

Edith Garrud at age 94, demonstrating jujitsu on the wrist of journalist Godfrey Winn.

Edith Garrud

1872   Edith Margaret Williams is born in Bath, Somerset, England.

1893   She marries William Garrud, an instructor of physical culture specializing in gymnastics, boxing, and wrestling.

1899   She and William Garrud learn jujitsu from Edward William Barton-Wright, the first European jujitsu teacher and inventor of a martial art called bartitsu.

1904   In the neighborhood of Soho, London, she and William Garrud begin following the teachings of Japanese jujitsu master Sadakazu Uyenishi. At the departure of the latter, the couple then takes over and teaches jujitsu and self-defense.

1908   Five hundred thousand suffragists demonstrate in London's Hyde Park to demand the right to vote. Emmeline Pankhurst, the head of the WSPU (Women's Social and Political Union), advocates for civil disobedience. Edith begins to give lessons at a suffragist self-defense club.

1909   Imprisoned activists begin hunger strikes.

1911   Edith Garrud choreographs fight scenes for the play *What Every Woman Ought to Know*, a photo-novel version of which is published in *Health and Strength* magazine.

1912   Faced with the silence of the British government and the repressive nature of its policies, the actions of suffragists become more radical, including setting fires and breaking storefront windows.

1913   The repressive policy of the Asquith government pushes the WSPU to form a self-defense unit known as the Bodyguard.

1914   This self-defense unit takes part in the Battle of Glasgow on March 9 and an attempted raid of Buckingham Palace on May 24. The group is dissolved shortly after the beginning of war with Germany.

1918   The Representation of the People Act extends the right to vote to women—but only to those over age thirty.

1925   Edith and William Garrud stop teaching jujitsu.

1971   Edith Garrud dies at age 99.

Historical Illustrations Included in the Narrative

Plate 41: Front page of *Daily Mirror* from November 19, 1910. Photograph by Victor Consul.

Plate 43: Forced feeding through the nose. Author unknown. Image from the book *The Suffragette* (1911) by Sylvia Pankhurst.

Plate 59: *Suffragettes In and Out of Prison*. Illustration adapted from a board game created by the WSPU in 1908.

Plate 62: Caricature of suffragist Theresa Garnett whipping Winston Churchill. Author unknown. Published in *Manchester Evening News* in 1909 or 1910.

Plate 74: *Nothing for their Panes*, an Irish political cartoon. Author unknown.

Plate 79: *One of the Suffering Yets*, a political cartoon dating between 1908 and 1914. Author unknown.

Plates 86 and 87: Scenes from a photo-novel published in *Health and Strength*, April 8, 1911. Photographer unknown.

Plate 98 – top: Pinfold Manor, home of David Lloyd George, 1912. Walton Local History Society. Author unknown.

Plate 100 – bottom: Kew Tea House Gardens, burned down by suffragettes. Bath News Service. Photographer unknown.

Plate 130: *The Suffragette that Knew Jiu-Jitsu. The arrest.* Political cartoon by Arthur Wallis Mills, published in *Punch Magazine*, 1910.

About the Authors

Lisa Lugrin and Clément Xavier are a pair of creators and storytellers, working through both the keyboard and the ink brush. The duo loves nothing more than tales of tangled and struggling bodies, as with their French-language graphic novel *Yékini, le roi des arènes*, which received the prestigious Prix Révélation (Debut Prize) at the 2015 Angoulême International Comics Festival. In 2016, they released *Geronimo, mémoires d'un résistant apache*, a combination of graphic journalism and biography. As a practitioner of wu dao, a martial-arts system similar to jujitsu, Lugrin also naturally jumped at the opportunity to tell the story of Edith Garrud.

About the Colorist

Albertine Ralenti is a colorist and graphic designer who has been collaborating with publishers, festivals, and organizations since 2003. Her work can be seen in graphic novels including *Brune platine*, *Genius*, *Koma*, and *Non retour*.

About the Translator

Award-winning translator Edward Gauvin specializes in contemporary comics and fantastical fiction. As an advocate for translators and translated literature, he has written widely and spoken at universities and festivals. The translator of more than 425 graphic novels, he is a contributing editor for comics at *Words Without Borders*. His past collaborations with Lerner, ranging in setting from Lebanon to World War II France to modern-day Beijing, have been honored by the American Library Association and the Eisner Awards, and he is thrilled to be working with them again.

About the Author of the Introduction

Elsa Dorlin is a professor of philosophy, most recently at the University of Toulouse Jean Jaurès. Dorlin is the author of *Self-Defense: A Philosophy of Violence*, *The Matrix of Race*, and *Sex, Genre, and Sexualities*.